UNCERTAIN MOTHERHOOD

UNCERTAIN MOTHERHOOD

Negotiating the Risks
of the Childbearing Years

editors

Peggy Anne Field
Patricia Beryl Marck

SAGE Publications
International Educational and Professional Publisher
Thousand Oaks   London   New Delhi

For information address:

SAGE Publications, Inc.
2455 Teller Road
Thousand Oaks, California 91320

SAGE Publications Ltd.
6 Bonhill Street
London EC2A 4PU
United Kingdom

SAGE Publications India Pvt. Ltd.
M-32 Market
Greater Kailash I
New Delhi 110048 India

Printed in the United States of America

Library of Congress Cataloging-in-Publication Data

Main entry under title:

Uncertain motherhood: negotiating the risks of the childbearing years/
    edited by Peggy Anne Field, Patricia Beryl Marck.
        p. cm.
    Includes bibliographical references and index.
    ISBN 0-8039-5564-2.—ISBN 0-8039-5565-0 (pbk.)
    1. Pregnancy—Psychological aspects. 2. Uncertainty.
    3. Motherhood—Psychological aspects. 4. Mother and infant.
    5. Pregnancy—Complications—Psychological aspects. I. Field,
    Peggy Anne. II. Marck, Patricia Beryl.
    RG560.U53   1994
    155.6'463—dc20   94-15629
                                                                CIP

94 95 96 97 10 9 8 7 6 5 4 3 2 1

Sage Production Editor: Yvonne Könneker

Contents

Preface

In this book we present the findings of six research studies that explored, from different perspectives, the experiences of women who found themselves faced with uncertainty during their childbearing years. Such uncertainty spans disparate groups of women, from those who wonder if they can become pregnant, through those who question what they will do about unexpected pregnancies, to those who do not know whether particular pregnancies can survive and result in children whom they will be able to mother. In pulling together chapters examining each of these problems as one body of work, this volume demonstrates that common insights can be drawn from women's varying experiences with uncertain motherhood.

Two qualitative methods, grounded theory and hermeneutical phenomenology, were employed in the research published here; they offer complementary insights into the women's experiences. Whereas each study focuses on a relatively small group of informants, the work taken as a whole represents a significant collective of women, one with much to teach us about their experiences of uncertain motherhood. Placed together, these women have a powerful story to tell about the ways in which women live through and survive uncertain outcomes in pregnancy and birth. This book is a place for these women and their stories to be together—a place for women to say, in their own words, what uncertain motherhood has meant for them.

The first work to be conducted in the series of studies reported here was undertaken by Barbara Brady-Fryer (1988), who looked at the experience of mothering a preterm infant. Although her research began with examination of the attachment behaviors of mothers of preterm infants, the nature of the interviews she conducted made her realize that attachment was not the mothers' focus of concern. Rather, what each mother in the research talked about was her need to find ways in which she could act as a mother to her baby: a need to *find a way to mother.*

In one manner or another, this search for a way to mother resurfaces with all the other women in the subsequent studies, where other aspects of uncertain motherhood are explored. For instance, like the women in Brady-Fryer's study, the mothers of Down syndrome babies in Gail Diachuk's (1989) research also searched for evidence of understandable, "normal" behavior from their babies, behavior that they felt would help them find feasible ways to mother their babies. For women in high-risk pregnancies, such as those in Ann Lever Hense's (1989) and Karen McGeary's (1991) studies, this search extended into pregnancy, where any sign of a normal trajectory of pregnancy reassured the women and moved them toward preparing for motherhood, whereas signs of an abnormal course seemed to hinder their projected sense of themselves as mothers.

Perhaps furthest back along the trajectory of uncertain motherhood are two of the most recent works: Rhonda Harris's (1992), which explores the experience of infertility, and Patricia Marck's (1991), which looks at unexpected pregnancy. Even here, however, either before or at the outset of pregnancies with very different meanings, all of the women sought ways to take on the possibility of mothering, if not the reality of giving birth. From the very dissimilar outcomes of not conceiving, enduring unsuccessful pregnancies, considering abortion or adoption, and giving birth to unexpected or much-yearned-for children, a common tie remains: Each woman found, through her fears and longings, her own personal way to mother in whatever way, real or imagined, full or limited, she was able to take it on.

The studies presented here in addition to Brady-Fryer's contribute to her initial work and advance our understanding of the similarities and differences in the ways women do or do not become mothers when faced with uncertain outcomes. Further, the validity of the findings submitted for scrutiny in this book is strengthened by the fact that many of the researchers had not read each other's work prior to collaborating on this project. Within this volume, the studies are organized to reflect the progression of pregnancy, from preconception to postbirth, rather than presented in the sequence in which they were conducted. This leads to a logical flow of information that we believe will help the reader to see the similarities in the concerns that women express when their life experiences across the childbearing years are uncertain.

Although the studies presented here were all conducted by nurse researchers, we are confident that they will be useful to students and practitioners in all of the helping professions who wish to understand more fully what women feel and how they cope when they are faced with uncertain outcomes in relation to pregnancy and birth. Many texts are available that describe the physiology and pathophysiology of uncertain maternal outcomes, but to date there have been few addressing what it is like to live through such events. Even in nursing and other texts that discuss psychological sequelae, uncertain maternal outcomes have not been placed within the experiences of the women themselves. The qualitative studies in this volume form a picture of motherhood when the outcome is uncertain that comes from women's own words and allows the reader to understand, from women's perspective, what the experience is really like.

Although the research presented in the following chapters was developed and conducted by the graduate students, members of the students' thesis committees provided guidance and assistance. These members were as follows:

- Rhonda E. Harris: P. A. Field, P. Valentine (cochairs), B. Munro
- Patricia Beryl Marck: V. Bergum, D. Forrest (cochairs), J. Dossetor
- Karen McGeary: V. Bergum (chair), P. A. Field, B. Munro
- Ann Lever Hense: P. A. Field (chair), I. Campbell, C. Stainton, D. Kieren
- Barbara Brady-Fryer: P. A. Field (chair), I. Campbell, C. Stainton, B. Munro
- M. Gail Diachuk: P. A. Field (chair), V. Bergum, B. Munro

In particular, we would like to acknowledge the insights of Colleen Stainton, professor, University of Calgary, who served on two committees. The typing services provided by Anita Wright and Tom Hall were critical in manuscript preparation. Rhonda Harris assisted with the preparation of the figures, the editing of the text, and the indexing. Anita Damsma, Carole Estabrook, Susan James, Judy Onyskiw, and Alice Rempel, graduate students in the Faculty of Nursing, all provided valuable input in the preparation of Chapter 8.

Research support for various studies was received from the Alberta Foundation for Nursing Research; the Alberta Association of Registered Nurses; the Division of Bioethics, Faculty of Medicine, University of Alberta (research associate support); the Dr. Jean C. Nelson Award for Public Health Nurses (scholarship support); a Province of Alberta Graduate

Scholarship; and a bursary from the government of Newfoundland and Labrador.

Peggy Anne Field
Patricia Beryl Marck

References

Brady-Fryer, B. (1988). *An exploration of maternal attachment to the preterm infant.* Unpublished master's thesis, University of Alberta, Edmonton.

Diachuk, M. G. (1989). *Maternal attachment to the infant with Down syndrome.* Unpublished master's thesis, University of Alberta, Edmonton.

Harris, R. E. (1992). *Pregnology: The process of getting pregnant through science.* Unpublished master's thesis, University of Alberta, Edmonton.

Lever Hense, A. (1989). *Livebirth following stillbirth: Maternal processes.* Unpublished master's thesis, University of Alberta, Edmonton.

Marck, P. B. (1991). *Women's experience of unexpected pregnancy.* Unpublished master's thesis, University of Alberta, Edmonton.

McGeary, K. (1991). *The process of connecting: The mother-child relationship in a high-risk pregnancy.* Unpublished master's thesis, University of Alberta, Edmonton.

1

Introduction

Peggy Anne Field
Patricia Beryl Marck
Gwen Anderson
Karen McGeary

What do we mean by *uncertain*? Our notion of the term and its connotation for women is limited at best. Yet uncertain outcome is a factor in many pregnancies, despite the societal values that motherhood is a desired state and that pregnancy is a normal, healthy process. Until one is faced with uncertainty, it is difficult to understand what this means. How do women who cannot become pregnant, or who become pregnant unexpectedly, experience their situations? How do women react when their pregnancies are labeled "at risk" or when they conceive again following a previous stillbirth? What is it like to have a preterm infant or a child with a genetic anomaly? Medical science provides increasingly sophisticated technology, but our ability to understand the feelings and emotional reactions of women who find themselves faced with uncertain outcomes to motherhood is very constrained. Stinson and Stinson's (1979) description of the life and death of their preterm infant in *The Long Dying of Baby Andrew* describes one traumatic personal experience of uncertain parenting. Do other people react the same way? How do they come to terms with their dilemmas? How can health professionals help? The studies included in this book were all designed to examine pregnancy when women were uncertain about motherhood or about the outcomes of

1

their pregnancies or the lives of their children. The chapters presented here describe the extraordinary personal experiences of these women.

A second source for those seeking to understand motherhood when the outcome is uncertain is the research literature. The literature on uncertainty is relatively wide ranging, as is the literature on maternal behavior and attachment, but rarely have the two been examined together. Women's reactions to uncertain outcomes when motherhood is an issue constitute a relatively new area of exploration.

The Concept of Uncertainty

In the broadest sense of the concept, *uncertainty* is defined in the literature as "the time of most doubt" (Robinson, Hibbard, & Laurence, 1984, p. 165). It is perceived as a multidimensional phenomenon. In the studies presented in the following chapters, there is evidence of reproductive uncertainty, waiting uncertainty, and diagnostic uncertainty. In a study by Anderson (1990) on parents awaiting the results of prenatal diagnostic testing, uncertainty meant difficulty in comprehending the information, ambiguity about what they might do once the results were known, and an expectation that testing would lead to the resolution of uncertainty.

Uncertainty in Illness

Uncertainty has been described as the "inability to determine the meaning of events"; it "occurs in situations where the decision maker is unable to assign definite values to objects and events or is unable to accurately predict outcomes" (Mishel & Braden, 1988, p. 98). The classic work on uncertainty in illness has been that of Mishel (1981) and Mishel and Braden (1988). Mishel has used work by Norton (1975) to develop and test a measure of uncertainty in illness. Norton suggests that uncertain events contain one or more of the following dimensions: vagueness, lack of clarity, ambiguity, unpredictability, inconsistency, probability (or lack thereof), multiple meanings, and lack of information. Mishel (1981) postulates that when stimuli are perceived as uncertain the perceptual tasks of recognition and classification are hindered and the individual fails to develop a clear picture of the situation, in this case illness. This leads to increased stress. Lack of a cognitive structure (a clear picture of the situation) results in appraisal of the situation and an identification of a threat to oneself. This leads to secondary appraisal that results in direct action (such as seeking further information), avoidance, or increased vigilance (Mishel, 1981).

From this model, Mishel (1981) developed an instrument that she validated on individuals hospitalized for medical and surgical conditions. Mishel and Braden (1988), in a study of women receiving treatment for gynecological cancer, found that those individuals who were able to construct patterns for their symptoms had clearer appraisals of their disease state. Patients who had fewer symptoms or were unable to identify change were less able to gauge their illness and experienced more ambiguity. Mishel and Braden argue that symptom pattern is supported as an antecedent to uncertainty when structure-providing variables—credible authority, social support, and education—are under control. These researchers posit that education enlarges the patient's knowledge base, thus allowing better interpretation of symptoms and a larger repertoire of references to enhance the familiarity of events. In addition, social support, particularly affirmation, will allow the exchange of opinions and views about a situation with others and one's own views may be respected and affirmed. Uncertainty itself may be influenced by both the ambiguity and the complexity of the situation.

Mishel's (1988) latest model of uncertainty in illness identifies symptom pattern, event similarity, and event congruence (the consistency between what is expected and what is experienced in illness-related events) as leading to uncertainty. The uncertainty can be altered through the structure-providing elements of credible authority, social support, and education.

Uncertainty itself may be perceived as a danger or an opportunity. Individuals cope with uncertainty by mobilizing strategies; these depend on whether the uncertainty is seen as an opportunity or a danger. One strategy is buffering, which serves the purpose of blocking new stimuli. Another coping mechanism may be the development of illusion, a belief in which emphasis is placed on the favorable aspects of a situation (Mishel, 1988). When coping mechanisms are effective, adaptation will occur.

Uncertainty in Childbearing

The concept of uncertainty in a woman's reproductive years has also been investigated. This work can be classified into three areas: reproductive uncertainty, waiting uncertainty, and diagnostic uncertainty.

Reproductive uncertainty. In a study by Lippman-Hand and Fraser (1979a, 1979b, 1979c), expectant parents identified three concerns related to uncertainty and decision making. First, there was concern related to how family and friends would evaluate the rationality of their reproductive decision making. Second, uncertainty was manifested as fear regarding the parents' ability to normalize the pregnancy experience. For example, if they knew the baby was abnormal following genetic investigation, would they feel normal prenatal attachment to the fetus and would they carry on with the normal tasks of parenthood once the child was born? In Lippman-Hand and Fraser's (1979a) study, the parents were also concerned about the decisions they would make once the child was born.

Waiting uncertainty. Waiting uncertainty has been described by Rice and Doherty (1982) as the feeling of tension and anxiety associated with the fetal diagnosis following amniocentesis. This can extend to other situations in the motherhood cycle in which waiting plays a role. For example, will the infertile woman become pregnant following treatment? Will the unborn child survive past the time when a previous pregnancy ended? In Rice and Doherty's study, the waiting period was frequently marked by hiding the pregnancy and not discussing it with others. This could be equated with the notion of *protective governance*, the protection of self from further hurt (Corbin, 1986).

Diagnostic uncertainty. Diagnostic uncertainty is related to the imprecise nature of tests and procedures, or the inability to predict outcomes accurately. Ambiguity and unpredictability are characteristics of this type of uncertainty (Black, 1979; Zuskar, 1987). Such uncertainty, focused on the long-term consequences of decision making, is reflected in most of the studies reported in this book.

Uncertainty can imply several similar concepts when applied to motherhood, but the experience of uncertain motherhood has many distinct characteristics. It may be that women cannot predict whether or not they will become mothers. It may be that they do not know whether or not they want to become mothers at this time. It may be that they are skeptical about the ability of tests and procedures to predict safe outcomes for their unborn children. It may be that their children's health status after birth is in jeopardy. A better understanding of what an uncertain outcome to motherhood means to parents will better prepare health professionals to help such parents through a stressful time in their lives.

Method

Five of the six studies included in this book were conducted using a grounded theory approach, whereas the sixth researcher (Marck, 1991) used hermeneutical phenomenology. The researchers used unstructured and semistructured interviews and field notes as the primary methods of data collection.

Grounded Theory

An assumption that underlies grounded theory is that there are unidentified concepts or constructs that, if identified, will enable understanding and thus, in this case, enhance health care. By definition, grounded theory is a method of discovering the reality of a given social setting (Stern & Pyles, 1985). It also allows the researcher to gain a new perspective in a familiar setting in order to generate theory (Stern, 1980). The goal is to generate a theory grounded in the reality of the functioning social system.

The origins of grounded theory are found in ethnography and symbolic interactionism. From ethnography came the methods of interviews, participant observation, and the use of case histories and field notes. Symbolic interactionism stresses the importance of the lived or experiential aspects of human behavior, which are developed through a process of negotiating and renegotiating the reality of the lived world. Symbolic interactionists believe that individuals define their world by processing knowledge in a variety of ways. These include negotiation and renegotiation of reality, encapsulation of knowledge, the development of patterns, and the rehearsal of situations. People construct their own reality from the symbols around them through interaction, rather than through a static reaction to those symbols. In this way, they are active participants in relation to the meaning they attribute to a situation. This leads to both a socially constituted self and a constituted environment. It is also assumed that individuals can describe the reality of the situation to others.

Grounded theory questions generally suggest a process, unlike phenomenological questions, in which the meaning and the lived experiences of the participants are important. Although Glaser and Strauss (1967) recommend that a literature review be done in the analytic phase of research based in grounded theory, it is difficult to justify such a review when previous studies have not been identified. It is equally important, however, that the researcher return to the library as concepts emerge, in order to link emerging theory with the work of other researchers.

Selecting Informants

When using grounded theory, the researcher recruits participants who meet the information needs of the study. This is referred to as *theoretical sampling.* With this type of sampling, the researcher strives to select participants who have the three qualities of a good informant: knowledge of the topic being studied, the ability to reflect on personal experience, and willingness to share that experience. Participants are selected based on the assumption that "all actors in a setting are not equally informed about the knowledge sought by the researcher" (Morse, 1986, p. 13).

Basic to theoretical sampling is the underlying canon that the selection of the study participants is an event that occurs simultaneously with the data analysis. The analysis then guides the selection of future participants through the evolving criteria for further development of the theory being generated (Glaser & Strauss, 1967; Strauss & Corbin, 1990). In the grounded theory studies presented here, the researchers deviated somewhat from this canon, in that although the participants were selected for their knowledge, they were generally recruited at the beginning of the studies. These researchers used newspaper advertisements to recruit respondents and then selected individuals who met the criteria of their respective studies. Thus, although the sample was purposive, it did not meet the total criteria for theoretical sampling.

The number of informants interviewed in the studies presented here varied from 5 to 17. It can be argued that data saturation was not achieved in the case of the study of mothers of Down syndrome babies (Chapter 7). Unfortunately, in that research community health nurses acted as gatekeepers, preventing access to mothers they believed to be stressed. In the majority of studies, primary informants were used to provide the initial data, and secondary informants were used to validate the emerging theory.

Generally, in grounded theory, data collection and analysis proceed simultaneously. This process of analysis is highly interactive between the emerging research and the interviews, with the interviews directing the coding. As far as possible, codes are taken directly from the interviews, using the language of the informants. In order to achieve this, the researcher must read the transcript line by line, highlighting important passages and creating theoretical memos. The next level of coding uses content analysis. At this stage, various portions of the text are coded and then compared with similar text across interviews. This process of constant comparison can be used across interviews of one informant as well as among interviews of different informants. Frequently, a computer program such as Ethnograph will be used to assist the process at this stage.

As greater understanding of the data emerges, the core variables or basic social process may become evident. Core variables may involve basic social psychological processes or basic social structural processes (Glaser, 1978; Strauss & Corbin, 1990). Theoretical coding follows, which is the establishment of hypothetical relationships or linkages between categories. For example, as Harris (Chapter 2) studied infertile women, it became evident that their lives revolved around the process of *becoming pregnant through scientific means.* This led to their being "under the microscope" as they underwent tests and procedures in hopes of becoming pregnant. Glaser (1978) lists the coding families as process, degree, dimension, type, strategy, interaction, identity-self, cutting-point, means-goal, cultural, consensus, mainline, theoretical, ordering, unit, and models. In the McGeary (Chapter 4) study, a causal-consequence model was used, with *uncertainty* as the causal condition and movement toward connecting with the baby as the consequence of that uncertainty. From the process of building connections, the framework for a grounded theory emerges.

The emerging categories are related to the core category by means of asking questions using the coding family described by Glaser (1978) as "the six C's": causes, contexts, contingencies, consequences, covariances, and conditions. The answers to these questions specify the relationship between categories. For example, in McGeary's study the question was raised: Is the category of *distancing* related to *guarding* as a strategy in response to the *perceived uncertainty?* This demonstrates beginning linkages among several categories. At this stage, diagramming and mapping are used to identify patterns and connections in the data. Many exploratory studies do not move beyond the description of process. Diachuk's (Chapter 7) study provides an example of this. This in itself is useful information, as it may identify the psychological or social process that was unanticipated by the researcher and thus can lead to further research. In five of the following chapters, descriptions of processes may be found, along with diagrams that illustrate the relationships among variables.

Phenomenology: A Method for a Purpose

In Marck's study (Chapter 3), four women were asked to speak about their experiences of unexpected pregnancy. To explore with women what it is like to be unexpectedly pregnant, Marck chose a hermeneutical, phenomenological method of inquiry. Her choice of method reflects

Gadow's (1990) observation that "we have a choice among ways of knowing" (p. 3). The questions Marck chose for her research did not seek to predict or control the phenomenon under study. Rather, they sought a deeper and fuller understanding of the nature and meaning of women's experiences of unwanted pregnancy and of our ethical comportment as caregivers in their experiences. They invited a dialogue between the researcher and each woman, for the express purpose of giving voice to their experience (Bergum, 1989a).

The method that corresponds with this understanding of the research questions is phenomenology. Where understanding another in order to take more thoughtful action toward him or her is the central aim of research, phenomenology offers a descriptive, reflective, interpretive, and engaged mode of inquiry that corresponds to that aim (Bergum, 1989a; van Manen, 1990). In the context of women's experiences of unexpected pregnancy, the phenomenological method represents an ethical means both to illuminate the nature of the experience and to stand faithfully within the experience with the women.

Activities of Phenomenological Research

The activities of phenomenological research include uncovering and recognizing the research question and searching out and carefully questioning one's own involvement in that question. Marck transcribed the taped and annotated conversations she held with her informants, and then asked the women to review the transcriptions in their entirety. She also used her research journal, field notes, and thesis development to undertake continued dialogue and reflection, hermeneutical interpretation, and meaning making and referred to them constantly in writing and rewriting the women's experiences. This set of activities constituted a discipline of thoughtful orientation to the research question throughout the research process (Bergum, 1989a; van Manen, 1990). Each undertaking contributed to both the data gathering and the data analysis phase and allowed Marck to question with each woman, at deeper and deeper levels, the nature of her experience of unexpected pregnancy.

Questioning With Women: Conversational Relation

Bergum (1989a) points out that the deliberate choice of conversation as a process of data collection assumes an attitude toward the research and the participants that is significant and different from the technique of interview. This difference may be that of a dependence on *tact* in creating

the conversation, as opposed to a reliance on the preconceived *tactic* of a structured questionnaire. Van Manen (1990) identifies this "conversational relation" (p. 98) as one of collaboration between the researcher and the participant as they orient themselves together toward the phenomenon in question. Conversations in this research therefore strove for a "hermeneutic thrust, oriented to sense-making and interpreting of the experience that drives or stimulates the conversation" (p. 98).

Interpretation: Bringing Experience to Language

The interpretive goal of bringing the women's experiences of unexpected pregnancy into writing began with dwelling in the talk of the women, by reading and rereading their stories. This activity proceeded from initial readings of each conversation as a whole to rereadings of the text, sentence by sentence, line by line. Marck identified recurring words and phrases and marked portions of the text that repeatedly stood out. She made notes about possible themes next to the text of each conversation, whether or not these potential themes seemed to have occurred in any of the other women's conversations. She adhered to this process, begun with the first woman, with the text of each conversation, for each woman.

As Marck identified themes appearing in all the women's talk over the six months of conversations, she recorded a separate developing outline of common themes in her research journal. She reflected on, validated with transcripts, and then rewrote this outline twice more before committing to an initial outline of themes common to all the women's experiences of unexpected pregnancy. She used the developing outline of themes to initiate further dialogue with the text of the conversations with each woman, with her thesis supervisors, and with her own thinking. Her interpretation of the women's experiences proceeded as she conducted additional reading of other research and nonresearch literature, traced the etymologies of significant words, searched for idiomatic phrases, and undertook the hermeneutical activity of writing and rewriting the women's stories. She continued to keep separate entries in her research journal to track the dialectic emerging in the written interpretation of the women's experiences. This separate writing activity provided a "second look" at the written account of the women's experiences as it developed and also helped Marck to reorient her reflective activity continually toward the women's experiences.

These activities assisted Marck with thematic analysis of the women's stories, where "the forgotten, hidden, mysterious, or ambiguous nature" of their experiences was sought (Bergum, 1989a, p. 51). In the words of van Manen (1990), through a deep interest in the question, the researcher "stands in the midst" (p. 43) of it, and by doing so, keeps opening up possibilities and deepening the questioning. Just as important, "standing in the question" maintained Marck's commitment to understanding the phenomenon and enhanced the likelihood of her differentiating essential themes from those that were incidental to the experience of unexpected pregnancy for these women.

As essential aspects of the women's experiences emerged, Marck searched for the existential themes of temporality (lived time), spatiality (lived space), corporeality (lived body), and relationality (lived relation with other) in the women's stories in order to evoke a stronger recognition of their experiences as they were lived. She then "wove" these existential themes into the writing (Bergum, 1989a, p. 52) to apply a rigor to the thinking and writing and to articulate unexpected pregnancy as these women felt that it was experienced (van Manen, 1990). Although in reality these elemental experiences of our being are not separable, differentiating them helped to clarify the descriptions of the women.

The "lifting up" of significant text to relate the women's experiences to the existential themes animated the reflective process of interpreting the women's stories. For example, initial recognition of one woman's experience of relationality was found in her expressive speech about never feeling, as an adopted child, that she "fit in," that she "belonged" with her adoptive family as who she truly was (Marck, 1991, p. 53). As Marck read and reread, wrote and rewrote this text, and informed by both other literature and etymological searches of words such as *fit* and *place*, her interpretation of Vanessa's words became stronger in relation to several existential themes. Themes such as not "fitting in," not feeling as if she was in "the right place," began to speak of never experiencing the lived space of "home," "where we can be who we truly are" (Bergum, 1989b, p. 75), and in turn, of her experience of lived time and lived other, in searching for knowledge about her birth mother.

The hermeneutical intention that animates phenomenological inquiry is thus one of breathing meaning into human experience (van Manen, 1990) and of gaining deeper insight into the values that underlie our actions. Marck's writing of these women's experiences for this research was an effort at such hermeneutical writing and rewriting activity, as the interpretations and questions developed both in her journal and in the other written text created their own dialogue. The women's stories were written "as a way to approach the knowledge" of their experiences (Bergum, 1989a, p. 50) and to offer us, through text, more direct contact with the true nature of both unexpected pregnancy and of choice. (For readers who wish to explore the method of phenomenology in more detail, we recommend the work of Bergum, 1989a, 1989b; Gadow, 1990; Johnson, 1987; Kristeva, 1981; van Manen, 1990.)

Rigor

Qualitative methodology is inherently different from quantitative methodology by virtue of its subjectivity. The purpose is not to objectify and measure the concept or to test theory, but rather to gain an understanding of the informant's experience. Sandelowski (1986) redefines the criteria used for evaluating rigor in qualitative research, suggesting that credibility (internal validity), fittingness (external validity), auditability (reliability), and confirmability (objectivity) should be considered.

Credibility. Credibility is enhanced when the researcher is able to spend time with the informant and can verify information from one interview to the next. The opportunity to conduct several interviews also allows the researcher to assess the impact of context on the phenomenon being observed or identified. In all of the studies presented in this volume, the informants were interviewed at least twice, with the interviews separated over a period of weeks or even months. It has been suggested that the greater the degree of intimacy and credibility the researcher establishes with an informant, the more accurate will be the information provided (Field & Morse, 1985). In addition, the researchers' relevant clinical experience enhances their credibility as investigators. For example, prior to undertaking their studies, Lever Hense (Chapter 5) was a regional perinatal nurse consultant, Brady-Fryer (Chapter 6) was a neonatal nurse, and Diachuk (Chapter 7) was a public health nurse who had been a genetic counselor.

Fittingness. To evaluate fittingness, one needs to know how the sampling was undertaken and the characteristics of that sample. Each of the chapters in this volume begins with a description of the study informants and the manner in which they were recruited. In all instances, both the informants themselves and the recruitment methods used were appropriate. In the case of Diachuk's study (Chapter 7), as noted above, the sample was small because of circumstances beyond the researcher's control. Given the similarities between the mothers in this study and those in the other studies reported in this book, we have chosen to include this chapter. We note, however, that the size of Diachuk's sample limits the appropriate application of the findings to mothers who are judged by health professionals to be adjusting to the birth of Down syndrome babies.

All of the grounded theory researchers used secondary informants to verify the emerging theory. These women were selected on the basis of their knowledge and experiences related to the phenomena being studied. If these studies have meaning and relevance for the reader, then the criterion of fittingness has been achieved (Sandelowski, 1986).

Auditability. This criterion refers to the ability of other researchers to follow the decision trail used in a particular study (Sandelowski, 1986). Auditability should be documented through the use of memos. In a book of this nature, rich description is used to illustrate the emerging theory; however, it may be necessary for an outside researcher to examine the original thesis of any given study before the decision-making process of that study's researcher is totally clear.

Confirmability. Sandelowski (1986) argues that "confirmability is achieved when auditability, truth value and applicability are established" (p. 33). Confirmability relates to the meaningfulness of the findings. Although it is the reader who must judge if this criterion has been met, the meaningful import of these works examined as a whole lends strong support to the confirmability of the researchers' collective findings.

Conclusion

In this book, we present the stories of women experiencing uncertain outcomes in relation to pregnancy. These stories are moving; they reflect the suffering and concerns of women facing uncertain motherhood. This volume represents only a beginning move toward an understanding of such women's feelings, and we are grateful to all the informants for allowing us to share their experiences. Further research must be conducted to identify the needs of these women on a broader base, and we hope that by sharing the insights we have gained through these studies we will assist others who will take and develop this knowledge. Continuing research will bring more of women's lives to our awareness and deepen our understanding of their experiences. Perhaps most critically, such inquiry will increase our ability to offer care that acknowledges that for many women, uncertain motherhood is the only reality available, a reality through which caregivers can and must work with women to find safe passage and meaningful outcomes.

References

Anderson, G. (1990). *Coping with fetal genetic risk: The parents' processes.* Unpublished master's thesis, University of Alberta, Edmonton.

Bergum, V. (1989a). Being a phenomenological researcher. In J. M. Morse (Ed.), *Qualitative nursing research: A contemporary dialogue* (pp. 43-57). Rockville, MD: Aspen.

Bergum, V. (1989b). *Woman to mother: A transformation.* South Hadley, MA: Bergin & Garvey.

Black, R. B. (1979). The effects of diagnostic uncertainty and available options on perception of risk. *Birth Defects: Original Article Series, 15*(5c), 341-354.

Corbin, J. (1986). Coding, writing memos, and diagramming. In W. C. Chenitz & J. M. Swanson (Eds.), *From practice to grounded theory* (pp. 102-120). Menlo Park, CA: Addison-Wesley.

Field, P. A., & Morse, J. M. (1985). *Nursing research: The application of qualitative approaches.* London: Chapman & Hall.

Gadow, S. (1990, October). *Beyond dualism: The dialectic of caring and knowing.* Paper presented at the conference "The care-justice puzzle: Education for ethical nursing practice," University of Minnesota, Minneapolis.

Glaser, B. (1978). *Advances in the methodology of grounded theory: Theoretical sensitivity.* Mill Valley, CA: Sociological Press.

Glaser, B., & Strauss, A. (1967). *The discovery of grounded theory: Strategies for qualitative research.* Chicago: Aldine.

Johnson, M. (1987). *The body in the mind: The bodily basis of meaning, imagination, and reason.* Chicago: University of Chicago Press.

Kristeva, J. (1981). Women's time (A. Jardine & H. Bicke, Trans.). *Signs: Journal of Women in Culture and Society, 7,* 13-35.

Lippman-Hand, A., & Fraser, C. (1979a). Genetic counseling: Parents' responses to uncertainty. *Birth Defects: Original Article Series, 15*(5c), 325-339.

Lippman-Hand, A., & Fraser, C. (1979b). Genetic counseling: The postcounseling period: I. Parents' perceptions of uncertainty. *American Journal of Medical Genetics, 4*(1), 51-71.

Lippman-Hand, A., & Fraser, C. (1979c). Genetic counseling: The postcounseling period: II. Making reproductive choices. *American Journal of Medical Genetics, 4,* 73-87.

Marck, P. B. (1991). *Women's experience of unexpected pregnancy.* Unpublished master's thesis, University of Alberta, Edmonton.

Mishel, M. H. (1981). The measurement of uncertainty in illness. *Nursing Research, 30,* 259-263.

Mishel, M. H. (1988). Uncertainty in illness. *Image: Journal of Nursing Scholarship, 20,* 225-232.

Mishel, M. H., & Braden, C. J. (1988). Ending meaning: Antecedents of uncertainty. *Nursing Research, 37,* 99-103.

Morse, J. M. (1986). Quantitative and qualitative research: Issues in sampling. In P. Chinn (Ed.), *Nursing research methodology: Issues and implementation* (pp. 181-191). Rockville, MD: Aspen.

Norton, R. W. (1975). Measurement of ambiguity tolerance. *Journal of Personality Assessment, 39,* 607-619.

Rice, N., & Doherty, R. (1982). Reflections on prenatal diagnosis: The consumers' views. *Social Work in Health Care, 8,* 47-57.

Robinson, J., Hibbard, B., & Laurence, K. (1984). Anxiety during a crisis: Emotional effects of screening for neural tube defects. *Journal of Psychosomatic Research, 28*(2), 163-169.

Sandelowski, M. (1986). The problem of rigor in qualitative research. *Advances in Nursing Science, 8*(3), 27-37.

Stern, P. (1980). Grounded theory methodology: Its uses and processes. *Image: Journal of Nursing Scholarship, 12,* 20-23.

Stern, P., & Pyles, S. (1985). Using grounded theory methodology to study women's culturally based decisions about health. *Health Care for Women International, 6*(1-3), 1-25.

Stinson, R., & Stinson, P. (1979). *The long dying of baby Andrew.* Boston: Little, Brown.

Strauss, A. L., & Corbin, J. (1990). *Basics of qualitative research: Grounded theory procedures and techniques.* Newbury Park, CA: Sage.

van Manen, M. (1990). *Researching lived experience: Human science for an action sensitive pedagogy.* London, Ontario: Althouse.

Zuskar, D. (1987). The psychological impact of prenatal diagnosis of fetal abnormality: Strategies for investigation and intervention. *Women and Health, 12,* 91-103.

2

The Process of Infertility

Rhonda E. Harris

At what point does a woman become uncertain of her ability to reproduce? To admit that one is infertile has implications for oneself, one's partner, and one's dream of a family. Infertility sets one apart from the mainstream of society, yet it is something that is beyond a woman's ability to control. Recognition of infertility may occur within months of seeking to become pregnant or it may take years. Once reproductive uncertainty is acknowledged, many women begin to seek help. At this point their private lives become public, and sex becomes a vehicle for procreation rather than an outcome of a loving relationship between partners.

The purpose of the study reported in this chapter was to generate a theory that would help explain the process women undergo when they undertake medical intervention because of their inability to achieve pregnancy on their own. I explored how the women in my sample decided it was time to seek intervention, the experience of undertaking medical treatment for infertility, and the reasons the women used in deciding it was time to terminate treatment. The informants' lives were frequently dominated by their experiences of infertility. The process of telling their stories was important for these women, as they believed no one understood their point of view.

Study informants were recruited through media advertisements and social networking, resulting in a purposive sample of 17 Caucasian women who had identified themselves as being infertile, ranging from 24 to 39 years old (mean 31.8 years). Of the 17, 14 of the women were experiencing difficulty achieving pregnancy for the first time (i.e., primary infertility); the remaining 3 had previously conceived but were having difficulty becoming pregnant a subsequent time (i.e., secondary infertility). At the time of the study, 10 of the women were experiencing infertility; the other 7 had experienced infertility 13 to 45 months prior to the study. With the exception of 2 informants, female physiological problems were the underlying cause of the infertile state; in 3 of these cases, fertility was further compromised by the women's mates' low sperm counts. For the remaining 2 informants, the cause of infertility had not been identified. Eight informants had conceived at some time, but the pregnancies had ended in miscarriages or ectopic pregnancies. Only 4 of the women became pregnant while receiving treatment, and 3 more became pregnant after terminating treatment; at the time of the first interview, 2 informants were pregnant and 2 had adopted children. All of the informants were married except for one who was in an ongoing relationship.

Of the 17 women involved in the study, 14 were primary informants (data were collected from these informants for the purpose of generating the theory); the remaining 3 were secondary informants (data were collected from these informants for the purpose of validating the generated theory). Primary informants were normally interviewed twice, but one was interviewed a third time because she was viewed as being a "really good" informant in terms of her (a) experience with the medical management of infertility, (b) ability to reflect and articulate on her infertility experience, and (c) willingness to be interviewed a third time (Morse, 1989). The secondary informants were used to validate the conceptual framework; because these 3 informants were "new" to the study, it was believed that they would provide verification without having been biased from previous interviews. All interviews but one were conducted in person, the exception being a telephone interview at the informant's request.

Becoming pregnant and having a family to raise were important for the informants. The importance attributed to pregnancy and parenthood provided the context in which the informants pursued pregnancy through medical intervention.

The Importance of Pregnancy and Parenthood

The importance of pursuing pregnancy and parenthood was embedded in the reasons informants cited for desiring these life events, in addition to the consequences of not being pregnant and/or being without one or more children. Inherent in these were intrapersonal and marital implications.

Intrapersonal Implications

Most of the informants wanted to become pregnant and have families to fulfill intrapersonal needs. For example, Greer "wanted to see what my husband and I could reproduce, what she/he would look like." Other informants sought life meaning through pregnancy and the parenting role. This was expressed in comments such as, "I want someone who I can take care of and raise and love" (Nora) and "To have the sense of accomplishment and the title of parents. I felt that having children would give us purpose and meaning to our lives" (Greer). For Hilary, it was important to have a biological child because she herself was adopted: "My [adoptive] parents don't look like me and they don't have my traits and my genes. I think being adopted ties into it all and it makes it all kind of necessary." Gillian, who had already adopted a child, wanted to become pregnant so she could experience the bodily changes that occur with pregnancy, in addition to being able to nurse a baby.

In contrast to the informants who were having difficulty "forming" families through having their first children, Jacqueline and Kate were trying to get pregnant with their second and third children, respectively. When reflecting on her current family size, Jacqueline stated, "I did have a sense that it wasn't a complete family. To me, having a complete family would be having one more child."

In addition to being able to relive her own childhood, Eve viewed pregnancy and raising children as a means of maturing and gaining entry into the adult world:

> It is important developmentally for an adult to have children, to go through recognized stages, rites of entry or passage in our society. If you don't enter into those, there's a sense of being an outsider. Children are really important to have a sense that we're part of the mainstream and help us feel that we've come of age, reached a level of maturation.

Eve's reference to being "an outsider" was one expressed by all the informants on various levels. On the first and most basic level, the informants felt different because they could not achieve pregnancy and other women could: "I felt like I was a woman, but when it came to getting pregnant, I felt, I'm not like other women. I can't do it" (Holly).

Seeing other women achieve pregnancy when they themselves could not often induced a mixture of feelings in the informants. For example, two of the women admitted to feeling bitter toward pregnant women: "[My friend] had two children and did not want any more. And she got pregnant. I did think, Well, that's certainly a rip off. I did feel some bitterness. For some people, it seemed to be so easy" (Jacqueline). "There would be moments where bitterness would hit me when you see other women getting pregnant and you're not" (Leah). In addition, the informants had feelings of jealousy when they saw other women achieve pregnancy: "I have a lot of friends who are pregnant right now. I'm really happy for them [but] a little part of me is jealous about their situation" (Hilary). When seeing other women pregnant, the informants would often question, "Well, why not me?" (Jacqueline) or "Why can't it be me?" (Gillian). Furthermore, the informants often felt a sense of unfairness when they saw "poor" candidates for motherhood getting pregnant:

> I'd find out that these young girls were pregnant and it really upset me because I thought, here's a young girl who's not married. She's not even finished school. She's having a baby, she's not ready to have one. Whereas me, I'm in my 30s. We're ready to have this baby. There'd be no problem having this baby, bringing it up and stuff like that. I really think it's unfair. (Holly)

The informants felt a further sense of intolerance as they saw their fertile peers complain about and/or mistreat their own children. This was expressed in comments such as, "This friend of ours has a baby. She's a real complainer. I feel like shaking her and saying, 'Don't you know how lucky you are to have what you do instead of complaining all the time?' " (Grace) and "I feel outraged by people who have children that abuse them" (Gina).

In addition to being unable to get pregnant, several of the informants felt different compared with their fertile peers on the basis of the age at which they had their children: "All my family had had kids at 19. And there I was, already 25 and then 28. . . . I turned 29 and I was still childless. None of my family in four generations had ever been that old" (Ruth). For Eve, this feeling of differentness continued even after she had achieved pregnancy: "Our friends' families are all five years older than us. We're not in the same situation at all. . . . Most of them are now getting back into the work force and we're still having babies." Eve elaborated on what this differentness entails for her now:

When I go visiting, I'm aware that my kids are in their messy stage and they're going to spill stuff on their floors. It's not such an issue if their kids are doing it, too. But when these people's kids have gone through that stage, their house is now relatively clean. So I don't know whether or not I should take my Dustbuster and mop with me!

The informants continued to be "outsiders" when their childlessness resulted in isolation from their fertile peers: "Once other people started having children around us, socially, we had fewer contacts with the same people. There is a kind of loneliness" (Eve). Several informants expressed feelings of isolation when their friends' children interfered with socializing, for example, "[My husband] and I can get up and go anywhere we wanted. Whereas with them they just couldn't go out all the time [because of their children]" (Holly) and "When I talk on the phone, I say, 'Do you guys want to come over for a barbecue?' And she goes, 'Well Ginny, we better not because your house isn't really that kid-proof.' "

Even when they were able to socialize with their fertile peers, the informants felt as if they did not belong or fit in. This "left-out" feeling was expressed when the informants described various social events they had with others. For example: "We're at these dinner clubs. People are always talking about their kids and I just felt really left out" (Leah) and "There was a Tupperware party that my friend had. There were two pregnant women and everybody else had children except me. I felt so left out" (Holly). Several of the informants also felt left out when they were unable to contribute to child-focused conversations: "I was sitting with my girlfriends. They were all talking about children. I try to get into the conversation . . . there isn't really much that I can say" (Ginny). There were several informants, however, who did not feel left out of these conversations because they had previously been pregnant and/or had had previous contact with babies/children: "A lot of my girlfriends that are pregnant or have been pregnant, I can relate to . . . because I've been pregnant myself. I talk about my experience with them" (Nora) and "I've been baby-sitting long enough. . . . We can talk baby-talk and I can be just as involved except that I don't have . . . the comparing [with my own baby]" (Tiffany).

The final level on which the informants felt different focused on their being denied the courtesy often shown to persons who have children. This differentness was noted by Eve:

You don't have any rights until you have children. . . . When you don't, you can't be busy. You can't be tired. You can't be worried. Your life isn't important. What you do isn't important. . . . There was a sense that we should be continually available. . . . All of our vacations were slotted out. "Eve and her husband have nothing to do. . . . We'll just go up and see them. They can entertain us." We were definitely, regardless of age, being looked upon as little kids with no rights, with no needs. . . . I find that now, with the children, people give us more leeway, more respect. We're big people now and we're acceptable. What we do is very important. We have a right to be tired. We have all these rights that we were denied before.

Marital Implications

Several of the informants wanted to become pregnant and raise families in order to meet marital expectations. This was expressed in comments such as, "My daughter's almost a teenager. I divorced her daddy when she was really young. It wouldn't be devastating to me not to have another child. I think it might have more of an effect on him [partner]" (Madeline) and "I want to be able to give that [children] to [my husband]. . . . That's something that he wants" (Tiffany). When they could not achieve pregnancy, the informants had the feeling of "I'm not fulfilling my role as a wife" (Tiffany).

Feeling that they had let their husbands down by not producing expected children led to informants' experiencing feelings of marital insecurity: "I was thinking, if we could never have children, would he leave me for somebody who could?" (Tiffany). When Leah attributed her inability to achieve pregnancy as a factor in the dissolution of a previous marriage, she questioned her worth as a woman:

My opinion is that my inability to conceive was a cause in the breakdown of marriage. Having lots of children was very important to him. I believe that his concern that I couldn't have kids was a large one and that was very painful. . . . It left me feeling less than adequate as a woman and like a failure. When I was finally divorced, I really doubted whether any other male would want me.

Leah is currently in a new marital relationship and, although she feared for the security of the relationship, she told her current husband prior to marriage about her previous experience with infertility. She did this in an attempt to protect herself from another marital dissolution:

We were deepening our commitment. I felt that it was very important that he knew. I absolutely did not want anything to happen again after the fact.

Having been through a marriage which had broke down because of it, it was a weighing of fear. Which was the greater fear? The fear that he would leave me now or the fear that he would leave me after we were married and feel betrayed that he wasn't told? . . . It was one of those things where you feel scared.

Rather than fearing that her husband would leave her because she did not become pregnant, Grace questioned herself: "Do I still want to be married if I can't have children?" Grace was unusual in that most of the informants did not question their own desire to remain married despite their inability to achieve pregnancy: "I didn't get married to have kids. I got married because I love my husband" (Hilary).

Attempting Pregnancy on Their Own

Although the informants knew they wanted to be pregnant at some time in their lives, they had initially decided to delay pregnancy by using contraceptive measures in order to "get ready" for the event and/or the subsequent raising of a child. For Eve, being "ready" meant "really wanting them, being emotionally in a state when you want them." The relationship the informant had with her partner was also an important element in the notion of getting ready: "We have been together for seven years and we felt, well, let's get married and start having a family" (Ginny). For Grace, the marital relationship had to reach a level of maturity before she and her husband felt ready to get pregnant and raise a family: "[My husband] thought it was better for us to spend time [a couple of years], just the two of us and get to know each other and getting settled instead of, all of a sudden, having a child."

Being ready also entailed addressing the practicalities associated with pregnancy and raising a family: "There are things I have to do to phase myself out of my job, to phase myself into a period of financial dependence, fix up the house, to satisfy the practical needs" (Madeline). For Ruth, being ready implied that "I was ready to [give up work]. I had got where I wanted in work. I had made a name for myself so when I applied for jobs in the future people would know me." In contrast, the balance between career and the parenting role was the reverse for Greer: "I had moved and was not working. Being a stay-at-home mom was the logical thing to do. Not until our infertility did my personal goals (i.e., education and career changes) start to become important."

Several of the informants assessed their readiness to start a family from a long-term perspective. This frequently involved the informants' own personal philosophies surrounding the parenting role, especially in relation to the age at which one would be a parent: "I didn't want to be having kids when I was 40. I would much rather have them when I was younger, so you could enjoy them a little more, keep up with them" (Rachel). For Ginny, in particular, getting ready meant dealing with the practicalities associated with the parenting role as they related to her own philosophy:

My husband was working on the oil rigs. I've seen [where] the husband works on the rigs, he goes away for two weeks and comes home for a week. I said, "That's wrong. I'm not going to raise a family on my own. I want you to get a job in [the city] so you can come home every night to see your kid instead of coming home for a week and then you're gone for two weeks and the kids will wonder, where's Daddy?"

Several informants also considered the needs of their current children when getting ready for another child. For example: "[My daughter's] at the age now where I could have that quality time with the baby and still have quality time with her. I didn't want to have children close together 'cause I wanted to have those years of quality time to spend with her" (Gillian).

Whereas most of the informants embarked upon achieving pregnancy when they felt ready for the task, Grace sought pregnancy as a treatment for endometriosis, even though she was not psychologically ready. Not knowing that she would have difficulty getting pregnant, Grace proceeded to attempt pregnancy on her own, following the medical advice.

Most of the informants embarked on the task of getting pregnant with the expectation that they would have little difficulty. This expectation was expressed in comments such as, "I always thought, have a baby, okay, that's it! Nobody ever looks ahead and sees any problem" (Tiffany) and "I went in and had my IUD [intrauterine device] removed. I thought, that's it! Next month, I'm pregnant" (Holly). Grace also noted the lack of preparation she had received for the infertility experience: "In the Catholic church, children are always the thing. . . . Nobody ever thought, what are you going to do if you can't have children? And all of a sudden you're affected with it. [It's] like, so what do you do now?"

This expectation that pregnancy would be easily achieved was often the result of the informants' having no knowledge of infertility. For most informants, this lack of experience was frequently felt in reference to their "fertile" peers: "I don't know anybody that is infertile. All my girlfriends . . .

have to do is have a guy sneeze their way and they're pregnant" (Ginny). In contrast, Kate's inexperience with the difficulty of getting pregnant was felt on a more personal level:

> [My son] was first try. And [with my daughter] we were away at the cottage and didn't have any birth control and it was like, "Could you get pregnant?" And I said, "Well, if I do, it doesn't matter. I'm ready for another one." And bang! I was pregnant. So to go two and a half years was a real switch. Usually, it was easy.

Tiffany believed that she would be able to achieve pregnancy easily despite previous gynecological surgery, as her doctor had told her that it would not interfere. Several informants, however, did suspect that they would have difficulty getting pregnant because they had experienced previous problems with their menstrual cycles: "I just knew that I was going to have problems. [When] I was fifteen, I ended up laying on the floor in school with such bad period cramps" (Ginny).

Pregnology: The Process of Getting Pregnant Through Science

Pregnology refers to the process the informants passed through as they pursued pregnancy through the science of medical intervention. It comprises four stages (see Figure 2.1). In the first stage, the entry into medical intervention, the informants were involved with three basic activities: suspecting that they had an infertility problem, seeking medical assistance based on their suspicions, and receiving confirmation that their inability to get pregnant was a problem requiring medical intervention. The second stage of pregnology is participation in medical intervention. Upon deciding that they would intervene with medical intervention, the informants then engaged in infertility work (i.e., the various activities involved in the medical management of infertility) in the hopes of achieving pregnancy. In the third stage, the informants experienced letdown when they did not achieve pregnancy. This stage of pregnology entails acknowledging the letdown, experiencing the emotional wound of the letdown, and responding to the letdown. The fourth and final stage of pregnology is the exit from medical intervention, either by achieving pregnancy or by deciding to discontinue medical intervention in the absence of pregnancy. Because these stages occur over time and in a sequential manner, pregnology is identified as a process.

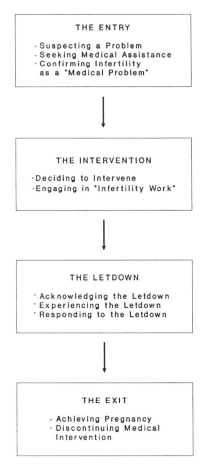

Figure 2.1. The Stages of Pregnology

Two distinct properties of pregnology were identified in this study. First, the informants played a very active role. For example, they responded to their inability to get pregnant by seeking medical help and then by participating in various activities demanded by the medical intervention. And second, the informants' pursuit of pregnancy was not linear; rather, it was ongoing and circular. This property was apparent when the informants repeated medical intervention because pregnancy had not been achieved.

When going through pregnology, each of the informants wanted to become pregnant but experienced difficulties in doing so (Figure 2.2).

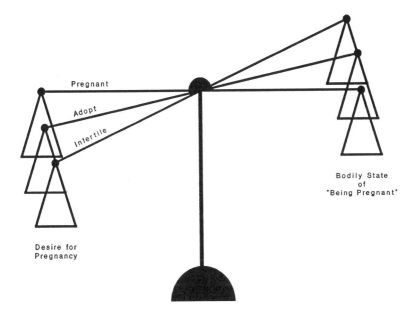

Figure 2.2.   Balance Between Desire and Bodily State

This, in effect, placed the informants in a state of imbalance: The desire to achieve pregnancy was not balanced with a bodily state of "being pregnant." Two of the informants "almost" achieved this state of balance when they adopted babies; although these informants had achieved their "end" desire of creating families, they had not achieved that end through pregnancy. Several of the informants reached a state of balance when they achieved pregnancy; however, this balance reverted to a state of imbalance when the achieved pregnancy was lost, either through spontaneous abortion or through ectopic pregnancy.

As the informants progressed through the stages of pregnology, they used two major strategies: balancing the scales and protective governing. They also lived as though under a microscope at various points throughout the process.

Balancing the Scales

Informants used the strategy of *balancing the scales* when they made various decisions about their infertility and its management. First, the informants made decisions about the management of their infertility in relation to the rest of their lives. Frequently, they would weigh various factors relating to their infertility (e.g., phases of the menstrual cycle, treatment protocols) with other aspects of their lives (e.g., energy level, employment, marital relationship). In balancing such factors, informants made decisions about whether their infertility or some other aspect of their lives would assume the primary or dominant role at a given point in time. When the informants' infertility played the primary or dominant role, the informants incorporated the rest of their lives into their infertility. Examples of this included (a) engaging in scheduled sex when they and/or their husbands were not interested in sexual activity and (b) taking time off from work for infertility-related appointments. In contrast, when other aspects of the informants' lives assumed the primary or dominant role, the informants incorporated their infertility into their lives. Examples illustrating this include (a) deciding not to fulfill the obligation of scheduled sex and (b) deciding not to intervene with medical intervention because of a perceived lack of the time needed.

The strategy of balancing the scales was also employed when informants made decisions to accept or reject various management options available for their infertility. Although some of the treatment options, such as ovulation induction with Clomid, were readily accepted, the informants used the strategy of balancing the scales when a particular option involved such factors as financial cost (e.g., in vitro fertilization [IVF], private/ international adoption), success rate (e.g., IVF), time commitment (e.g., IVF), and genetic continuity (e.g., artificial insemination using donor sperm [AID], adoption). When making decisions, the informants often assigned these various factors differing weights, ranging from "very important" to "not really important." This ranking of importance was highly individualized. For example, the factor of genetic continuity was considered to be very important to some informants, whereas others considered it to be unimportant.

The acceptance or rejection of a given management option was often determined through the weighing of factors surrounding that option. For example, the informant would balance the factors that were "in favor" of the option with the factors that were "against" the option in question. The informant would either accept or reject the option depending on which side of the scale was outweighed. As decisions were made over time and under different conditions, the weights assigned to the involved factors frequently changed. This change in balancing the scales sometimes resulted in different decisions being made from one time to the next (e.g., one informant initially accepted ovulation induction with Clomid but later rejected it when she gained experience with the side effects of the medication). The decision to accept an option contributed to the informant's state of balance by moving her closer to the goal of becoming pregnant and/or creating a family. On the other hand, deciding to reject an option would not contribute to the informant's state of balance because the decision would not move her closer to the goal of pregnancy and/or parenthood.

Protective Governing

When making decisions about the management of their infertile state, informants sometimes employed a second strategy, protective governing. This term is borrowed from Juliet Corbin's research pertaining to pregnancy complicated by chronic illness (see Corbin, 1986, 1987; Strauss & Corbin, 1990). In this study, *protective governing* was defined as a strategy whereby the informants protected or shielded themselves and/or others from a perceived risk. The informants identified numerous risks as they progressed through medical intervention. For example, several of the informants felt that the privacy surrounding their sexual relationships was invaded when they had to document on basal body temperature (BBT) charts the times that they engaged in sexual activity and later show their doctors the charts. To protect against this invasion of privacy, the informants used two strategies of protective governing: (a) not documenting on their BBT charts when they had engaged in sexual activity and (b) marking when they had engaged in sexual activity during the suspected time of ovulation only (that is, they did not record any sexual activity that took place at other times during the menstrual cycle).

The informants also used variants of the strategy of protective governing when responding to risks associated with the letdown. These variants (and the perceived risks) included changing doctors (risks: continued inability to achieve pregnancy because of inadequate or suboptimal medical care; not receiving "the best" medical care, in terms of either medical/technological or emotional/psychological factors), releasing oneself from the responsibility (risk: being responsible for the nonachievement of pregnancy), feeling better off in comparison to other people (risk: feeling the full impact of infertility), compensating (risk: not reaching the goal of parenthood at any level of attainment), parenting vicariously (risk: living a life that excluded children), ventilating feelings and concerns (risk: not dealing with one's feelings and concerns regarding the infertility and its management), normalizing (risk: being different from either fertile or infertile women), and escaping from infertility (risk: confronting one's infertility).

As they progressed through medical intervention, there were times when the informants did not protect themselves and/or others from the perceived risks (e.g., the risk of multiple births associated with ovulation induction, the risks associated with general anesthetic when undergoing a laparoscopy). This decision often was reached through the informants' balancing of the scales: The perceived risk was outweighed by another factor, most commonly by the high desire for pregnancy.

Living Under the Microscope

While the informants' were "living under the microscope," their infertility and its management were meticulously scrutinized. This examination generally involved three basic aspects. First, the anatomical and physiological factors involved in conceiving a pregnancy were examined; the informant underwent an extensive infertility workup involving numerous diagnostic procedures. Second, personal and private information became public knowledge; for example, health professionals, most often strangers to the informants, were involved when the informants told them, through BBT charts, when they had engaged in sexual intercourse. And third, the informants themselves examined particular aspects of their infertility and its management in microscopic detail; this included watching for bodily signs indicative of ovulation (e.g., reading the BBT chart, observing the presence of mittelschmerz, observing cervical mucus, using ovulation detect0ion kits) as well as for signs of the achievement of pregnancy (e.g., late menstruation, breast tenderness, lack of premenstrual symptoms, pregnancy testing) or the nonachievement of pregnancy (e.g., onset of menstruation, reading the BBT chart, symptoms of premenstrual tension).

The Stages of Pregnology

Stage 1: Entry Into
Medical Intervention

The entry into medical intervention occurred in three phases: First, the informants suspected they were experiencing problems with achieving pregnancy; second, they sought medical assistance for this perceived problem; and third, they received confirmation that they had a problem with fertility requiring medical intervention.

Suspecting a Problem

All informants identified "a problem" when they were unable to achieve pregnancy after a period of trying. The time frame was variable, ranging from 8 months to 10 years of unprotected sexual activity.

Seeking Medical Assistance

Most of the informants sought medical assistance when they first suspected that they may be having fertility difficulties. Kate and Eve, however, delayed seeking medical assistance despite their inability to achieve pregnancy. For Kate, this delay was related to the reason she identified as being responsible for her lack of pregnancy: "We were living down East at the time. We just decided, now, and it didn't happen. We were moving back here so I said, oh well, it's just the stress of moving." Eve had several reasons for purposefully delaying seeking medical assistance. The strategies of balancing the scales and protective governing underlie Eve's explanation:

> I would have liked the baby to have happened naturally. I really wanted that magical experience of finding out, "Oh my god, you're pregnant! When did it happen?" I held off from seeking medical assistance for that reason. I was sorting through an awful lot of personal problems related to my career; in that sense, I wasn't emotionally ready to be pursuing yet at another front. This [infertility] was another battle. I was just recovering from the last one. And so I didn't really feel I had the emotional strength to head off into that.

Eve's reluctance to seek medical assistance was also influenced by her philosophy that "I wasn't going to go run to the doctor every time I thought there was a problem. So I was trying to be patient and take things in stride."

Seeking medical assistance for infertility was initiated by the informants, with one exception. In Kate's case, she and her husband sought medical assistance for infertility after her husband saw a urologist because he was experiencing scrotal pain. Following her husband's inquiry, Kate sought further assistance from her own doctor.

Because of a geographic move, Nora did not have access to a doctor from whom she had previously received medical care, so she asked a friend for the name of a doctor. However, in balancing her desire to seek medical assistance with the effort involved in obtaining that assistance, Nora rejected this referral, as the doctor lived outside the city and she judged the driving time necessary to make a visit to be too long. Instead, Nora sought medical assistance through a medical center, because, as she noted, "there are good and bad doctors everywhere. I can go into a regular practice and find crummy doctors I don't like. It's like a hairdresser. You can go to a $6 haircut place and find the best hairdresser in the world. You just never know when you're going to find one [a doctor] or where." Nora presented her infertility as a "secondary" concern when she did visit a doctor: "I'll go for my sixth-month checkup or whatever. I'll just go and see Dr. K [about it] whenever I have something go wrong." Nora did not provide a rationale for seeking medical assistance for her infertility in this way.

Confirming Infertility as a "Medical" Problem

Once the informants had sought medical assistance, they passed into the third phase of entering into medical intervention. In this phase, the doctor determined if the informant's inability to get pregnant was a problem requiring medical intervention. This was usually done on the basis of how long the informant had been unable to achieve pregnancy. Frequently, the inability to get pregnant was defined as a problem if the informant had failed to conceive for at least one year.

There were often differences of opinion between the informants and their doctors when the doctors assessed that a year wasn't "that long" to try; for example, Holly responded this way: "What do you mean a year's not very long? That's a long time, because in my mind, if I wanted to get pregnant this month, I should have got pregnant this month, not a year later or two years later." When giving this medical assessment, the doctor often rationalized that the informant's inability to achieve pregnancy was a result of "poor timing"; that is, her sexual activity was not coinciding with her fertile periods (i.e., during the ovulatory phase of the menstrual cycle). Thus informants were advised to "try longer." Although several informants simply accepted this advice, Hilary chose an alternate course of action, seeking a second opinion from another doctor, to whom her mother had referred her. On the basis of Hilary's menstrual history (irregular menstruation) and BBT charts (indicating anovulation), this second doctor confirmed that Hilary's inability to get pregnant was, indeed, a problem requiring medical intervention.

Stage 2: The Intervention

Once their inability to get pregnant was determined to be a problem requiring medical intervention, the informants entered the second stage of pregnology. This stage, the intervention, comprises two phases: deciding to intervene and engaging in infertility work.

Deciding to Intervene

Once infertility problems were diagnosed, the informants had to decide whether or not they should undertake intervention. Because most of the informants viewed medical intervention as a means of achieving pregnancy, they decided to proceed. Ginny, however, had ambivalent feelings toward medical intervention, especially at the infertility clinic: "[There] was a period where I was saying, oh, should I really go to the infertility clinic? Or should I just say to heck with it and get pregnant on my own? 'Cause I'm deathly scared of doctors and needles and all that kind of stuff." Despite these ambivalent feelings, Ginny proceeded with treatment. Her decision illustrates the strategies of balancing the scales and protective governing: The emotional pain associated with not pursuing medical intervention (putting herself at risk for the continued inability to achieve pregnancy) was greater than the unpleasantness associated with medical intervention (physical pain); Ginny attempted to protect herself from her continued inability to get pregnant by deciding to accept intervention.

Every informant except Nora decided to proceed with medical intervention. The first reason Nora gave for her decision not to take that step was related to balancing her infertility with the rest of her life: "I've been so busy lately with company and everything else. So I haven't really been doing anything [about my infertility]." Nora had previously conceived a pregnancy that ended in a stillbirth, and she also balanced the consequences of undertaking medical intervention and not getting pregnant with the chances of achieving pregnancy:

> Dr. K says, "Don't get your hopes up. Chances are very slim that you'll have another baby." When you get that said to you it's like, should I bother anymore? 'Cause . . . I get excited about it and hopeful. I don't like building up my hopes and having them fall [when I don't get pregnant]. I've had so many doctors just say like, "It took you [over ten years] to get pregnant the first time and that was kind of a fluke. So don't get your hopes up 'cause chances are like one in a million that it'll ever happen again." If I had little better odds, like a hundred out of a million, I would probably try a little harder [and undergo medical care].

In this example of balancing the scales, the strategy of protective governing is also present: by not pursuing medical intervention, Nora is protecting herself from experiencing the excitement and hope surrounding the possibility of getting pregnant only later to suffer a letdown when pregnancy is not achieved.

Engaging in Infertility Work

Upon deciding to intervene, the informants began to engage in numerous activities aimed at overcoming their infertility. As Leah commented, undertaking medical intervention represented hope: "I remember reading about the birth of Louise Brown, the first test-tube baby. And so I thought, well, science and technology will find some way to rescue me from this peril of infertility." Despite the hope that medical intervention offered, the informants still felt much uncertainty surrounding their achievement of pregnancy. For example:

> "Hang in there." Yeah, I remember Dr. J saying that. . . . The concept was time, like, how long do I have to hang in there for? I thought, this could be years. It could be months. It could be weeks. Like who knows? (Holly)

> It's almost an added torment that I have a uterus and a functioning ovary. So I've always had this possibility [of getting pregnant]. If I did have a hysterectomy, it would be final. Uncertainty is really about the whole thing. I don't know if I'm going to be 60 years old and childless or not. (Leah)

Kate noted that permanent sterility would almost be preferable to the uncertainty of not knowing whether pregnancy would occur: "I say to [my husband], 'Well, why don't you get a vasectomy? And then the decision is made and we won't have to think about it anymore.' "

For several informants, living under the strain of uncertainty interfered with life plans. While balancing their infertile state with the rest of their lives, the informants routinely entertained the thought of being pregnant. For example: "[My husband's] sister is getting married. The months would get close and I'd think, if I got pregnant now, I could still wear that [bridesmaid] dress" (Kate); "I delay scheduling annual leave [for holiday time] because I'd like to save it for an eventual extension of a maternity leave" (Madeline).

The uncertainty surrounding *when* pregnancy would be achieved also interfered with the informants' plans to pursue their careers. For example, Eve made the conscious decision not to pursue a career in an attempt to protect both herself and a prospective employer from a possibly short-term employment situation. Grace avoided a career change: "I kept saying, oh, I'm going to wait till after I have children. And now, I'm still waiting. Like how many years have I wasted? Like I probably could have had two careers by now." In contrast, Jacqueline attempted to advance her career by going to college while receiving treatment, because "we might not have this child so I thought that I should get on with something. I worked really hard but my soul and spirit were not in it. . . . What I yearned for was the baby, not the degree."

Many of the informants found that the infertility work became the central focus in their lives, and other aspects assumed a more peripheral nature. This concentration on getting pregnant was expressed in comments such as, "Baby. Baby. Baby. That's all I think about" (Tiffany) and "Everything in my life revolved around this business of trying to get pregnant" (Jacqueline). During this time, they would often dream about getting pregnant and having children. The content of such dreams often focused on "being pregnant, me and my big, fat belly" (Holly), "being at home on maternity leave with a baby" (Tiffany), "having a baby and putting this birth announcement in the paper" (Hilary), and "wonder[ing] what my kid would look like. Would he have [my husband's] nose or my toes?" (Ginny). The informants would also visualize their future parenting experiences, such as "taking [the baby] out and buying clothes for it and taking it out for walks and things like that" (Holly).

Going to Infertility Appointments

Deciding to pursue medical intervention resulted in the informants' need to attend numerous appointments with their doctors and other health professionals (e.g., laboratory and X-ray technicians) (see Table 2.1). The purpose underlying a particular appointment was the foremost consideration in its scheduling. When the purpose of the appointment was to undergo various diagnostic procedures or receive infertility treatment, the appointment was scheduled during the appropriate time of the informant's menstrual cycle. For example, appointments were scheduled during the ovulatory phase of the menstrual cycle when the informant was undergoing a postcoital test (PCT) or when she was receiving intrauterine insemination (IUI). Although scheduling appointments was not problematic for most informants, Gina stated that at one point she "had to forget about it [IUI] because my ovulation had occurred over the weekend." Appointments to obtain test results were made according to the informant's own time preferences and the availability of appointment slots.

Most of the informants prepared themselves cognitively for their appointments by thinking of questions that they wanted to ask their doctors and either "writing them all down, probably the evening before" (Kate) or keeping them "in their heads." Grace noted that, depending on the

TABLE 2.1 Infertility Appointments

Purpose	Scheduling	Preparation
Diagnostic testing	Related to menstrual cycle; office hours; available opening	Sexual intercourse (PCT); prepare questions to ask doctor
Treatment	Related to menstrual cycle; office hours; available opening	Obtaining Lupron prescription (Lupron treatment); scheduling of sexual intercourse (IUI); prepare questions to ask doctor
Test results	At woman's convenience; office hours; available opening	Prepare questions to ask doctor

purpose of the appointment, this type of preparation was not always necessary because sometimes "there wasn't really anything to ask. You just go in and have your procedure [IUI] done and you go home."

Although some of the appointments required the informants simply to "show up," others demanded that they do some form of physical preparatory work. For example, when having a PCT done, the informant had to engage in sexual intercourse prior to testing. To meet the time restriction associated with this particular test, Ruth noted that she had to incorporate her life (i.e., the time when she would engage in sexual intercourse) into the management of her infertility (i.e., having the PCT done): "They book the test for 11 o'clock. You're kind of [like], 'That's not going to work, doctor. My husband's at work.' So at 8 in the morning you have sex because at 9, you're having the test." Ruth also recognized that this type of preparatory work was compulsory in nature: "You have to have sex . . . your test is booked. So you have to go at a certain time. You can't phone the doctor and go, 'I didn't feel like it this morning. Can I rebook for another morning?'"

Other types of appointments required different activities to be done in advance. For example, Ginny was responsible for obtaining a Lupron prescription needed for a treatment appointment. In most cases, Ginny did not find it problematic to obtain this prescription from the university hospital, although she noted that "you [might] have to run all the way across town" to get it at another health care facility. Twice, however, when she was not able to fill the prescription at the hospital, Ginny coped in the following ways:

> The hospital is the cheapest [$365]. . . . The first time they didn't [have it], I had to change my appointment. Every month after that, I'd phone ahead to make sure they had it. The last shot I had, they didn't have it again until

the day after my appointment. I said, to heck with it, I'm not going to wait another day and miss another day of work. I'm just gonna go get it for $407 at [another pharmacy].

Thus Ginny incorporated infertility into her life as she balanced her work life (i.e., losing time at work to attend her infertility appointment) against the cost of the medical treatment for her infertility.

Informants who worked outside the home at irregular hours (e.g., shift work) or on a part-time basis generally attended their appointments during their time off from work. In contrast, informants who worked full-time and during standard working hours had to leave work to attend their appointments. Although most of these informants were willing to incorporate their work lives into the management of their infertility, Judith was not. Rather, she decided to quit work so she could attend her infertility appointments with a clear conscience. As the following illustrates, Judith used the strategies of balancing the scales and protective governing when making her decision:

> [It] got to the point where I was taking so much time off work. . . . It wasn't fair to everyone else at work because they were always covering for my work. So I quit. I would have a doctor's appointment once or twice a month. I had laparoscopies and a laparotomy. You take six weeks off at one time and then each laparoscopy is a week off.

When the informants took time off from work to go to their appointments, some explained to their supervisors why they were missing work and others did not. The decision to tell or not to tell was related to concern that supervisors suspected the informants were missing work without legitimate reason. Holly, who worked within a small organization, told her supervisor because "I went there [infertility clinic] five or six times. So I thought, well, how am I going to explain this? . . . I just wanted [my supervisor] to be aware so he didn't think that I was just missing work." On the other hand, Madeline, who worked within a large organization, did not tell because "I don't go that often enough that they could suspect abuse, so no explanation is required." Although Madeline did not routinely give information about why she left work, she was prepared for a possible confrontation:

> If there were some questions I could say, "Yeah, I'm going to have a D&C." At my age, that kind of thing isn't unusual. The people I work [with] are within my approximate age bracket. Sometimes, we make off-the-cuff, tongue-in-cheek comments about the body's falling apart when you get to 35. I put it in that same general light.

When attending their appointments, the informants waited to see their doctors; waits varied from a minimum of 15 minutes to more than two hours. Most of the informants accepted this; Holly, however, "ask[ed] for the first appointment in the morning so I wouldn't have to wait very long." During this waiting game, the informants would sometimes talk with other infertile women who were also waiting or "read a bit, [a] raunchy novel to keep my mind occupied" (Holly). In addition, the informants often watched other patients in the waiting room, observing various characteristics, such as the fertility status of the other patients, "You have people . . . who have two or three kids with them. And you think, what are they doing at the infertility clinic?" (Ginny). As Ginny explained, watching the activities of the other infertility patients would sometimes generate feelings of uncertainty:

> You're sitting and watching all those people come and go and they are all carrying little vials and some are carrying boxes. . . . You're sitting there, thinking, well, I wonder if I'm going to have to do that. I wonder if that costs anything. And then you see the sign on the wall saying, "Semen washing, $80," and you're thinking, . . . should I bring money next time? . . . So you're sitting there going, I don't know if . . .

Several informants also observed the age differences between themselves and the other patients as they waited for their appointments. When this happened, they often felt a lack of normality. This was expressed in comments such as, "I'm younger than most patients that are there. . . . There might be some people my age [26 years old], . . . but most of the people there are 30, 35" (Ginny) and "A lot of people look . . . a way older than I am. . . . I'm 31. They look 35-ish . . . if not older" (Grace).

Optimizing Reproductive Factors

For conception to occur, the anatomical and physiological functioning of both the female and male reproductive systems must be intact to some degree. The optimization of reproductive factors was accomplished through four strategies: (a) undergoing an infertility workup, (b) undergoing infertility treatment, (c) increasing the sperm count, and (d) engaging in scheduled sex. Figure 2.3 presents a taxonomy delineating these strategies.

Undergoing an infertility workup. As the informants embarked upon medical intervention, efforts were undertaken to discover the underlying causes of their infertility. This was accomplished through infertility workups, which consisted of various diagnostic procedures, such as BBT charting, hysterosalpingogram (HSG), endometrial biopsy, laparoscopy, and hormonal assays. The workup also involved two additional tests, the PCT and semen analysis, both of which demanded the involvement of the informants' husbands. Having to undergo some of these diagnostic tests represented abnormality to Holly, who stated, "Dr. J recommended that I take my temperature [BBT] and chart it. The thought kept coming to my mind, why can't I be normal? Why do I have to take my temperature every morning and chart it?" When undergoing these tests, the informants began to "live under the microscope" as their doctors and other health professionals (laboratory and X-ray technicians) scrutinized their reproductive systems.

The informants generally greeted the tests with excitement, because they believed that the tests would identify the causes of their infertility and move them closer to the desired pregnancy: "I'm so excited. We're going to do these tests. Dr. J is gonna tell me what's going on. Maybe [with] this [test], Dr. J will find something. It was like, I'm getting a step closer to my dream" (Holly). Many of the informants approached the workup with an attitude of "hoping that one of my tubes were blocked. They'll blow it open and we'll get pregnant. It's like, if your leg's broken, they put it in a cast and they fix it" (Tiffany). For Holly, however, no underlying cause for her infertility was discovered. As a result, she "didn't feel very good about it because when there's nothing to correct, then you feel lost. Like, how can I correct this problem if I don't know what it is?" Not knowing the underlying cause of her infertility resulted in much uncertainty for Holly. Even when a cause had been identified, uncertainty remained for several of the informants. From Hilary's perspective, undergoing additional testing was viewed as a way of removing this uncertainty: "I'm ovulating [while on Clomid], but maybe the tubes are blocked. If I had the laparoscopy, then a lot of questions would be answered."

Most of the informants found it traumatic to undergo the various diagnostic procedures. Of all the procedures involved in the workup, the informants focused mostly on how they were affected by the BBT charting. This procedure, which is done to determine ovulatory function and requires the woman to take her oral temperature every morning prior to rising, was often viewed as being "kind of a drag" (Grace) or "a pain in the butt more than anything else" (Rachel). Although most of the informants simply endured the inconvenience of BBT charting, Ginny looked for ways to make the task easier, such as using a digital thermometer:

> You turn it on, stick it in your mouth, and go back to sleep. It'll beep three times when it is done. All you do is press the off button and put it away.

OPTIMIZING REPRODUCTIVE FACTORS				
	Scheduled Sex	Fulfilling the Obligation	yes	avoid confrontation avoid a missed opportunity temporary means to an end
			no	not interested not available
		Managing the Need	avoiding unpleasant situations erotic messages left for partner erotic clothing going to a hotel scene nights romantic dinners showing affection	
		Identifying the Time	ovulation-detecting kits (commercial)	
			bodily symptoms	mittelschmerz cervical mucus cervix
			BBT chart	
	Sperm Count	Avoiding Activities	smoking sports tight undershorts/pants hot baths	
		Scheduling Sexual Activity	abstaining 3 or 4 days before IUI every other day	
	Infertility Treatment	Therapeutic	in vitro fertilization (IVF) artificial insemination with donor sperm (AID) intrauterine insemination (IUI) surgery Lupron Danazol Clomid baking soda douche	
		Prophylactic	Clomid	
	Infertility Workup	With Husband	semen analysis postcoital test (PCT)	
		Solo	hormonal assays laparoscopy endometrial biopsy hysterosalpingogram (HSG) basal body temperature (BBT) chart	

Figure 2.3. Taxonomy of Optimizing Reproductive Factors

Then when you get up in the morning, it's got a memory on it. You press a button and then you can record it. You don't have to get out of bed at 6 o'clock in the morning to record your temperature.

As the informants did the BBT charting over time, it became part of their normal routine: "I've been doing it for so long" (Ginny); "It's just a force of habit. You do it when you wake up in the morning without even thinking" (Kate).

There are several factors that may affect the accuracy of the BBT chart, such as the informant's sleeping patterns (e.g., having a late night), rising prior to taking the temperature, the taking of medication, and the presence of illness. Rather than simply acknowledging the potential for inaccuracy by indicating the occurrence of these situations on the chart, as most informants did, Kate changed her lifestyle habits so the accuracy of her chart would be maintained: "You take it [BBT] before you stand up and do stuff. I know that if I got up in the middle of the night, maybe that's going to throw me off. So when I'm in bed, I don't get up even if I have to go to the bathroom. I wait until morning." The informants who worked shift work frequently had concerns about the accuracy of their BBT charts, especially as it related to when they should be taking their temperatures:

[When] I was working shift, I was never too sure when I was supposed to be taking my temperature. Working days, it was no problem; you'd wake up in the morning. But when you were working nights you didn't wake up in the morning. You went to bed in the morning. So I would just take my temperature when I woke up because it was the temperature after you had rested. And then when you switched over, you'd be taking your temperature within twelve hours of one another. You'd kind of wonder how accurate the picture was, especially if I was working nights right around the time when I was supposedly ovulating. (Rachel)

In addition to marking their temperatures on their BBT charts, the informants were requested to record when they had engaged in sexual intercourse. Giving this information to their doctors often made the informants feel as if they were under the microscope: "[Dr. Q knows] when my husband and I make love because I have to record it. So it's kind of like you are under a microscope. Even when you're in your bedroom, you're still being monitored" (Ginny). Many of the informants perceived this request as an invasion of privacy, an intrusion into their sexual relationships. Eve stated: "It was very invasive. Not everybody has to check in and tell people when they've made love." Showing the doctor her chart extended into a "confession of wrongdoings" for Eve: "You were supposed to have intercourse every other day. When you had it two days in a row, it was like a confession."

The informants employed several strategies to protect the privacy of their sexual relationships. For example: "I never marked intercourse on my chart. I figured, everybody knows that's when you're going to do it. So I thought, I'm not going to put it on. I wasn't anxious to let everybody know when I had sex" (Rachel). "We only kept [a] chart of that one week [during ovulation]. Nobody really knew if we had intercourse any other time during the month because we only kept track of that one little segment" (Eve). Although Eve did not want to record when she had engaged in intercourse on her BBT chart, she did comply with her doctor's request. The rationale underlying Eve's decision involved the strategy of protective governing:

> I knew that they [doctors] were going to ask us to prove it. I wasn't going to have anyone telling me to do it again. Dr. A would say, "They don't know for sure. They can't tell for sure. Go back and do it for two or three months and come back." That would've put us behind a few months because they would have asked me to do that.

There were informants, however, who did not mind letting their doctors know when they had engaged in sexual activity. Holly expressed this in a way that was typical of this group of women: "I felt, this is a medical thing. Dr. J needs to know this. It was like, Dr. J knows that we had intercourse but Dr. J wasn't there. So Dr. J doesn't know what happened. Dr. J just knows it happened. So no, it didn't really bother me to let Dr. J know that."

Eve also perceived another diagnostic procedure, the PCT, to be an invasion of her privacy: "I felt like a laboratory specimen. The only thing worse would have been [if we had been] asked to do it in a laboratory where people were watching through a window. Being instructed when to [have sex] and then coming in with the evidence was the aspect that was most difficult." Eve elaborated further on this perceived intrusion: "You have to make love that morning and then you come in. They know you've done it. We normally don't do that, go around with banners saying 'We just made love' to the world. That's very, very private, very personal."

The informants also found it traumatic to undergo other diagnostic procedures. For example, Kate expressed financial concern involving the HSG: "It's not covered by [health insurance]. My husband is up in arms against paying anything extra. We discussed it, like, do we want to pay to have this done?" The strategy of protective governing is evident in Kate's further explanation of her financial concerns surrounding the HSG: "If they don't find that the tubes are blocked, then they'll do another procedure. Since there's a fee for this, there'll probably be a fee for everything else. I'm not about to start spending dollars and dollars and dollars." Despite these considerations, Kate considered having the HSG done. However, that decision in turn involved deciding in which menstrual cycle she would have it done. Kate used the strategies of balancing the scales and protective governing when she made this decision: "Last month, I just pushed it by because I thought with the wedding coming up, in case there's really bad cramping, I didn't want it to ruin my month."

Undergoing the HSG, as well as the endometrial biopsy, often involved the endurance of some physical pain: "Some of those tests are incredibly uncomfortable. Ouch! The one test that I really absolutely hated is the endometrial biopsy. It was incredibly painful" (Gina). Rather than feeling physical pain with such tests, however, Leah felt more emotional or psychological discomfort: "Some people said that it [HSG] was painful; it wasn't. The actual surgery stuff doesn't bug me so much as what's going to be the outcome." It was also common for informants to feel embarrassed or humiliated when procedures involved the public viewing of their normally private parts: "Sometimes you're in X ray and they're putting dye in and watching it go up your tubes. You're lying there in stirrups and people are going in and out of the room. I found that humiliating" (Ruth).

Undergoing a laparoscopy was particularly traumatic for some of the informants because they perceived a threat to their lives from general anesthesia: "It's the fear of being put under. You can think of all these things that could happen. What if my heart stops? What if I stop breathing? I don't want to die" (Gillian). For Ginny, the fear of dying was so great that she was unwilling to repeat the laparoscopy. The rationale Ginny used illustrates the strategies of balancing the scales (the fear of death was greater than the desire to pursue diagnostic testing) and protective governing (Ginny was protecting herself from the perceived risk of death by purposefully deciding not to undergo general anesthesia):

> I don't feel that I would do it again. I am scared of the surgery [laparoscopy]. I had a scare last time. I remember laying [in the recovery room] thinking, My blood pressure is going down. I'm going to die. That really scared me. That's weighing a lot on me, going in for another surgery 'cause I'm scared that if they put me out again, then my blood pressure's gonna go down and that I'm gonna die.

In contrast to Ginny, several informants found that their stress levels were usually reduced when tests were repeated and they gained familiarity with them: "The first one [laparoscopy] was the worst. The two after that weren't as bad. . . . You kind of knew what to expect. It was the fear of the unknown, going under the first time" (Gillian). The tests also proved to be less stressful if the informants had had previous experience with other surgical procedures. This was expressed by Leah and Tiffany, respectively: "I'm kind of a veteran around surgery now. So that [laparoscopy] didn't scare me" and "Surgeries really don't scare me because I've been through so many. I was scared when I first started going for them. I know what to expect now; the unexpected is always the worst." The informants' perceptions of the diagnostic procedures were also influenced by the conditions under which the tests were done: "[Laparoscopy is] day surgery. Like to me anything you go for in day surgery, it can't be too complicated. Otherwise, they wouldn't be doing it on a day surgery basis" (Grace).

Informants had feelings of normality when they discovered that their reproductive systems were functioning properly. This did not happen when their reproductive systems were found to be malfunctioning:

> Dr. Q says I'm on a really long cycle. A supposedly normal female does it every so many days [28 days]. I take 43 or 44 days. So this is a lot different. Dr. Q says that most normal females ovulate between the eleventh and fourteenth day. Well, here I am ovulating on my eighteenth and nineteenth day. (Ginny)

This feeling of abnormality was reinforced in the literature read by the informants: "There is a little sheet that comes with the thermometer. My BBT chart was certainly a way more spazzy than that sheet led me to believe" (Jacqueline). Ginny described a similar experience:

> This book [*Insights Into Infertility*] tells you this is the way your [BBT] chart should look. . . . Maybe it is just an exaggerated model of it. A bunch of crap for me. They should also show, don't freak out, don't phone your doctor like I did and say, "What's going on with this chart? How come my temperature is dropping below what is on the chart and I have to write my own numbers on the chart?"

For all but two of the informants, physiological factors underlying the infertile state were discovered in their own bodies (i.e., endometriosis, anovulation, tubal blockage). This discovery often made the informants take ownership of their infertility, which was expressed in comments such as, "I felt like it was my problem, because medically, it was my body" (Jacqueline); "It was my problem. [My husband] had had his sperm count and it was all fine. The laparoscopy had shown there was a blockage. It was clear that something was wrong with my system" (Eve); and "As far as I know, [my husband's] fine, just from those sperm counts he's had. So it's me" (Gillian). Gillian supported her belief that the infertility was "her" problem further by observing her husband's potential fertility with another woman: "I know the problem is with me. If [my husband] was married to somebody else, he'd probably have his 'own' children." Leah, in particular, expressed feelings about the burden of physiologically owning the infertile state: "[My husband's] sperm sample last time . . . was really low. His count has always been very, very high. I said, 'Oh well, so the problem could be yours.' I was almost grateful that someone else could share the problem and that it was off my shoulders for a while."

Although many of the informants owned their infertility at the physiological level, they did identify their infertility as being a combined problem that they shared with their husbands. This combined ownership was expressed in comments such as, "It's both of ours in the sense that we can't have a baby. You have to deal with it as a couple, but it's my body that has problems, not his" (Grace); "It is a shared problem because together, we can't have the children. Even if it's physically mine it involves both of us as a couple" (Gillian); and "It's our problem 'cause I wouldn't be doing this if I was single. If I was single, I wouldn't want to have a baby by myself. It's something that he and I both want together" (Ginny). Several informants also defined the ownership of the infertility in terms of which partner was responsible for carrying out the activities associated with medical intervention. For example:

I feel that it was my project. It wasn't something that we were doing together. Physically, it meant that I had to go for all the testing, take the Clomid, take the progesterone, and I was the one who kept track of the calendar. I was the one that always had to go to the doctor. My husband didn't once go to the doctor except for his sperm test; he just carried on [with] what he was doing in life and I didn't. (Jacqueline)

When the underlying causes of their infertility were discovered, the informants began to put themselves under the microscope as they examined the circumstances surrounding the causes:

My mom had a hard time getting pregnant. . . . It took her four and a half years to get pregnant with me. And then it took her four and a half years on hormone pills to get pregnant with my sister. . . . My grandmother had a hard time, too. So, in my case, it looks like it's hereditary. (Ginny)

I just wonder, why? Like where would these problems [come from]? Like how do they arrive there? How did I end up with both a mucus problem and endometriosis? Another thing about endometriosis, [the doctor] said it could be hereditary. But nobody else in my family has it. That's the one thing I can't figure out, like there are three other sisters and then plus my mom; they've all had kids. What happened in the chain of kids? (Grace)

In the most basic sense, the underlying causes of the infertile state meant that the informants' ability to achieve pregnancy was compromised. For several informants, however, the underlying causes of their infertility held additional meaning. For example, the informants who had endometriosis experienced painful menstruation. In contrast to this "invisible" pain associated with endometriosis, Madeline exhibited "visible" manifestations associated with Stein-Leventhal syndrome (i.e., polycystic ovarian disease). Madeline discussed what these manifestations meant to her:

> My spouse asks me, "Why do you spend half an hour in front of the mirror every day?" I don't tell him that I'm plucking little hairs off my chin. "Why are your legs so bristly?" I have quite a thin spot on top of my head. I have to spend an extra 10 minutes in the morning blow drying my hair in a particular way and using particular products so that the physical manifestations of masculinization are buried. There are those practicalities about dealing with the effects.

Most of the informants felt that they were healthy despite the discovery of the underlying causes of their inability to get pregnant: "I still think I'm healthy. I'm not going there [infertility clinic] 'cause I'm sick" (Grace). Rather than believing herself to be completely healthy, Hilary expressed being "borderline healthy, borderline sick." In contrast, Eve perceived herself as being sick rather than healthy because the underlying cause of her infertility had extended to body parts other than her reproductive system:

> If the endometriosis had been confined to the reproductive tract, I would've regarded myself as healthy. When the doctor told me that it was involved with my bowel and that I might be looking at surgery, that was the point when I felt that I wasn't healthy. That was the critical part for me because the reproductive tract can be taken out and discarded and you can continue. When we're talking about the digestive tract, we're talking about some pretty important stuff here.

Having to undergo bowel surgery for the endometriosis resulted in Eve's feeling "trapped by the body. These things are happening in your body. You've got to go through this [treatment]. This isn't something you choose to do but the rest of your existence is dependent on it."

Undergoing infertility treatment. For most of the informants, pursuing treatment was specifically directed at the achievement of pregnancy. For Madeline, however, the rationale for the treatment alternated between reasons pertaining to the infertile state and gynecological reasons. Madeline balanced the scales between issues relating to life and death:

> I'm going to Dr. H and having the D&Cs more for gynecological than obstetrical reasons because I have the propensity to develop uterine cancer. . . . My doctor says, "Well, a hysterectomy's something that we won't consider right now because she wants to get pregnant." I get the feeling that Dr. H's actively treating my uterine condition if there is one or assessing me for the development of it. . . . The pregnancy is sort of a residual issue that he uses to consider in how he treats me. A person who's going to have uterine cancer makes a deal of their own mortality rather than their own motherhood first.

In the informants' experiences, the acceptance or rejection of the various infertility treatments at the medical level was generally determined by the underlying cause of the infertile state (see Figure 2.4). However, Eve deviated from this guideline when she pursued ovulation induction prophylactically, that is, when an anovulatory state did not exist. Eve employed the strategy of protective governing in viewing ovulation induction under these circumstances as "insurance":

> It's six months after you're off the danazol [for treatment of endometriosis] when the peak number of pregnancies happen and then it declines after that and this was [my] sixth month. Since I wasn't pregnant, and now coming on the decline, I started taking Clomid. It was an insurance that I would ovulate that month just in case I might not.

Once a cause had been discovered, treatments that would either rectify or overcome the cause were identified. For example, inducing ovulation through Clomid administration was a medically appropriate treatment for anovulatory informants. When appropriate treatments were identified, they were then further evaluated by the doctors in relation to the individual informants. Acceptance or rejection of a treatment by a doctor was most often based on the informant's health status: "My [doctor] won't give me Clomid until I'm down below a certain weight. [My doctor] said that it just complicates things and that it's not going to work anyway" (Madeline).

Once the treatments were identified and had received medical acceptance, they then had to be accepted or rejected by informants themselves. In most cases, the informants readily accepted treatments because they believed that they would, indeed, result in pregnancy. There were times,

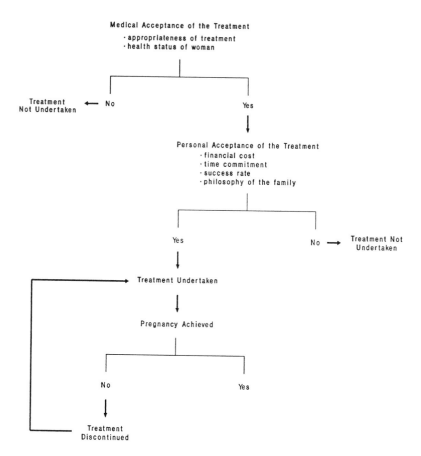

Figure 2.4. Undergoing Infertility Treatment

however, when informants were hesitant to accept suggested treatments. In these instances, the informant would examine the various factors involved with a particular treatment and, through balancing the various factors, accept or reject it. One factor that was weighed included the personal philosophy that the informant and/or her husband had surrounding family. For example, Grace stated:

They asked me if I want[ed] to go on the sperm donor list. . . . We decided that there was no way. [My husband] said, "If you're going to do that, you might as well hop into bed with somebody else." I wouldn't be comfortable. We want something that we could create together. Not anybody else's, whether it's adopting or someone else's sperm.

In addition, informants routinely questioned their acceptance of high-tech treatment options, such as IVF and gamete intrafallopian transfer (GIFT), primarily on the basis of financial cost: "There's in vitro. That all costs money, $4,000 or $5,000. Like that's just for the initial attempt and then, down the road, you can go again. That's not just the extra kind of money we have sitting around" (Grace); "Medically, [GIFT] was an option, but it wasn't financially an option. The procedure would cost thousands of dollars; it was just out of the question. We didn't have that kind of money" (Eve). Grace also looked at the financial cost of IVF from a long-term perspective: "If you have a baby and then you can't afford to take care of it, then that isn't fair." Grace was also cautious about accepting IVF because it was costly in other ways: "They don't do it here. I would have to take time off from work and go [to another city to have it done]. . . . So we didn't know if we'd put ourselves through that."

The informants also considered the success rate of a treatment option while deciding whether to accept or reject it. When the success rate was low, the treatment was often rejected: "It [IVF] doesn't have a very high success rate. I'm not that big a gambler" (Eve). In contrast, a treatment was more likely to be accepted by the informants when it had a higher success rate. The consideration of this factor is illustrated by Grace's assessment of her chances of getting pregnant through Lupron treatment in light of balancing the scales (i.e., before and after treatment; her own chances of achieving pregnancy versus that of other "normal, healthy" women):

> [My doctor] did tell me after this [Lupron] treatment stops, my chance would be about 50%. I think that's pretty good because nobody's chances are ever 100%. I can't remember if it's 60 or 70% [for a normal, healthy female]. So when [my doctor] told me 50%, I thought, oh, well, it sounds good to me; let's do it.

Several informants viewed the pursuit of very expensive treatments having low success rates, such as IVF, as being "the thing of desperation" (Holly) or "grasping at straws. It's your last resort" (Eve). Although she was not undergoing medical care for her infertility at the time, Nora approached the high financial cost and the low success rate associated with IVF by using the strategies of protective governing and balancing the scales:

Every time you try it [IVF], it's thousands and thousands of dollars and there's only a 10% chance that it will work. That's a lot of money for that kind of a success rate. We just don't have that money to spend. Every time you try, you pray that it's going to work and it doesn't work; that's such a big letdown every time you do it.

Once an informant decided to accept a particular treatment, the next step was to take that treatment. Several of the treatments were short-term in nature. For example, ovulation induction with Clomid is a treatment that is completed over five days of the menstrual cycle. Informants using Clomid treatment attempted to achieve pregnancy by engaging in scheduled sex during those five days. If pregnancy was not achieved, they repeated the Clomid in their next menstrual cycle. Another example is IUI, which is done during the ovulatory phase of the woman's menstrual cycle. As with ovulation induction with Clomid, the IUI was repeated in the following menstrual cycle when pregnancy was not achieved.

In contrast to these treatments, there were two informants who pursued long-term infertility treatment with Lupron administration. These informants took monthly injections of Lupron over a period of six months, during which time they did not attempt to get pregnant, through either sexual or technological means. Once the Lupron treatment was completed, the informants attempted to achieve pregnancy.

The treatments discussed thus far were all pursued on an outpatient basis; that is, the informants were not hospitalized. Several informants, however, were hospitalized when they underwent surgery for the treatment of blocked fallopian tubes and/or endometriosis. For two informants, parts of their reproductive systems (e.g., ovary, fallopian tube) were removed. Although one informant did not express concern about this loss, the other did:

Losing the left side was no issue to me. My attitude was, it wasn't doing me any good anyway. So it wasn't of any value. My doctor had assured me that I could function quite well without it. What did concern me were the long-term effects because I was in my early 30s at the time. I had raised that with Dr. A, "Does this mean that you go into menopause instantly?" Dr. A said, "Well, you can go on the hormones." I've been reading lately about different hormones; there are certain concerns about that. (Eve)

Although several informants had undergone surgical treatment for their infertility, Ginny was the only one who focused on the side effects experienced with such treatment:

When I had my operation I couldn't figure out why my brain seemed to be so far away. I kept asking the doctor, "Why do I feel so brain dead?" [My doctor] said that it could have been a combination of the anesthetic and a steroid, plus they also had me on morphine [and] this Lupron. I was just an unbelievable airhead. I couldn't drive a car; it was scary.

Ginny also noted that this surgical treatment left her with a six- to seven-inch scar on her abdomen that "actually makes my body look unattractive."

Rather than focusing on the side effects they experienced with surgical intervention, many of the informants described those associated with ovulation induction through Clomid administration: "I've gained about 10 pounds in the last seven months. I get really severe hot flashes. . . . It's probably closer or worse than when you're in menopause. I'm kind of testy sometimes, like snappy and moody and kind of PMS-y" (Hilary); "I had incredible mood swings. I would get the most incredible hot flushes. . . . My periods were a lot crampier, a lot heavier, a lot more breast tenderness. A lot more fluid retention, an exacerbation of premenstrual syndrome" (Rachel). As Hilary noted, these side effects were often felt in all parts of their lives, including at work: "I find them [hot flushes] very, very uncomfortable especially when I'm working in an office where the heat is intense and the air conditioning doesn't work. I have to walk around or just leave the room 'cause it is unbearable."

When pursuing the various treatment options, the informants some-times incurred financial expenses. Medical treatments, such as ovulation induction with Clomid and danazol treatment for endometriosis, were partially covered through the informants' health care insurance plans or their husbands' plans. Ginny, however, was responsible for the entire financial payment for her Lupron treatment, which was very expensive, ranging anywhere from $365 to $545 "for one shot of it." In contrast to Ginny, Grace, who was planning to pursue Lupron treatment in several months' time, was informed that the financial cost of Lupron was covered by her health care plan.

In contrast to these medical treatments, several informants were re-sponsible for paying the financial costs involved with more extensive treatments, such as IUI and IVF. For example: "Having all of these IUI done, I'm paying for all of this out of my [own] pocket. Like you don't get no funding for any of this" (Grace) and "[IVF] is about $6,000 to $8,000 [as a total figure]. We paid that one [first attempt at IVF]. It was about $6,000, that one" (Leah). As they undertook medical intervention, several informants anticipated attempting IVF at some time later in the future; when entertaining this possible treatment option, these informants considered ways in which they would cope with the financial expenses associated with IVF. For example, Ginny stated: "It's $8,000 one try. [The doctors] said to plan to spend $20,000 'cause it usually takes two times. And plus your . . . food and living expenses [when you're having it done in another city]. We can get the money in our RRSPs [Registered Retirement Savings Plan] or just take out a loan."

After they pursued their treatments, especially surgical treatments, several informants had the expectation that they would be able to achieve pregnancy immediately. This expectation, however, was not fulfilled for Ginny, who stated: "I get out of surgery thinking, it's all over and done with; now we can start trying to get pregnant. And then they slap this six-month hormone shot [Lupron] on us." Nora, who had undergone surgery for blocked fallopian tubes several years previous, also described a similar experience: "The doctor said to me after surgery, 'You'll never be able to have kids on your own.' It was like, What?! I was under the impression that I was going to be able to start having kids right away."

Undergoing infertility treatment was one way in which the informants optimized their reproductive functioning. Although, as noted above, ill effects were frequently experienced with the various treatments, the informants were usually willing to pursue them because they believed that they would achieve pregnancy by doing so.

Increasing the sperm count. Optimizing the male partner's reproductive capabilities involved increasing the sperm count. An attempt was made to increase or at least not lower the count further by having the informants' husbands avoid particular activities that are known or believed to lower the sperm count: "We knew that he had a low sperm count. The interventions to manage that included no hot baths and avoiding tight shorts and tight pants and things like that" (Rachel). When her husband did not avoid these activities, Rachel experienced marital disruption: "He knew the reasons for not taking hot baths and things like that. And yet, he continued to do it. And I thought, 'You just don't care.' That really made me angry." Gina expressed a similar concern:

> You're angry at your husband because there always seems to be some things that he is doing that could be possibly handled a bit differently that might affect the outcome. For example, having lots and lots of hot baths or playing soccer three or four times a week and smoking too many cigarettes.

The man's sperm count was also optimized by having the informant and her husband not engage in intercourse for a certain length of time prior to uniting the gametes, through either sexual or technological means (e.g., IUI). This was explained by Eve and Grace, respectively: "We had that week [during ovulation] slotted off and you're timing. Every other day, you have to wait [to have intercourse] for the sperm to build up"; "When you go for the IUI, you're not supposed to do it three or four days before so there were lots of sperm." Other informants further explained the need to time sexual activity in an attempt to increase the sperm count in comments such as, "If you do have a moment where you feel that you might want to have intercourse you have to check and see if that is a day that you're allowed to" (Ruth) and "We're both in the mood and then you think, well, jeez, maybe we better wait a day 'cause I might ovulate tomorrow, to make sure your sperm count's up" (Ginny).

Engaging in scheduled sex. Most informants attempted to unite the gametes through sexual intercourse. For three informants, however, there were factors involved in their reproductive functioning (i.e., cervical mucus incompatible with husband's sperm, blocked fallopian tubes) that presented barriers to uniting the gametes in this normal way. Thus these informants attempted to unite the gametes through technological means (i.e., IUI, IVF). One of these informants, Grace, did not believe that she could successfully achieve pregnancy through intercourse: "We still had intercourse, but I didn't think of it as a way that I'm gonna get pregnant. From what I understand about this [incompatibility of cervical mucus and sperm], it's impossible." Although her case also involved incompatibility of the cervical mucus and her husband's semen, the second informant, Gina, attempted to unite the gametes through intercourse when her ovulation occurred over the weekend and she was unable to receive IUI at the infertility clinic: "The specialist said to me, 'Why don't you neutralize yourself and try this baking soda douche? At least that way, you can feel like you're still working toward it.' So we did." Similarly, the third informant, Leah, believed that she could possibly get pregnant despite the knowledge that she had blocked fallopian tubes: "There's always a little part of me that thinks, I know there's no miracle. But there's a part of me that goes, every period counts. So I do try to make love around that time." Although Leah engaged in intercourse during her ovulation time, she acknowledged that the procreative element in her sexual relationship was diminished or absent. Leah explained what this did to her feelings toward sexual activity:

It's taken something out of our sex life. It's lost a very special meaning.
It's great to have sex when you're not trying to get pregnant. But to always
have that possibility, "Oh, I forgot my pill." Or even [to] have it back-
burnered for some time that, okay, now we'll have it just for the sake of
sexual passion but we can introduce the element of procreation. When
that's not there it's just sex. Its purpose is questioned.

Uniting the gametes through intercourse implied that the informants
would engage in such activity during the suspected time of their ovulation.
This time was usually determined through use of the BBT chart; thus the
engagement in sexual activity became "sex by the calendar." Several
informants also identified their suspected time of ovulation by observing
other bodily signs indicative of ovulation: "I know because I get very
nauseated. I have mittelschmerz, pain in my side. My mucus is very thin
and very stretchy. And my cervix is very soft and open" (Gillian). Other
informants, such as Madeline, "knew exactly" when they were ovulating
because they used commercial ovulation detection kits.

Once the informants identified the suspected time of their ovulation,
they would then schedule sexual activity during that time. Although
several informants were advised to engage in intercourse every day, most
were instructed to do so on an every-other-day basis during this time "so it
would be days 11, 13, 15, 17" (Rachel). None of the informants but Greer
admitted to planning other aspects of their lives around these days of
suspected ovulation, when sexual activity was scheduled. Greer stated,
"Educational or social commitments were either rejected or postponed and
vacations and business trips were synchronized by ovulation schedules."

There were times when an informant was unable "to circle the date
when I actually ovulate" (Hilary). When this happened in relation to the
BBT chart, the informants would "cover" that time of suspected ovulation. Hilary described how she did this: "To be on the safe side, [my
doctor] said to do it [have sex] from [days] 12 to 17 of my menstrual
cycle." Kate also covered her suspected time of ovulation: "If I've had
sex on this day and the temperature drops the next day, then that night,
wow! 'cause I would not have wanted to have missed that day and maybe
the next day, it'd be too late. So you might do it twice in a row just to
make sure you got the time covered." In addition to being advised by their
doctors as to when they should engage in sexual activity, Holly was also
told to "make it fun"; Rachel was told to "have fun trying."

For many of the informants, the need to engage in scheduled sex often
occurred when they and/or their husbands were not interested in engaging
in sexual activity. This situation was emphasized by Kate: "When you're

ovulating, it's kind of like, it's time to perform. You have to have sex when you're really not wanting to or you're not quite in the mood." Losing control in their sexual relationships was further described by two other informants:

> It didn't matter how tired you were or how bad the day had been. It was the concept of having to. There was no consent; it wasn't something that you could decide to do or you would like to do. "Like" never came into it. (Eve)

> You feel like you've lost control. You have to do something that you really don't want to do. There were times when we were supposed to have sex and we really didn't want to, but I would force [my husband] and then force myself. (Rachel)

Rachel observed a further loss of control in her sexual relationship when her engagement in sexual activity was driven by the knowledge that she had taken Clomid: "You have no control over your sex life anymore. It seemed that way because you weren't having sex because you wanted to. You were having sex because you took these pills."

The informants employed various strategies to help them manage the need for scheduled sex. Rachel acknowledged the importance of these strategies by saying, "You think, well, jeez, I'm going to have to do something to make sex more exciting tonight. You have to try and do something so that it's more pleasant." The most common strategy that informants used was the creation of a social setting that would facilitate their engagement in sexual activity. Sometimes, this was created simply through the showing of affection: "As soon as he'd come home from work, I'd rush up and give him big kisses and hugs. . . . He'd sort of get the idea" (Rachel). At other times, the informants created the setting through more extensive plans. For example: "With our Polaroid camera, I took some pictures in a negligee. When he came home, he was like, 'Wow!' " (Kate); "I'd cook a nice dinner and we'd have a little wine with dinner. I'd try to make it more of a romantic event" (Rachel). In addition to going out to dinner and sometimes a hotel, Ruth managed the need for scheduled sex by having "scene nights": "One night, [when my husband] came home, I had a beach set up. I moved all the furniture to the dining room. And I had a sun lamp and I was in a bathing suit and we had a picnic." Rather than using strategies shortly before the time of scheduled sex, Kate attempted to heighten her husband's libido several hours before the anticipated time of sexual activity: "Sometimes just getting things ready. Leave a little note stick-it in his lunch. I'd just say like, 'When you get home be ready to turn the oven on' or 'Get warmed up' or 'I'll be waiting for you.' " In contrast to these strategies, Eve attempted to make a pleasant social environment by avoiding situations that would decrease the likelihood of engaging in intercourse: "It doesn't matter what he says. It doesn't matter what happens. We can't have a tiff. Tonight's the night!"

There were times when informants purposefully decided not to fulfill the obligation of scheduled sex. In this situation, the informants incorporated their infertility into their lives. This is illustrated by Kate's comment: "This month it was 11 o'clock before [my husband] got home and I had a bad day with kids. I didn't wait up for him. I went to bed and said, 'Tough!' " Rachel provided a similar example:

> I'd come home from work and I'd just be exhausted. You'd think, tonight's the night we have to have sex and the last thing I want to do is have sex. You try to get your husband interested and he's not interested at all. And you kind of say, to hell with it.

In most cases, deciding not to fulfill the obligation was acceptable to both the informants and their husbands. Rachel, however, experienced marital disruption: "We ended up fighting about it more than we ended up doing it. He just wouldn't be up to it or didn't want to. Quite often, I would get very angry with him." There were also times when Rachel was unable to fulfill the obligation because "we were changing back and forth between working my shift and [my husband] was working some shift work, too. So it was hit and miss."

When they did not fulfill the obligation of scheduled sex, informants frequently felt that their participation in medical intervention had been wasted. This was expressed in comments such as, "I always had to visit the doctor when I was on Clomid to make sure that the ovaries weren't getting too big. So that was kind of a wasted visit" (Jacqueline) and "When our schedules didn't mesh, we never did have sex. You kind of wasted these [Clomid] pills. Going through all this havoc and side effects for nothing" (Rachel). A sense of a "missed opportunity" was also felt by the informants: "Some months ended up getting really lost. There was a sense of missed opportunity; maybe that gambling mentality of, this might have been the only chance." Eve also noted that "to not fulfill our obligation that night, you might lose a whole month; the pressure was on. If we don't, then it'll be another month." Rather than simply accepting this consequence, Kate, in particular, attempted to recapture the missed opportunity:

I knew that if we had sex tonight that was a day I could get pregnant. But we were just too exhausted. You just don't feel like it. Even though you know it's the crucial time you let it slip. And you don't mind letting it slip to the next morning. And then you think, jeez! Missed it. And then you would have sex that next night thinking, well, jeez, maybe this is okay. Do you think the egg's still hanging around?

At other times, informants and their husbands simply accepted the need to engage in scheduled sex in order to avoid missing an opportunity for conception to occur. This was expressed in comments such as, "You have a horrendous day and you're just wiped out and you still have to. That could be the one day that I'm going to ovulate and I wouldn't want to miss it" (Hilary) and "I'd say, 'Yeah, we have to do it because otherwise, what if this is the right day?' So we decided to go through the motions even though you really didn't feel like it" (Jacqueline). In these instances, the informants incorporated the infertility into their lives. Ruth was also motivated to fulfill the obligation because "this is something we have to do; it is a temporary [means to an end]. We both knew it wouldn't last forever. You can live with anything for a short period of time knowing there's an end to it." In contrast, Ginny fulfilled the obligation of scheduled sex in order to avoid a confrontation with her doctor:

It is hard when you are under a microscope and Dr. Q is going like, "You ovulated here. You should have been doing it here." When you're under the microscope that's when you're sitting back thinking, hmmm. Well, if we don't do it here, the doctor's going to say that we should have been doing it here. So let's go to the bedroom and let's do it.

Fulfilling the obligation of scheduled sex implied that the informants and their husbands engaged in intercourse for the primary purpose of procreating rather than for pleasure. Thus sexual activity was often viewed as the means to the end (the achievement of pregnancy). This was expressed in comments such as, "You're not having sex just for the pleasure of having sex and being close to someone you love. You're doing it because you want to procreate" (Rachel) and "You want to conceive a baby out of it. So it's not just lust and passion" (Hilary). When engaging in sexual activity for "making a baby," informants often viewed sexual intercourse as "a chore because you're not making love to show your love to each other anymore. You're making love to have a baby" (Tiffany).

When intercourse was being engaged in for "making a baby" rather than for "making love," it became a mechanical task to be accomplished at a specific time. Informants experienced a loss of spontaneity in their sexual relationships: "When we were supposed to have sex, it was so forced. Neither one of us really expressed much interest in it. It wasn't the spontaneous and loving thing that it had been before" (Rachel). When the sexual relationship was approached from this perspective, a sense of depersonalization surrounded it because the sexual partners were valued for their procreative attributes rather than their humanity. As Rachel commented, "One night, [my husband] said to me, 'You want me to perform just to have kids. That's it.' " The informants' desire to engage in sexual intercourse was sometimes absent during the nonovulatory phase of their menstrual cycles " 'cause it didn't mean anything. Even if you had it, you weren't going to get pregnant. It was kind of like, what's the point?"

Initially, engaging in scheduled sex was not problematic for many of the informants. Over time, however, this task became more difficult to complete. This was expressed in comments such as, "For the first few months it was sort of a game. After a while, it lost its novelty" (Rachel) and "You might view it as a bit of an adventure or something funny, originally. But you don't after you've done it for 12 or 13 months. There's nothing very humorous about it" (Eve). In contrast, Jacqueline found fulfilling the obligation of scheduled sex to be more stressful in the beginning than toward the end: "Initially, I think it put some pressure on us like, we have to do this for this result rather than just spontaneously because you want to. We found after a while it would be the right time and we would just think, oh, that's nice!" The informants acknowledged that engaging in scheduled sex was more difficult for their husbands than it was for them. Despite this, they denied that their husbands experienced difficulty with sexual performance (e.g., erectile difficulties). Jacqueline, however, admitted that "the only time [my husband] had trouble was when I had to go in for the PCT and we had to have intercourse at 7:30 in the morning."

Fulfilling the obligation of scheduled sex permeated every aspect of the sexual relationship. For example, there was frequently a role reversal about who would initiate sexual activity. This was described by Hilary and Rachel, respectively: "I'm the one initiating it, while before, it was the man always did the initiating"; "It was always me instigating sex. It was never him, which is abnormal because both of us seem to initiate sex equally as the other does [when infertility was not being experienced]." Kate noted that "if you know you're going to ovulate that particular day and he's not in the mood at all, then the woman does all the foreplay to get sex." Kate added that penile-vaginal intercourse was the focus of sexual activity, rather than other forms of activity such as fellatio or masturbation:

When you're trying to get pregnant, like if you have oral intercourse or whatever you stop just before; it has to be intercourse. Like you don't want him to ejaculate when he's not inside because then you think you waste it. If you're not trying to get pregnant, then it wouldn't matter.

The experience of being sexually active was also different for the informants when they were seeking pregnancy compared with when they were not seeking pregnancy. Holly described this: "Sometimes, we didn't even kiss. That was how bad it was. It was just, let's just do this." Kate also noted that "the passion's not there. You go to bed and it's man on top of woman and you go through [the motions] and it takes five seconds and it's over. With other times it can be an hour long." Holly also stated that the thought "a baby, please; a baby" would often fill her mind as she engaged in intercourse.

After engaging in intercourse, the informants frequently changed their activities in order to increase the likelihood of conception occurring. These changes were identified in comments such as, "They say to put pillows underneath yourself after. Don't get up. I've done all that stuff so the semen doesn't run out" (Gillian) and "I would always stay in bed on my back when I was trying to get pregnant. You have to keep the semen inside of you so you just lay there" (Jacqueline). Immediately following intercourse, it was not uncommon for the informants to think about conceiving a pregnancy and having a baby. For example, after intercourse Nora would pray, "Please God, let it happen now"; Tiffany would just "lay there and talk about babies."

Stage 3: The Letdown

When the informants initially began medical intervention, they generally expected that they would, indeed, become pregnant. Thus they were not prepared for the event of not getting pregnant. When this happened, however, they experienced a letdown: "I really hope for it and then when it doesn't happen, it's a letdown" (Nora). This led the informants to acknowledge the letdown, experience its emotional wound, and respond to it.

Acknowledging the Letdown

For the informants, the most obvious sign that pregnancy had not been achieved was the onset of menstruation: "There's nothing more real than bright red blood. It's pretty undeniable [that you're not pregnant]" (Leah). Many informants were consumed with the activity of "looking for blood

. . . to see whether or not you're getting your period" (Jacqueline). Ruth noted that "every time when I went to the bathroom, I was afraid to wipe because there might be red on the tissue." The meaning of menstrual blood remained with the informants even after pregnancies had been conceived and delivered. This was especially true for Ruth, who stated: "Every time I menstruate or go to the bathroom, I still look at that tissue. My first day of menstruation is an unsettling day for me; it brings back all those feelings." Ruth elaborated on her feelings surrounding menstruation:

I don't even mark my menstruation down on the calendar anymore. When I went for my checkup, I had no idea when my last menstrual period was. I knew I had had one but I really didn't know what days. I had to guesstimate. It's almost like I've gone back the other way. I'm not going to keep count at all. I grew to just absolutely hate my menstruation.

Bodily signs other than menstrual blood also indicated to the informants that they had not achieved pregnancy. For example: "I had all the other symptoms; I get premenstrual cramps and I get cranky. And my face breaks out. And I gain a pound or two" (Kate). The nonachievement of pregnancy was also acknowledged when the informants received a negative result on a pregnancy test. Finally, informants knew that pregnancy had not been achieved "because you missed having intercourse during those days [of suspected ovulation]" (Kate).

As time passed and they did not get pregnant, the informants came to realize that achieving pregnancy was not guaranteed by medical intervention. Having this experience of "failed" intervention, informants began to prepare themselves for the event of not achieving pregnancy. This preparation often entailed approaching the suspected time of menstruation with an attitude of guarded optimism in an attempt to protect themselves from the emotional hurt that was usually felt when the letdown occurred:

I'm not gonna get my hopes up. It's not worth it. It's hard on me. When Dr. F finally says to me yes or no, then that's when I'll believe. But until then, it's not worth it to get all excited because I've been let down so many times. (Hilary)

From about the 27th or 28th day on, I'd be looking for it [menstrual period] and it wouldn't come. And I'd think, Ah! Wow! Well, maybe I'm pregnant, and get a little bit excited. Not really excited because I'd had too many disappointments in the past. I figured, I'm not going to get excited. I'm not going to worry about it because it's not going to do any good. So I'll just wait and see if I get my period. (Rachel)

Whereas these informants appeared to have reached a state of guarded optimism toward the achievement of pregnancy, Tiffany demonstrated a continued ambivalence:

I don't get myself as worked up anymore; when it [menstrual period] comes, it comes. I kind of think that way but I kind of don't. You have to say like, I'm not going to worry about it. But yet, I am. Even to go for a pregnancy test or making love, in my heart it's just like, we're going to make a baby, or it's going to be positive. But yet, my mind is saying, Don't do this to yourself. That's something that I found was very hard trying to decipher on which feeling to go with. Do I try to relax and try to calm myself down or do I just go with the excitement? It's just a feeling that I kind of got, like I'm going, okay, well, it's negative. But I keep thinking, in the back of my mind or in my heart, this other feeling: well, I could be pregnant.

Although many of the informants prepared themselves emotionally for the letdown, none but Leah prepared herself physically:

This time [third attempt with IVF], I set up a plan for myself in case I did get my period. I bought a really nice pair of panties and had a pad in it already. I was preparing that if my period comes, that I'd have something to take care of myself.

When the informants acknowledged the letdown, they became aware of the consequences of the letdown: "I have to try again" (Holly); "I've got to take those [Clomid] pills again" (Rachel).

Experiencing the Emotional Wound

When pregnancy was not achieved, all the informants experienced the emotional wound of infertility. Most often felt with the onset of menstruation, this stage included feelings of depression, frustration, devastation, and hopelessness. These feelings were expressed in comments such as, "It got depressing and frustrating after you got your period" (Grace); "That period is just like devastation. It's like hitting rock bottom. Everything you've hoped for is gone" (Tiffany); and "When your period came you'd cry. I would be so cranky. I'd be so down in the dumps" (Gillian). The informants also felt the emotional wound of the letdown when a pregnancy test was negative: "I thought for sure it was positive. They [staff at doctor's office] said, 'It's negative.' And I was like, ah! I can't believe it. I tried not to sound too disappointed even though I was devastated inside" (Hilary).

The emotional wound of infertility went beyond the events of menstruation and negative pregnancy tests. For example, many of the informants felt a sense of failure because "all the success would be measured by is if you get pregnant. Everything else is a failure. Each month, you're no closer to your goal than you were the day you started" (Ruth). Informants often directed this sense of failure at their bodies and at their lack of control over their bodily functioning. This was expressed in comments such as, "I felt like my body had failed me. I felt like my body and my mind were not quite in sync" (Jacqueline) and "It's the powerlessness to deal with something that most people can and I can't. I can deal with a lot of things, legal matters and difficult people and technical questions, but I can't [deal with] that" (Madeline). Eve, in particular, felt a sense of betrayal when experiencing the letdown: "I definitely felt that I had been betrayed someplace along the line by some supernatural force. There's no reason why I should be picked out or singled out; they could have dealt the cards a little bit more evenly." Several informants perceived their infertility as a punishment for ill deeds done in their pasts. Eve noted: "That's part of my upbringing that if something bad happens to you, it's your own doing. For me, it was related to premarital sexual exploits. I may have been messing around when I shouldn't have been messing around." Greer also expressed anger when reflecting on her past: "I was angry at myself for everything [previous relationships, use of birth control pills for extended periods of time] I did in my past that may have contributed to our infertility."

Responding to the Letdown

When the informants did not achieve pregnancy, they routinely repeated medical intervention. As time passed, often months evolving into years, many became more desperate as they were caught up in the vicious cycle of repeating the various activities. For many of the informants, this desperation was often felt in response to "being up against the clock" in terms of their ages: "It took [my mom] five years between my eldest sister and my middle sister. But I keep thinking, I don't have five years. Not at 28 years old and not when my husband's in his mid-30s" (Tiffany). The informants stated that they were able to persist with medical intervention simply because "there's a light at the end of the tunnel and it'll all work out in the end" (Hilary) or "there was an end in sight and we knew that we wouldn't have to continue with this forever" (Eve). Although not explicitly stated by many informants, the persistence with medical intervention was undergirded by the hope that their participation would, indeed, be worth it in terms of achieving a pregnancy. For example, Grace stated: "We'd say, like, why are we doing all this? Like hopefully, it's worth it." Many of the informants were willing to experience the ill effects associated with the interventions simply because they wanted to get pregnant so badly. The informants' willingness to do this was guided by the strategy of protective governing:

> There's something that can help my problem [anovulation]. If that's what it takes, that's what it takes, even if I have to go through these hot sweats. I hope that it will be worth it. If it doesn't happen, at least I tried. I can't live my life thinking, "If I could've . . ." So that's just the facts of life if you want to have a baby. (Hilary)

In addition to repeating medical intervention, informants responded to the letdown with a variety of strategies: (a) changing doctors, (b) releasing themselves from the responsibility of the infertility, (c) feeling better off in comparison to other people, (d) adopting, (e) parenting vicariously, (f) ventilating their feelings and concerns surrounding their infertility, (g) normalizing, and (h) escaping from their infertility. The informants employed the strategies of repeating medical intervention and changing doctors in attempting to achieve pregnancy; they used the remaining strategies in attempting to change their personal responses to their inability to achieve pregnancy. Many of these latter strategies can be seen as examples of protective governing.

Changing doctors. Changing doctors frequently occurred when the women were referred from a general practitioner to a specialist or from one specialist to another. However, there was some evidence of "doctor hopping," or moving from one doctor to another because of dissatisfaction with care or failure to achieve pregnancy. Gillian provides one example: "The infertility specialist put me on danazol; it's not working. So I switched to another specialist. I thought, well, another opinion. I had heard that this other [specialist] was really good." Gillian switched doctors again later when pregnancy was still not achieved with the second specialist.

Although the informants recognized the value of a technological focus to infertility management, they were also concerned about their need for emotional support. In attempting to balance these components of medical care, they sometimes changed doctors.

The women were also influenced by the ages of their doctors. Some preferred older doctors, as they found this less embarrassing, but for informants who had always had younger doctors this was not a factor. Another characteristic that was important was whether or not the doctors were willing to spend time talking with them. However, for these women, medical-technological expertise was more critical than bedside manner in their choice of doctors.

Releasing oneself from responsibility. Some informants provided explanations as to why they did not get pregnant. By placing the responsibility beyond themselves, it seemed that they were protecting themselves from the letdown of not being pregnant: "There was a sense of someone taking the responsibility for you. Dr. A has given you a drug, timed your cycle for you. If it doesn't work it's not something I've done wrong; either the body's failing or someone else has miscalculated" (Eve). Other informants gave the responsibility for pregnancy to God. Kate said: "I really believe that God has our lives planned out and He's in control. And if it's not in His plan for us to have a baby, then there's not much I can do about it." When giving God control over their fertility, some informants attempted to bargain: "With my PID [pelvic inflammatory disease], they said I might have to have a complete hysterectomy. I remember making one of those pacts with God. I said, 'If You let me keep my uterus I'll start believing in You' " (Leah). Hilary also commented, "If God would grant me just one kid then I'd be happy." Some informants also expressed anger at God when they did not become pregnant: "I get really mad at God; it's kind of up to God to give me a baby and why won't God give me a baby?" (Leah). There was also concern that God was unfair, in that women who do not want babies are able to conceive, whereas these informants were left barren.

Feeling better off. Some informants coped by comparing themselves with others who are less fortunate and finding themselves better off. Jacqueline said: "It's like Ann Landers used to say, 'You shouldn't feel bad if your feet are misshaped; look at the person who can't walk.' There's always someone worse off than you." By thinking of the ways in which they were better off than others, the informants minimized their emotional hurt and protected themselves from feeling the full impact of their infertility.

Adopting. When pregnancy was not achieved, informants began to change their goals. Some moved to compensate for the lack of a child by deciding to adopt. However, they needed to be sure, in their own minds, that it was impossible to achieve pregnancy before they took this step. Thus adoption was definitely a compensation, not a primary choice. Nora said, "Before we go through adoption I wanna know that there's no way I can get pregnant myself and have our own kid." Hilary made a similar comment: "If we've tried every angle to conceive and have a child and we can't, we can adopt." Holly was afraid pregnancy would be a major health risk, so she applied for adoption while seeking infertility treatment. Her previous health history made Holly unique in the study group.

Adoption was rejected by some informants for a variety of reasons: The wait for public adoption was too long, private adoption was too expensive, the partner was not supportive of adoption, or the couple already had one child. When a couple had previous experience of adoption—for example, if they themselves or their own siblings had been adopted—they tended to accept the process more readily: "My husband was adopted by his stepfather; we don't have a problem with adoption" (Tiffany). The informant's desire for pregnancy versus desire for a child was also influential in determining whether adoption would be accepted: "It's great being pregnant, but the outcome of being pregnant is the point we're trying to get to. . . . If adoption's the only way we can have a family, then that's the way we'd go" (Nora). When considering adoption, Leah likened pregnancy and the parenting role to a wedding and marriage: "Pregnancy is nine months and motherhood a lifetime. It's like a wedding is a day and a marriage is a lifetime. What I really want is to be a mom."

Two informants did adopt babies. This process also put them "under the microscope" in that they had the "feeling you have to prove you will be worthwhile parents" (Greer). Gillian was concerned that one had to expose one's own and one's family's values in order to adopt, but that this was not required of parents who had a child naturally. Feelings of anger, differentness, and unfairness were all expressed by the women who had adopted. They continued to experience feelings of loss of control and powerlessness as others decided whether or not they should have children. For example, Leah stated:

> When you get pregnant and have your own kid, no one's checking your home or how you live or what your values are or your opinions on disciplining children. [When you adopt] you have to get permission to be a parent from someone else. It's just one more case where parenthood is in the hands of others. If I could get pregnant on my own I'd just be pregnant.

Parenting vicariously. To protect themselves from a life that did not involve children, several informants experienced the parenting role vicariously. Nora noted, "If I can't have kids, it's great being around other people's kids." Grace attended her niece's ball games and became a godmother; Ginny joked that she "rented a kid" when she invited a friend's daughter to share a meal with her and her husband. Many informants also baby-sat their friends' children, although some, such as Eve and Judith, found it painful to be taking care of other people's children when they had none of their own. Rachel enjoyed the parenting role vicariously when she worked as an obstetric nurse: "I was getting a lot of satisfaction working with these mothers and helping them breast-feed and helping with their babies. 'If I couldn't have a baby I'm sure going to help this woman.' " Ginny, in particular, noted that she experienced pregnancy vicariously: "It's just like I'm going through [my girlfriends'] pregnancies with them, because I'll sit with my hand on their stomachs, feeling the baby move." In another form of vicarious parenting, Leah compensated for her lack of a child by lavishing affection on her two cats. All the women appeared in some way to experience childbearing or parenting vicariously as a means of compensating for their own loss.

Ventilating feelings and concerns. Most of the informants had told others about their infertility. This allowed them to vent their feelings and concerns: "It's not so much letting people know about it but talking about it. If I didn't have anybody to talk to I would be eating myself inside out" (Ginny). All but one of the informants, Madeline, talked to their husbands about their infertility. Madeline lived in an ongoing relationship with a partner but was afraid her infertility "would be the determining factor in our continuing relationship." She further explained, "I'm protecting my place in the relationship."

The informants found it valuable to talk with other infertile persons, because they understood the problem and could either sympathize or empathize. As Ruth said: "I felt the most support from people who I met in the infertility clinic or someone who had been through it. I had a girlfriend who had [been infertile], so she knew what I was feeling." Jacqueline also felt close to other infertile women: "We had something to share and here was someone you could talk to about it. You just don't understand unless you go through it. It's like if someone experiences a death in the family, you can feel sympathetic but you don't feel empathetic unless you've experienced it." Grace's mother had a hard time understanding the problem because "every time she turned around she was pregnant." It was easier to seek understanding from a "kindred spirit." Despite this, none of the informants took part in a formal peer support group, although Madeline believed such a group could be a useful source of information.

Rachel and Gina knew other women who were having problems getting pregnant. They talked together as a group, comparing treatments and discussing the effects on their husbands, their marriages, and their lives. Eve and Madeline, in an effort to protect themselves, did not talk about their infertility with others. Eve noted: "We didn't want to open ourselves up to everyone else's doctoring. So we primarily avoided the topic." Madeline, who had Stein-Leventhal syndrome, attempted to protect herself from being seen as abnormal:

> It's just another indication that you're a little abnormal. I have enough indications that I'm not exactly normal—the manifestations of hormonal imbalance. The extra hair here [chin], thin here [top of head]—the masculinization features. It's that kind of thing that distracts from your physical wholeness. Why should I talk about the negative aspects of my health? People have enough reason to stereotype you or to pigeonhole you or to be prejudiced. I'm not going to give them anything more to fuel the fire.

Normalizing. In attempting to protect themselves from being different, the informants sought normality in two ways. Leah avoided associating with other infertile women to protect herself from the infertility identity:

> I didn't want anything to do with other infertile women. If I hang around with them, then I'm one of them. So I held them at arm's length. I refused to be supported by them when I was in the IVF clinic. They'd talk to me and I was just like an ice princess 'cause I was trying to be different. I was going to be the one who was going to get pregnant. If I was looking at them I'd be looking at myself. Like their pain is my pain.

In contrast, others sought a sense of normality through associating with other infertile persons. These informants found it easier to live with their infertility when they knew others who had similar status. They compared the resemblances they observed between themselves and other infertile women through talking with them. Gillian, in particular, sought to normalize her own infertility experience by having indirect contact with other infertile women through her involvement in this study: "I was interested to know what other women have gone through, how other women feel about it, how they deal with it; to see if their experiences are comparable to my experience."

Several informants also sought to normalize their infertility experiences by reading about infertility. Grace noted that this happened for her: "That book I read, it's really helped. It's very normal for what I'm going through to have these feelings; it's not abnormal. Before I was thinking like, what's the matter with me?" On the other hand, it was sometimes difficult for informants to find literature specific to their own physical problems so they could gain a sense of physiological normality: "I've read eight books on infertility; by the fifth book they all say the same thing. There's nothing new here. You're looking for something different so you can say, ah, that's my problem!" (Kate).

Seeing other infertile women achieve pregnancy created feelings of hope in the informants: "There were patients that I took a lot of comfort from because they were having babies and they had had fertility problems. I'd get this glimmer of hope and think, well, maybe it will happen to me" (Rachel). Despite gleaning hope from the news of pregnancy, it could also be a source of pain. As Jacqueline said: "I wanted them to tell me about it but it did make me feel kind of crummy because I'd think, well, why not me?" Hope was also generated when they saw women who had adopted become pregnant. This happened to Ginny and Nora, who both reacted by thinking, "Why not me?" When Rachel achieved pregnancy, she noted that it created distance between her and her nonfertile peers:

> I had moved on to another stage and they were still left behind. . . . We weren't quite on the same wavelength anymore. . . . I feel more empathy toward them . . . because I've been there. But I also know what it's like to be a mother now and to have gone through a pregnancy and the delivery. . . . [I've gone] the whole nine yards.

Escaping from infertility. Informants found relief by distancing themselves from their infertility in a variety of ways. For example, several informants found escape through their employment: "It keeps my mind off of this infertility" (Hilary); "Nobody knew all that [infertility]. You could just, for a while, pretend or just forget about that part of life" (Jacqueline). However, several informants stated that they were reminded of their inability to achieve pregnancy when coworkers became pregnant: "This young girl at work, when she came in and announced her pregnancy, I had to leave the office because I was going to cry" (Tiffany).

At her place of work, Hilary noted that "all the girls have either had babies or are pregnant. So you sit at lunch and that's all you hear. I feel like saying, 'Can we change the subject?' " Several informants who worked within a hospital setting were also confronted with their infertility when they saw women pregnant who did not want to be pregnant and/or women who had had previous therapeutic abortions. For example: "It is hard to think that these people [teenage moms] are coming in and they really didn't want to have these babies and I'd really like to have a baby and I was having trouble having one" (Rachel); "When you have a patient who's had several therapeutics and now they have this baby, you think, 'How many babies did you just throw away?' I could squash them. I feel very angry, like, 'What have you done?' " (Gillian).

The informants also escaped from their infertility by becoming involved with other things in their lives. For example, when taking an educational course, Kate thought, "If I'm busy studying all the time it'll take it off my mind. It's keeping me busy. It gives you something to do during the day. So your mind is preoccupied some of the time." Holly found that taking vacations was a great way to escape her infertility because "you were in a little dream world. You didn't have to worry about the infertility. You forgot about everything." Although vacationing allowed Holly to escape physically from the management of her infertility, it did not always necessarily provide a mental escape: "When I was going to bed, I'd be laying there. I'd toss and turn and I'd touch base again with what was happening."

Informants also escaped from their infertility by socializing with friends who did not have children, because "if you did go out with someone who had children, they'd be talking about them even if the kids weren't there" (Holly); further, childless friends "don't have to worry about [getting a baby-sitter]" (Grace). In addition to avoiding friends who had children, Grace avoided her mother-in-law, because "I'm sick with trying to explain things to her. I thought, it's better to stay away from her than always having to try to explain things to her." Greer described her use of the avoidance tactic: "I would avoid baby showers, parties, and family outings when I knew children would be present. I became very good at avoiding situations and people who would remind me of my infertility."

Stage 4: The Exit From Medical Intervention

The fourth and final stage of pregnology is the exit from medical intervention. According to the informants' experiences, there are two basic avenues of exit: The first and most desired involves the informant's achievement of pregnancy; the second involves the informant's decision to discontinue medical intervention despite not achieving pregnancy.

Achieving Pregnancy

When they undertook medical intervention, the informants lived under the microscope as they looked for bodily symptoms implying that pregnancy had been achieved. For all the informants, a late or missed menstrual period suggested pregnancy. It was also suspected when other bodily symptoms were experienced, such as "really full breasts, tenderness, any kind of nausea" (Gillian). In contrast to these signs of pregnancy, Grace focused on the lack of symptoms associated with menstruation: "With my period I get a lot of pain. I wasn't getting any of that. And then you get all these positive thoughts."

When suspecting that they were pregnant, most informants had urine pregnancy tests done, either in a health care facility (medical center or doctor's office) or in their own homes (commercial testing kits). There were two informants, however, who did not do this. Rachel, for example, did not pursue pregnancy testing immediately upon suspecting pregnancy because "I figured you'd have to wait at least two weeks after your missed period before you got an accurate test. I didn't want to get my hopes up. There was no sense in going before it would show anything." On the other hand, Leah purposefully underwent an early pregnancy test prior to observing signs of pregnancy because "I hated the waiting so much. I didn't want to wait and have my excitement build with each day. . . . I was prepared for the worst when the blood did come. That was better than getting the excitement built up." Note that both Rachel's and Leah's decisions as to when to go for a pregnancy test were guided by the strategy of protective governing.

When the informants got the "Big P"—that is, when the pregnancy test was positive—they received objective information that they had probably achieved pregnancy. For these four informants, achieving pregnancy meant that their dreams had come true. It also meant that medical intervention could be discontinued; however, one informant continued with medical intervention (i.e., progesterone suppositories) to maintain the conceived pregnancy. For the informants who passed through the final stage of pregnology this way, the achievement of pregnancy was a very happy and joyous event.

Of the 17 informants, 8 achieved pregnancy while under medical care but lost their initial conceived pregnancies, either through spontaneous abortion (7 of the women) or through ectopic pregnancy (1 woman). These 8 informants reentered pregnology when they began to repeat medical intervention following their reproductive loss. Of this group, 4 have subsequently made permanent exits from pregnology by achieving, maintaining, and delivering subsequent pregnancies; 1 of the remaining 4 is continuing with intervention, and 3 have discontinued it in the absence of pregnancy.

Discontinuing Medical Intervention

Of the 17 informants, 5 discontinued intervention in the absence of pregnancy. Several informants who are currently in the stage of pursuing medical intervention anticipate discontinuing treatment at some time in the future, even if they have not achieved pregnancy. In addition, several informants who exited from pregnology by achieving pregnancy described times when they entertained the thought of discontinuing their treatment in the absence of pregnancy. On the basis of the informants' experiences, it appears that they had to pass through a phase of *letting go.*

Letting go of the pursuit of pregnancy through medical intervention was extremely difficult for the informants. Jacqueline commented: "You're caught up in the process [of medical intervention]. You continue because the more energy you put into it, the more you want to resolve the infertility and the more you don't want to abandon what you have already done." Leah also found it difficult to let go because "as long as you have the possibility [of getting pregnant], it's very hard to turn your back on it regardless of how small the possibility is."

Deciding to terminate the intervention without achieving pregnancy meant that the informants could "get on with their lives" by making plans that excluded having a family. When anticipating a "future" child-free life, the informants would sometimes speculate on what it would entail for them. For example: "I'll make a career change. We both enjoy sports. So we thought, we should buy season tickets to hockey or football games or start planning holidays. Like all the things that people who have kids can't do" (Grace); "[After quitting medical intervention,] I registered to go back and do my degree. I just said, forget it. We'll work our buns off, make big bucks, retire early, and travel. To heck with having kids" (Rachel). Although Ruth was planning to adopt a child, she chose to live a child-free life while waiting for the adoption to be realized:

> I had put it behind me that I couldn't have kids. [My husband] and I had planned to go to Europe. I got accepted at the university. I had made these

new plans. I knew that at the end of the tunnel, I was going to get a little baby, but in the meantime, I had made plans.

To discontinue medical intervention, the five informants simply stopped their participation in the required activities. For four of them, termination of treatment was done quickly. Rachel, however, made the "mental" decision to terminate intervention but continued to participate. The inconsistency between Rachel's thoughts and her actions continued for several months, until finally she abruptly stopped the medical intervention. Her terminating intervention in this fashion was influenced by outside forces: "I had just finished a 35-day cycle. The day before my period started, my sister-in-law had a baby. I just said, forget it. It's bad enough to get your period and then here's this sister-in-law and she had a baby. I'm just going to quit trying."

According to the informants' experiences, letting go of the pursuit of pregnancy through medical intervention involved three factors: doing everything possible, perceiving risk, and committing to pregnancy.

Doing everything possible. The first factor that influenced the decision to let go was whether the informants had attempted all medical interventions that were available and acceptable to them. This was reflected in comments such as, "I'm not there yet [terminating] but I do feel closer. If this [third attempt at IVF] doesn't work, I'll know I'll be one step closer to saying that. This is the way that I'm doing it [letting go]" (Leah) and "A doctor would have to tell me, 'There's nothing else we can do for you.' There'd have to be some kind of closure, that's for sure" (Jacqueline). Holly stopped medical intervention simply because she perceived continuing to be a fruitless activity, as no treatment options were available. AID was available to Ruth, but she found it unacceptable; this resulted in her discontinuing intervention: "We weren't going to have that [AID]. If I was going to have someone else's child, I might as well adopt and we would both have somebody else's child."

Perceiving risk. The second factor in letting go involved the informant's deciding to terminate medical intervention in order to protect herself and/or others from perceived risk resulting from the continuation of intervention. The informants identified various risks associated with continuing medical intervention. For example, the cost of IVF was high and Leah decided to protect her husband and herself from financial risk. She also anticipated further attempts would be discouraged by the IVF team: "After three times [of IVF], they do sit down and talk with you about further attempts, 'Maybe this is not working for you. We don't recommend you do this again.' " Leah also terminated treatment in an attempt to protect herself from the negative psychological effects associated with IVF:

> It's always devastating when it doesn't work. I carried this feeling, why do I keep wanting something that I can't have? Why do I keep banging my head against a brick wall? So I decided to shelve it for a while. I'm not going to try again; it's been very painful and unsuccessful. It's time to pursue other things where I can feel some success.

Rachel accepted ovulation induction initially, when she lacked personal experience with the Clomid administration. However, once she gained experience with the ill effects associated with the treatment (i.e., marital disruption experienced as it related to fulfilling the obligation of scheduled sex, mood swings), she rejected it because she believed it threatened the stability of her marriage; terminating intervention for this reason was an attempt to protect her marriage from further instability. When making this decision, Rachel balanced the scales: The importance of maintaining her marital relationship outweighed her desire to achieve pregnancy through intervention.

Several informants also entertained the idea of terminating medical intervention in order to protect themselves and/or others from the risks associated with becoming pregnant and/or parenting at an older age:

> If I don't have children by the time I'm 35 then I'm not having any. I want to, at that stage of my life, to be able to go out and do things with the kids. I don't want to be pushing 40 and just beginning to have children; there's more medical problems then. (Gillian)

> I'll be [31 years old]. My other kids were born when I was in my mid-20s. So I'm wondering if I'm going to run out of energy this time around. Being a little older puts you [at] a little higher risk and problems with the child. Down syndrome is one of the major ones. And then just being older, weight gain. The last one was over nine pounds at birth and they say they keep getting bigger and then going through another cesarean and taking longer to heal. . . . I'm looking at them leaving home. When they're 20, I'll be 45. By the time the next one's 20, I'll be 52. (Kate)

As noted above, terminating intervention was often considered as a strategy to protect oneself and/or others from a perceived risk. In contrast, for Grace the decision *not* to terminate was a protective governing strategy: "You don't know when to quit. If you do, will you regret it years down the road? Like, why didn't you try everything?" Jacqueline took a similar position: "I didn't want to give up the hope of having another child. I had to continue or say that I'm not going to have any more children. Since I couldn't do that, I had to stay in this process."

Committing to pregnancy. While undergoing infertility care, the informants' levels of commitment toward pregnancy and having babies fluctuated. For example, the level of commitment was often high when the informants experienced "positive" feelings toward the parenting of a baby. At other times, when the informants experienced "negative" feelings, the commitment decreased:

> When I was assigned to the nursery and I'd get to spend a whole evening walking these babies, I thought, I don't wanna have any kids, because they'd all be screaming. When you had one and they'd be all snuggled in and you'd be rocking them you'd think, jeez, it would sure be nice to have one of my own. (Rachel)

Kate's commitment to getting pregnant a third time was influenced by the other priorities in her life. When balancing these priorities, Kate used the strategy of protective governing:

> It's one of those nice-to-have things. If you had a list, you want this or that, the baby's way up there. But it's not the only thing like groceries. My thoughts right now are, I'm really looking forward to the honeymoon [celebrating my wedding anniversary] next year. So having a newborn would interfere with that. . . . It's kind of like, I'd rather go on a honeymoon than have a baby.

In contrast, Jacqueline became less committed toward achieving pregnancy when she observed that a future pregnancy would have resulted in a long, almost "unacceptable" age spread between her last child and the "future" child: "It was really important for our son to have a sibling; the older he got, the less pressing that need seemed. . . . The time factor would have become really relevant at some point. We would have said, well, it's just not worth it anymore because he's too old." Despite these feelings, informants persisted with medical intervention regardless of their level of commitment toward pregnancy.

The Typologies Involved in Pregnology

Informants highlighted the support they received from their husbands during the process of seeking pregnancy through the science of medicine. They also recognized the worth of medical intervention they had already undergone even though they had not (yet) achieved pregnancy. The analysis of these data revealed several typologies; these are discussed in turn below.

Support From Husbands

The informants in this study received two types of support from their husbands. First, most informants felt supported emotionally when their husbands spent time with them, listening to their feelings and concerns surrounding the infertility and its management. They also received instrumental support when their husbands were actively involved in the activities associated with the medical intervention. A typology of support was developed, identifying the degree of the husbands' involvement (see Figure 2.5). According to the informants' descriptions, the husbands' levels of support fluctuated during the infertility experience.

The Activist

The husbands designated as activists (Figure 2.5, cell a) were very willing to listen to their wives express feelings and concerns surrounding the infertility. Several of the informants stated that although their husbands did not always understand their feelings (e.g., why their wives cried when they got their menstrual periods or when pregnancy tests were negative), they still felt emotionally supported when their husbands simply listened to them express their feelings.

These husbands were also very willing to provide instrumental support in various ways, such as becoming actively involved in the planning and/or initiation of scheduled sex. The informants also reaped this type of support when their husbands drove them to and from their appointments. This support was especially needed when physically invasive procedures, such as laparoscopy, had been performed. Ginny, in particular, found it helpful when her husband bridged the communication gap between her and the doctor after a laparoscopy: "Dr. Q talks to you after. . . . You're not really coherent because you're so screwed up from being put out. So my husband always goes and he'll scribble down whatever Dr. Q is saying. He'll write it down so that when I get home he can tell me what Dr. Q said."

Several of the informants noted that they were also emotionally supported when their husbands accompanied them to the infertility appointments. The informants felt that they required their husbands' emotional support during the appointments when something "major" was being done, such as a laparoscopy. In contrast, most informants felt that it was unnecessary to be accompanied by their husbands when they were having other procedures done, such as reviewing the BBT chart, because these procedures were things they could cope with themselves:

> If I'm just having a test to see if my ovaries are swollen . . . [or] if Dr. Q is just taking blood and looking at my BBT chart, he doesn't have to come. But if Dr. Q is going to say, "Okay, I want to do another lap on you. I want you to come in," I'll say [to my husband], "Can you come with me please?" (Ginny)

In this instance, the strategy of balancing the scales was present: The husband's presence at the appointment was considered to be more important than the loss of time at his employment and the potential loss of wages.

The Sideliner

Another type of husband very similar to the activist was the sideliner (cell b). This type would provide emotional support to his wife through listening when she expressed feelings and concerns. However, he did not provide instrumental support, although he may have wanted to do so; instead, he sat on the sidelines. On the basis of the informants' situations, only one husband fit this typology. Ruth's husband was unable to engage in scheduled sex because he was out of the city for several months at a time because of his employment. During that time, he provided Ruth with emotional support by keeping in contact with her by telephone.

The Cooperator

A third type of husband was the cooperator (cell c). These men were similar to the activists by virtue of offering instrumental support to their wives; however, their levels of active support differed. For example, there were several informants whose husbands would participate in scheduled sex only when asked to do so by their wives; they would not assist in the

Husband's Instrumental Support

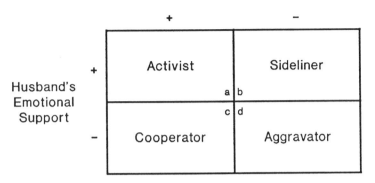

Figure 2.5. Typology of the Relationship Between Husband's Instrumental and Emotional Support as Perceived by the Participant

planning of scheduled sex and/or initiate sexual activity. Two informants, in particular, stated that their husbands would provide semen samples for analysis through masturbation, but the women were responsible for delivering the samples to the infertility clinic. In this group, the wives did not report talking with their husbands about the infertility.

Rather than receiving emotional support, wives of cooperators got comments from their husbands that negated their concerns about the inability to conceive. This was expressed in comments such as, "When I was getting a bit upset, [he] would say, 'Don't worry about it' or 'Just forget about it' " (Holly); "[He] sort of says, 'Well, if we can't get pregnant, we can't.' He says like, 'Don't worry about it' " (Gillian); and "[He] just doesn't want to get serious about it. He'll always say to me, 'Don't worry about it' " (Hilary). In addition, the wives in this group stated that the desire for a child was unequal between the partners, with the wife having a greater desire for a child than the husband. This perception was noted in comments such as, "We both want children, but he accepts [the infertility] a lot easier. If we don't have them, it's no big deal. Like he can go one way or the other" (Grace) and "I do worry. It doesn't seem to matter to him" (Gillian). Although not explicitly, it appeared that these husbands were simply going along with their wives' wishes regarding fertility.

The Aggravator

The fourth and final type of husband has been classified as an aggravator (cell d). This type displayed two basic characteristics: First, he did not give any emotional support to his wife, refusing to listen to her talk about her feelings and concerns surrounding the infertility; second, he did not provide instrumental support to his wife, and this lack of support actually aggravated the management of the infertility. For instance, fulfilling the obligation of scheduled sex was negated by Rachel's husband, who either unwillingly engaged in such activity or refused. The fertility of two informants' husbands was potentially reduced when they continued to engage in activities (e.g., hot baths, smoking) that are believed or known to reduce the sperm count. Further, Madeline felt that her own fertility potential was negatively affected when she did not receive her partner's support about lifestyle habits as they related to her weight problem:

> There's a lot about [his] lifestyle that I've absorbed and accommodated that is contributing to my weight problem. I put it to him in an ultimatum sort of fashion that, "Hey, I've talked to you many times over the past year about eating at 11 at night and never going anywhere for a walk. If you really are interested in having a child you have to stop these things." . . . I've tried to tell him, fat women do have problems getting pregnant. He doesn't believe it's true. He's just calmly waiting for me to get pregnant. Each time he brings home a barrel of ice cream, I see another roadblock to eventually achieving a weight that would accommodate pregnancy. He just sort of glosses over my references to, "This weight is going to be a problem for us. Help me get rid of it."

The Worth of Medical Intervention

When they did not achieve pregnancy, the informants felt that their participation in medical intervention had not been worth it to date, "but it'll all be worth it in the end when I get the baby" (Tiffany). When balancing the worth of intervention in terms of time, the informants placed greater weight on the future (i.e., long-term) worth when they anticipated the achievement of pregnancy, and lesser weight on the present (i.e., short-term) worth when pregnancy was not achieved.

Although many of the informants had not achieved pregnancy, several of them acknowledged that the management attempts undertaken thus far had contributed to the possible resolution of their infertility. Hilary noted:

"I've gone over these hurdles. I might be halfway there or a quarter-way there but at least I've accomplished this much. I've done much more than I would've a year and a half ago." Similar feelings were echoed by other informants:

> It's worth it to me now 'cause I know that my insides could have a baby. . . . Dr. Q cleaned out both my tubes, whereas before it didn't matter whether an [egg] flowed down there because it couldn't get through. My tubes were blocked. So now, at least I know that they're going to flow down. (Ginny)

> It has furthered me in seeing that I may not get pregnant. I'm closer to it, knowing that I gave it everything. So if I let go of this it's complete. There's no, "I could've." It's knowing that I gave it everything. So that makes it worth it. (Leah)

There were other benefits from medical intervention, even when pregnancy was not achieved. For example, there were positive effects in relation to an increased closeness in the marriage and the adoption of a daughter that gave an added dimension to the life of both partners. It also made partners more aware of their own physiology:

> If I had been able to get pregnant, we never would have adopted. There's that extra special bonus in our life. It has brought us together in a way that some couples don't get to experience because they don't have that problem; it makes another extra bond between you. (Gillian)

> It's brought us closer together. I can say to [my husband] like, "My cervix is opening. I'm shedding out all the lining of my uterus" and he knows exactly what I'm talking about. Whereas years ago, a female would never say that to her husband. It's made me more aware of my body more so than I ever knew before. (Ginny)

Kate found that experiencing infertility "makes you think more about yourself and what you really want out of life, for yourself and for your family, where your priorities are and what you really want." Through experiencing infertility, several informants also came to know the full value and appreciation they had for children: "I came to realize that being home with kids probably meant more to me than what I thought. Before, I never really understood how important having children was to me" (Ruth). This particular benefit of the infertility experience was reiterated by Leah: "Going through this, I've certainly seen the value of mother-hood. Having had it taken away from me, its value and appreciation are much more enhanced than what I thought was just some inconvenient part of my life that I'd have to fit in with my career." Several informants saw the infertility experience as beneficial, because "we can now have [compassion] for other people in similar kinds of situation[s]. Not just infertility but anything that's that big of a struggle" (Eve); "It does help to develop some feeling of empathy for other people in the struggles that they have in their everyday life" (Gina). Finally, Ruth felt confident about her ability to meet future life challenges simply because she "made it through" the infertility experience: "I have been through something really tough and I made it. And I don't think that anything will really knock me down again."

Figure 2.6 presents a typology of informants' views of the worth of medical intervention in terms of achieving pregnancy and other benefits. All the informants viewed their participation in medical intervention as being ultimately "worth it" if and when they achieved the goal of pregnancy. In addition to getting pregnant, these informants reaped other benefits from the medical intervention, as noted above. Thus the ultimate worth of their participation in medical intervention was surpassed when they achieved pregnancy and experienced additional benefits from the intervention (cell a). One informant achieved pregnancy through medical intervention but did not experience any additional benefits (cell b). This informant realized the ultimate worth of her participation in the intervention, but that worth was not surpassed. Many of the informants have not yet achieved pregnancy, but have experienced other benefits of medical intervention. Thus these informants have not yet realized the ultimate worth of their participation within medical intervention, but are continuing to engage in the various activities of medical intervention in hopes of eventually achieving pregnancy (cell c).

The final element in this typology (cell d) is the questioning of the ultimate worth of medical intervention. Informants who fall into cell d include those who have experienced neither the achievement of pregnancy nor other benefits from medical intervention. Those in this group did one of two things. First, two informants discontinued intervention when they experienced various ill effects (i.e., marital disruption, emotional hurt felt in response to the letdown) rather than benefits other than pregnancy. One informant continued treatment while at the same time questioning its ultimate worth.

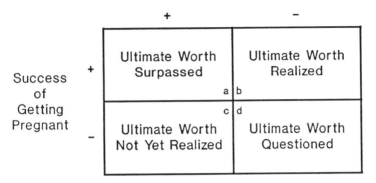

Figure 2.6.   Typology of the Relationship Between the Success of Achieving Pregnancy and the Effects of Medical Intervention

Conclusion

In this chapter I have described the process of getting pregnant through science, or pregnology. The name of the process is derived from the combination of *pregnancy* and *technology* and is meant to convey the concept of "scientifically getting pregnant," a phrase used by several study informants. The drive of the informants to give birth was so strong that they were willing to include various outside parties (physicians, nurses, technicians), who were often strangers to them, in their attempts to achieve the goal of pregnancy. In this they differed from most couples; the achievement of pregnancy is generally a very private matter, shared only between partners (Grayshon, 1989; Sandelowski, Harris, & Holditch-Davis, 1990).

Pregnology is a process consisting of four stages: entry into medical intervention, the intervention, the letdown, and exit from medical intervention. As the informants progressed through these stages, they used the strategy of balancing the scales in two particular ways. First, they balanced their infertility and its management with the rest of their lives. For most of the informants, their infertility and its management became the central focus in their lives, while other aspects assumed a more peripheral nature; this was particularly noted when the informants invested much of their time, energy, and financial resources in infertility work—that is, when they pursued the various activities of medical intervention. And second, the informants balanced the scales when they weighed the pros and cons of given management options in the process of deciding whether to accept or reject them. When informants perceived that treatment risks outweighed their desire for pregnancy, they frequently used a second strategy, protective governing. The informants also lived "under the microscope" as they progressed through the stages of pregnology. This was most pronounced when private information became public knowledge and in the activity of "looking for blood."

The findings of this study indicate that the current management of infertility focuses on the physiological, medical, and technological aspects of human reproduction. Health professionals can help infertile women endure the quest for pregnancy through the science of medicine in numerous ways, such as by providing emotional and informational support. Professionals can help clients to make decisions surrounding the management of infertility by providing them with clear, accurate, and complete information in language they can understand.

The phenomenon of living under the microscope can be minimized for these women if nurses and other health professionals create safe environments for the performance of infertility procedures (e.g., having a third party present during all procedures, especially when bodily exposure is required; employing appropriate draping practices). In addition, nurses and physicians can demonstrate greater respect for the privacy of these women's personal lives by not routinely advising them to document all sexual activity on BBT charts; it can generally be assumed that clients will engage in sexual activity during the appropriate times in their menstrual cycles, especially because infertile clients are highly motivated to participate in any activity that will help them achieve pregnancy. It may be better to advise women to keep "private" records of their sexual activities; in special circumstances surrounding infertility management, they may be asked to share that information with particular health professionals. Further, health professionals can help to take some pressure off of their clients by giving them permission to let the obligation for scheduled sex go unfulfilled in times of low sexual desire.

When pregnancy is not achieved, health professionals can provide support for their clients by giving them some different options, such as taking a break from medical intervention, or by helping them to decide if they should terminate medical care in the absence of pregnancy. Health professionals can also help infertile women to redefine *success* in terms other than the achievement of pregnancy.

References

Corbin, J. M. (1986). Coding, writing memos and diagramming. In W. C. Chenitz & J. M. Swanson (Eds.), *From practice to grounded theory: Qualitative research in nursing* (pp. 102-120). Menlo Park, CA: Addison-Wesley.

Corbin, J. M. (1987). Women's perceptions and management of a pregnancy complicated by chronic illness. *Health Care for Women International, 8,* 317-337.

Grayshon, J. (1989). Special delivery? *Midwives Chronicle and Nursing Notes, 102,* 12-13.

Morse, J. M. (1989). Strategies for sampling. In J. M. Morse (Ed.), *Qualitative nursing research: A contemporary dialogue* (pp. 117-131). Rockville, MD: Aspen.

Sandelowski, M., Harris, B. G., & Holditch-Davis, D. (1990). Pregnant moments: The process of conception in infertile couples. *Research in Nursing & Health, 13,* 273-282.

Strauss, A. L., & Corbin, J. (1990). *Basics of qualitative research: Grounded theory procedures and techniques.* Newbury Park, CA: Sage.

3

Unexpected Pregnancy

The Uncharted Land
of Women's Experience

Patricia Beryl Marck

For many women who find themselves unexpectedly pregnant, it seems that almost everyone has at least one idea of "what should be done." Advertisements on buses urge women to telephone agencies that will arrange adoption, and pro-choice and antiabortion activists disseminate their rhetoric in the media. On the street, clinics have been bombed, chained closed by protesters, and set ablaze. As Callahan (1981) notes, activists on either side of the abortion debate do not seem to want to listen to anyone; they only want to hear "one's final 'position' " (p. 15). A cacophony of other voices variously vilify, glorify, and even try to sanctify what women do or do not do, or should or should not do, about pregnancy (Condit, 1990).

But what do we hear from women? Where are their voices? Among the women who reach nurse counselors at one reproductive health clinic, many report that the clinic visit is the first time that anyone has asked them, "What is this like for you?" (MacKay & Marck, 1990). Surrounded by others' thoughts on their experiences, few women, it seems, are asked to voice their own.

In the research discussed below, four women with current or recent experience of unexpected pregnancy were asked, "What is this like for you?" Drawing on the previous work of Bergum (1989b) with first-time mothers and van Manen (1990) in human science research, I have explored several foundational questions about the experience of unexpected pregnancy with each woman. These questions included the following: What does it mean to move into or not move into motherhood? What does it mean to imagine or not be able to imagine oneself as mother? What does it mean to accept or not accept a relationship with a child-to-be? What constitutes ethical comportment for each of us as caregivers when we encounter women with unexpected pregnancies? The goal of this questioning was to bring to speech, and begin to sense and make sense of, what the experience of unexpected pregnancy may mean for women who are trying to make choices about the relationship of pregnancy, and who consciously consider and question the possibilities of mothering or not mothering, birthing or aborting, keeping or giving up an imagined child.

Private conversations with each woman were taped in their entirety after the woman gave informed consent to participate in the research. The initial meetings took place during the first 12 weeks of a medically diagnosed pregnancy for Mary and for Katherine, 11 months after an abortion for Maggie, and 3 weeks after childbirth for Vanessa. Each woman and I mutually decided upon the number of conversations in response to the need either of us felt to clarify and validate interpretations of the talk as they emerged. The taped conversations ranged from one to three in number for each informant, and all initial conversations lasted three or more hours; others lasted anywhere from 20 minutes to 90 minutes. I then reviewed and annotated each transcript during further personal or telephone conversations with the woman concerned before undertaking the process of interpreting the transcripts.

My research journal, recorded in both handwritten notes and transcribed tapes, informed my continuing examination of the research process from the outset of the project to its completion. Within its notes, I set down the thoughts, stories, and questions stemming from sources other than the women for retrieval after conversations with the women were completed. The journal thereby facilitated a careful and continual questioning and bringing to awareness of my own involvement in the research question (Bergum, 1989a).

The tension between my own involvement in the question and my efforts to attune to the words of the women in the research created a dialectic (Bergum, 1989b; Drew, 1989) that surfaced in the interpretation of the women's experiences. A continued reorienting to the research question helped that tension to emerge in the interpretation in a way that deepened, rather than detracted from, my understanding of the women's experiences (Bergum, 1989b). Always, through all the activities of the research process, I returned to the stories of the women and asked, What does this tell us about their experiences?

When facing unexpected pregnancy, women must make choices that are often difficult. This is true both of women who, before pregnancy, could not countenance any choice in pregnancy but birth and motherhood and of women who always felt that such choices were theirs to make, or at least should be. Within many pregnancies that are unexpected, however, as well as in many planned ones, "choice" changes from scripts based on abstract principles to a call for action grounded in experience: the experience of pregnancy. This belies the notion of choice as understood from outside of pregnancy. Once pregnant, women sometimes take different actions from those they might have envisioned beforehand. In the experience of pregnancy their understanding of choice changes.

Regardless of their eventual choices, what remains largely unexplored is the actual experience of pregnancy for these women. Indeed, women's experiences as a whole remain largely uncharted land. The word land means, among other things, "the solid ground of the earth, especially as distinguished from the sea"; it also can mean "to cause to arrive, set down, place" (Morris, 1978, p. 735). For women, the metaphor of land can expand our understanding of the purpose of our search for knowledge. Gadow (1990) notes that the meanings situated in human experience are analogous to places that "cannot be drawn on a map but that define the nature of the land as markedly as its geography, meanings that are its geography for people whose lives are bound up with it" (p. 10). We seek knowledge of human experience not to order the world but to "recover the world and our place within it" (p. 7). Yet in the case of unexpected pregnancy we do not know what the ground of women's experiences looks like, feels like, or means; few women in this situation have ever been asked. We remain at sea in assisting women who feel the need to make choices about their pregnancies; we do not know what it is like for them.

The purpose of this research was to increase our knowledge about the experience of unexpected pregnancy by seeking the perspectives of women who had gone through it, in their own words. A phenomenological, hermeneutical method was used to ask four women with current or recent experience of unexpected pregnancy, What is it like for you? This question represented a commitment to explore the nature of unexpected pregnancy for the women as well as our place as caregivers with them during their experiences. To pursue a shared understanding of the experience of unexpected pregnancy with these four women was to begin to chart, together, one small corner of women's land.

Unexpected Pregnancy: Bringing Women's Voices to Speech

Let a body venture at last out of its shelter, take a chance with meaning under a veil of words. WORD FLESH. From one to the other, eternally, broken up visions, metaphors of the invisible. (Kristeva, 1986, p. 162)

The talk of the four women who participated in this research is the foundation upon which this interpretation of unexpected pregnancy is built. Each woman's voice took distinctive forms and underscored the life experiences that she brought to her unexpected pregnancy. Mary looked at the question of another child from the vantage point of mothering teenagers, whereas Katherine considered the possibility of motherhood after previous abortions. Maggie reflected back on her experience of choosing abortion over a hoped-for child and Vanessa considered placing her newborn son for adoption.

From the words of four very different women, the collective speech that coalesced in the research process yielded several common themes about their experiences (see Table 3.1). These common themes of unexpected pregnancy, validated with each woman, spoke of needing a place to be listened to by others, of entering a dialogue between her body and self-as-pregnant that informed her actions, of attaining a place for a real or imagined child that corresponded to the place in her world that she experienced as a woman, of finding unavoidable pain where a real or imagined child came into being, and of searching out the meaning of her experience through the pain that accompanied imagining or taking on motherhood.

The theme of needing a place to be heard in unexpected pregnancy resounded throughout all of the themes identified in this research. Each woman, in becoming unexpectedly pregnant, found herself displaced, unseated in her world. Each talked of finding the right place for her pregnancy in her life, the place where it should be or could be. In seeking that place for their pregnancies, the women seemed above all to be searching for a place for their voice, a place where they could speak as they truly were.

Place can be defined as "an area occupied by or set aside for someone or something." This notion of place allows us to begin a discourse on what it means to these women to look for a place for their own voices and to

TABLE 3.1 Themes of Unexpected Pregnancy

A place to be heard: A place to be heard during unexpected pregnancy was a place where each woman felt that she would be accepted for herself as she truly was and listened to in her own words. From such a place, it seemed that each woman could then hear herself and begin to find the place of her pregnancy in her life.

Pregnancy as dialogue: Pregnancy as dialogue was a constant communion between body and self for each woman, a "body talk" that informed her understanding of herself-as-pregnant and that founded or negated the place from which a relationship with a developing fetus could come into being.

A place of self, a place for a child: The place that each woman experienced for herself in her world of relationships seemed to mirror the place she was able to imagine or eventually provide for a real or possible child, either during or after pregnancy. It was here that the ground of the body-self dialogue came into view, as each woman sought a place for her real or imagined child that reflected her own experience of place, in relation to others in her life.

Mothering pains: Mothering pains were the inevitable cost that each woman bore in her unique search for a place for a real or imagined child, a place that fit with her experience of pregnancy and that allowed her to give voice to her pain.

A place for pain, a place for nurturance: Where a woman felt allowed to voice the pain of her experience, a place to nurture her understanding of herself and her unexpected pregnancy was created. Pain itself was inevitable, but that each woman would draw meaning from it that assisted her was not; only pain listened to and accepted by others became a nurturant force in each woman's interpretation of her experience.

---

look for the place of their unexpected pregnancies in their lives. Another meaning of *place,* as a verb, perhaps extends the manner in which we consider each woman's experience. This meaning "always implies care and precision in bringing something to a desired position" (Morris, 1978, p. 1000). For these women, this research was that place, a home for their voice. Here they could speak to the question no one had asked them: What is this like for you? Thus, despite the real risk of pain that accompanied our intimate conversations, these women identified one overriding benefit in our talk: a place, finally, to voice their own experiences of unexpected pregnancy.

As the women talked, significant aspects of their experiences came from different roles in their lives and from their different voices. It was in the voice of woman-as-self that the dialogue between body and self-as-pregnant was uncovered, and it was in the voice of woman-in-relation that the context of the body-self dialogue became apparent, the context of the place she experienced for herself in the lives of those who mattered to her. From these voices, a narrative for each woman took shape, completing its features with the words of each woman as she imagined or took on motherhood and met the pain of mothering a real or possible child. Johnson (1987) advances the notion that we seek a structure and unity of narrative in our experiences of the world, both within our own lives and within our larger human community. This interpretation of unexpected pregnancy is one structured narrative of four women's experiences. To the extent that a unity of understanding about their experiences is achieved, the pedagogic value of each woman's experience has been attended to. In that attending, we can hope to further our questions about women's needs during this experience and others. The narrative begins as we turn to women's voices.

Fleshing Out Women's Experiences: Women's Stories

> The Muses are said to inspire mortals with their voices. They sing to those they love and bestow talents that make these humans happy, wise, and respected. Surely the image of the Muses is derived from infancy and early childhood. This is the time when the sound of a woman's voice means nearly everything to nearly everyone. (Goldenberg, 1990, p. 208)

Goldenberg (1990) asks us to consider how it is that women's voices, so central to our first understanding of the world as infants and children, become so difficult to locate in our experiences of adult discourse. Of the largely hidden experience of unexpected pregnancy we have heard little from the voices of women who feel that they face a need to choose. This research suggests that women simply do not expect to be asked. Mary expressed her sheer relief at the discovery that the purpose of the research was to understand, rather than to deliver "some pitch" for either the pro- or anti-choice camps: "It was so nice to hear it was a research project that was unbiased either way." The women had not found many nonjudgmental reactions when revealing their unexpected pregnancies to others. In Katherine's past experiences of being pregnant, "everyone is either have it or don't have it." Vanessa said that "everybody just told me what to do." Like Mary, she found it gratifying just to be asked; she "never felt that anybody would."

Maggie, whose lover said that he would be there for her even though their romance was over, passed her fetus alone at home after taking an antiprogesterone given to her by a physician friend. She said that she wished she had never told her lover about the pregnancy. In her eyes, doing so merely opened her to the devastation of hearing him say, "It's your body, I can't tell you what to do." For Maggie, the lack of caring that judgment implied contained the same message as the one perceived by the other women in this study: that her experience was not sought and taken into account. Rather than what pregnancy meant to them, these women found repeatedly that what seemed to matter most to the majority of the people they confided in was what they were "going to do."

To counter this negation of the value of their experience, each woman continued to search for someone who would invite her to speak. Maggie sought to speak for both herself and the child-to-be she aborted by going to a priest after she learned the sex of her fetus from laboratory testing. She had a blessing said, and named her. Her child "that was supposed to be" is noted in the priest's personal log. "I had to do that. And it was peaceful, we put it at rest. As far as I was concerned, well, I've done for her all that I can."

For Katherine and Vanessa, the talk of their experiences that began in the research continued afterward in conversations with the men in their lives. Resolving to choose for this pregnancy on her own, regardless of her boyfriend's opinion, Katherine stated, "I have made a decision about one thing and that is [it is] going to be *my* decision." Standing firm on that promise to herself, she found herself in new relation to her boyfriend: "Putting my foot down and saying, 'Look, you are not going to influence me this time so don't even try' has made him see me in a different light and he has given me more respect." Perhaps even more critically, she sees herself differently: "I feel better about myself . . . without him and with him." To Vanessa, her husband's fear of her participation in the research sparked a dialogue of a kind she had not experienced with him "since we've been together." She felt listened to, and for the first time since disclosing her pregnancy, she felt that "he's really trying to understand me, to understand my situation and how I feel." As their new way of talking continued over the following weeks, she said that she noticed a difference in how she feels toward both her husband and her newborn son. More able to respond to both of them since she has felt heard, Vanessa now is involved in two dialogues that seem to be unfolding: one with her husband in words and one with her son in other ways.

Mary found a change in many of her relationships as well since making a choice about this pregnancy. Always mindful of many others all her life, Mary saw some of her friends and family in a new light after her upsetting spontaneous abortion of this pregnancy, one she had chosen to continue over her husband's objections. Finding out who was there for her when she miscarried, her teenage daughters, she finally felt able to leave the others behind. She moved to an isolated community where she is one of only six nurses, and she loves it: "I know that what I do is important. I'm important and that's nice." She feels liked and respected, "not for what I can do for them but for who I am." She has found a place where she feels affirmed for herself, not just for the next favor she performs for an endless legion of relatives and friends. With that confirmation of self, she goes on doing for others but in a much more gratifying way, receiving appreciation and realizing that she deserves it.

Mary's father and sister, both of whom Mary had previously accommodated at every turn of their lives, are "livid." Her ex-husband, who had stayed with Mary in town whenever he was sober, has begun drinking heavily again. Although Mary recognizes the difference her leaving has made in their lives, she has experienced a profound change since this pregnancy. After a lifetime of mothering family and friends since her own mother's progressive illness throughout her childhood, she is now no longer taking responsibility for their upsets. Her previous responsiveness to all their needs has found a better expression in a new responsiveness to herself, an attunement brought about by her experience of this pregnancy and its loss. In choosing to carry this pregnancy and its attendant hopes for a child, Mary stopped carrying the responsibility for relationships that did not nurture her or her daughters, her "core family." Even after losing her pregnancy to spontaneous abortion, Mary remains committed to her new relation with self and others. Since this pregnancy, Mary's relationships are shared as opposed to carried: "I'm going to live for who's giving to me and that's who I'm going to give to."

For all the women in this research, voicing their experiences of unexpected pregnancy to others was paramount. Perhaps the foundation for this need was best described by Katherine when she considered what her pregnancy and the opportunity to talk about it meant to her: "It was my time to be heard." Even more significant than being heard by anyone who would listen, Katherine thought, was value in the fact that this research represented "women listening to other women." Believing that what she had to say was valuable enough to share in the research, Katherine also seemed to value her voice enough at this time to stand up to her boyfriend. In considering the worth of that standing up for herself to others, Katherine has become a woman listening to her own voice. Now that she has given herself voice, no one can take away what it has revealed to her. In the strength and respect she discovered within as she listened to herself, perhaps Katherine says what we all need to realize. The most important event that occurs when someone listens to us is that we can finally hear ourselves. In making a choice about an unexpected pregnancy, each woman needed to hear her own voice, to make sense of her experience, and to begin to find what she sought to understand.

The First Voice: Woman as Herself

Finding one's own voice in the world begins with the location and knowing of self. But how do we find and know ourselves? In the most fundamental sense, many scholars talk of the embodied self, our way of physically being in the world, as the primary basis for our understanding of ourselves (Benner & Wrubel, 1989; Johnson, 1987; Merleau-Ponty, 1962; Sacks, 1985). These bodily ways of knowing proceed unconsciously for us much of the time, and our experiences remain largely unarticulated, unreflected upon, and "taken for granted" (Benner & Wrubel, 1989, p. 81). However, Johnson (1987) has built a strong case for the notion that these bodily experiences concurrently engage us, through imaginative structures, in shaping the forms of language and reasoning with which we reflect, articulate, and form our conscious understandings of ourselves and our world.

These distinctive "ways in which the body is in the mind" (Johnson, 1987, p. xxi), so central to the meanings we create in our lives, take shape in "the sense we make of being in the world through the experiences of moving, touching, feeling, speaking, hearing, and seeing" (Etches, 1990, p. 260). Pregnancy, as a profound physical transformation, is frequently delineated in medical and nursing texts by its physiology and its signs and symptoms, but such explanations of pregnancy do not address the complex and interwoven nature, for a woman, of her bodily experience and her sense of changing self.

In a different account, one that recognizes pregnancy from the perspective of women's experience of it, Bergum (1989b) describes the altered experience of self that accompanied the women in her study as they realized their pregnancies: "She was taking naps in the afternoon and her moods were very labile. She said, 'I was not myself' (J1). Women wonder 'just who they are' " (p. 55). To still be oneself, and yet somehow not so, speaks of the pregnant woman's "experience of being thrown onto awareness of one's body" (Young, 1984, p. 51). The descriptions of unexpected pregnancy that follow attempt to articulate this experience of bodily awareness in pregnancy for four women. They are accounts of each woman as she comes to know her pregnancy and herself-as-pregnant.

Woman Embodied: Dialectic With Self

Gadow (1980) argues that the embodied way of knowing can be described as a dialectic between body and self that generates self-knowledge throughout several stages of body-mind dialogue. In the primary stage she ascribes to the "unbroken immediacy . . . of the lived body" (p. 173); we receive and generate our knowledge through a body that is "ready-to-hand" (Heidegger, 1962, p. 98). "Ready-to-hand" means that in an "unnoticed" (Benner & Wrubel, 1989, p. 81) mode of being, we as-our-bodies proceed to act on the world in a nonreflective fashion. Gadow (1980) contends that in this fundamental mode of relation between body and self, we come to understand our capabilities in the world and our vulnerabilities to it. Such unity of self-knowledge allows us to proceed unself-consciously through our daily lives, perhaps providing what Johnson (1987) calls "narrative unity" (p. 172) at a preconceptual level. Our stories to ourselves about what we are doing, unexpressed, "make sense" to us.

Gadow (1980), however, asserts that, in illness, aging, fatigue, or other faces of a changed capacity to act on one's world, a new or second relation between body and self emerges: "disrupted immediacy" (p. 174). When I no longer experience existence from my previous bodily understanding of the world, the nature of the relation between my body and self becomes adversarial. In this relation, my body's differences threaten my sense of self as known and the unity previously lived in my state of primary immediacy is gone. In its place, I struggle with "myself" as body and self pull me in disparate directions. My former story of "what is" no longer creates understanding for me, and I must try to interpret the new text that this unfamiliar bodily experience provides.

The physical onset of pregnancy for Maggie evokes an image of this mode of the dialectic. In the final semester of her graduate program, Maggie attributed her fatigue and "lousy" feeling to the stress of her studies and her first fight with her lover. With an intrauterine device (IUD) in place, she did not consider the possibility of pregnancy until her period was long overdue. Then, as her relationship with her partner deteriorated, the realization hit: "I didn't feel pregnant but I knew I was." She was out of town on a business trip as the early days of her pregnancy ensued. Weight fell off her and the pregnancy physically felt like one part of an entire life under siege. Her overwhelming feelings were ones of bodily vulnerability, real frailty, and escalating fear.

Back in town, Maggie faced the end of her relationship with her lover at the same time she contemplated a choice for her pregnancy. This pregnancy, although unexpected, was supposed to be in her future: She and her lover had planned marriage and a child together. They had talked in the past about what she would look like pregnant, what a child of theirs would look like, and even what names they liked. From that vision of a secure relationship and a wanted child, Maggie suddenly found herself placed in a disintegrating world of no relationship and a man who said, "It's your body." She continued to lose weight, couldn't sleep, and cried all the time. A physician friend expressed alarm at her overall health; she was down to almost 85 pounds. The friend gave Maggie an antiprogesterone abortifacient at Maggie's request, ensuring that she would be available to Maggie if she was needed. Maggie told her lover what she was going to do; he told her that he had to go to a tennis tournament. Alone, she labored and passed her fetus at home.

Maggie's body-as-pregnant seemed to symbolize a greater disruption of her very being. In the struggle between body and self, pregnancy seemed to reinforce to her the vulnerability and complete aloneness that her severed relationship represented to her. Although Maggie agonized over a project that she had imagined in her future, a child, she could not see a present with that child; she could not even take care of herself. Her physical appearance alarmed her friends, and they tried to feed her. She began counseling and determined that she would have an abortion. Afterward, she continued counseling, took antidepressants, and eventually began to eat again.

In this pregnancy, it seemed that Maggie's body-self dialectic threatened her very being and could not give her a way of seeing herself in the world as mother. The dialogue and a hoped-for child were both aborted, not far from a point of impending physical and emotional self-destruction. Incomplete for now, the dialogue instituted with pregnancy may return for Maggie when she is able to entertain it safely, without fear of losing herself in it. Recently, she bought the perfume that she used to wear in that relationship; she now feels able to wear it again. It is a special freedom for Maggie to do so: "That perfume is me, and it's so nice to be able to wear it again. I'm getting back what is mine." What is good for her and about her is hers again. Slowly, she reclaims herself.

Mary's experience of discovering her pregnancy represented a disruption of another kind, but also one attended by fear. Her early symptoms of fatigue and nausea convinced her that the cancer she had fought previously was out of remission. Pregnancy did not even enter into consideration as an explanation: She had undergone radiation and chemotherapy for cancer two years prior, and had been told that she was sterile.

Her trepidation turned to shock and then relief as she interpreted the positive pregnancy test as an indication that she was "healthy enough to be pregnant." After reassuring her that she did not have cancer again, her physicians told her that she could continue the pregnancy if she wished. Mary declared, "I don't feel pregnant. If I decide not to terminate, then I'll feel pregnant." Her choice would rest on many factors, including her husband's reaction and the results of an ultrasound. Of her first children, premature twins who died within hours of birth, she recalled how her growing excitement turned to pain on their untimely arrival: "When they were born at six and a half months that was just, don't count on anything. It was just reinforced that . . . until you can put your hand on it and say, 'Here it is,' it's not. It's a 'might be,' but it's not a definite."

Two weeks later, after a normal ultrasound, Mary entered her pregnancy physically. Morning sickness was "no big deal—you just smile. . . . it's nice being pregnant. You just get this smile on your face." She sewed material for a baby blanket as we talked and debated on styles of diapers. There was time for such things, baby things, now that she had decided to carry on with her pregnancy. Her daughters marked "due date" on the calendars in the house and there was a lottery among friends and family to guess the birth date. The winner would buy the christening layette: "Once I knew I was pregnant and going to have the baby, it was wonderful. I really enjoyed it. . . . There was a baby coming."

Mary's doctor ordered a second ultrasound to verify her baby's gestation. This time, Mary saw something in the face of the technician who performed the exam that "gave her away." When Mary asked, the technician insisted that nothing was wrong: "Just go see your doctor and don't worry about things." After getting home, Mary started to have mild cramps; the clinic called her back for another ultrasound. When the doctor did it, moving the probe around her tummy, she could see on the screen that "everything was textbook perfect except for the heartbeat. It just wasn't there." When she asked him why there was no heartbeat, he asked if she had any children at home and she said, "Yes." Then he asked her about miscarriages, abortions, and again about her children—were they healthy?

I said, "Yes." He said, "Then this probably won't be so hard." . . . But why wouldn't it be hard? . . . I said, "There is no fetal heartbeat there, why not?" "Well, it's something you have to talk to your doctor about," he said. "No," I said, "that's something you can tell me, you're a doctor, you're performing this exam, you can tell me." "There is no heartbeat," he said. And I said, "I'm getting cramps, I'm miscarrying, aren't I?" And he said, "Well, yes." And those cramps intensified so bad.

Within a few more hours, Mary's flow was frank bleeding. Still, she clung to a hope that things would be okay: "It didn't matter what kind of physical signs there were. Up till then I just kind of drew a blank. . . . You can find all kinds of things about why you can be pregnant when you're not." Baby blankets, the diapers she had made, and the little baby shoes from a friend all told her that a child was coming, that she was *with child.* While she was in the hospital, waiting for surgery, a tactless remark about her medical history from a student intern unleashed her grief: "I just cried and cried. . . . It wasn't just a fetus that got carried away with a D&C, that was my baby."

When Mary arrived home after her miscarriage, she found that a friend had delivered a beautiful crib. A few weeks later, she and her daughters were out shopping in a department store: "Sometimes, I think I'm still pregnant. They had all this baby stuff and they had this great baby sale going and we stopped, you know, and the three of us were looking and [we said], 'Oh, look at this.' And it was kind of simultaneously."

Bergum (1989b) notes that "it is through her pregnant body that a woman comes to know herself as mother" (p. 53). Being *with child,* Bergum suggests, is a "commingling, an entangling, an interlacing that goes beyond companionship. It is a mysterious union, unlike any other" (p. 53). Like the women in Bergum's research, the women in this study did not express a sense of understanding the meaning of their pregnancies instantaneously or of knowing themselves as mothers immediately. Rather, with communion over time between body and self, each woman moved toward or away from a vision of self-as-mother. Mary's experience also suggests that just as a woman's knowledge of being with child develops over time in pregnancy, an understanding of the absence takes time as well. It seemed that for Mary, choosing for the pregnancy began a dialectic between body and self that created a knowing of her child. This knowing stayed with her after its death, giving her both pleasure and pain as she looked at baby things with her daughters.

At home with a 3-week-old infant, Vanessa perhaps presented another manner of dialectic between body and self in pregnancy, one that continues even as she mothers her son. Recalling her initial attunement to her body-as-pregnant, she vividly expressed the profound shock that came over her as a friend described her own pregnancy symptoms: "She told me how she was feeling and I thought, oh my god! I feel the exact same way. . . . My heart just dropped out of me. All of a sudden reality hit me. I thought, I'm pregnant, I know I'm pregnant."

On oral contraceptives and just newly reconciled with her former boyfriend, Vanessa stated that "there was no way I wanted to be pregnant."

She had important plans for her life, and she was working and saving to go back to school. Neither marriage nor children were in her plans; she "never, ever wanted children or to get married when I was growing up. . . . I knew what I wanted to do." She had avoided pregnancy successfully for six years while taking the pill, and being pregnant seemed impossible to her now. Yet, as she listened to her girlfriend over the telephone, she knew: "I felt more in touch with my body, like something is different. . . . All of a sudden, I felt what was there all the time but I'd never felt it the same way. It was in a different way once you knew."

Her first thought was, "I've got to get rid of this; I wanted to have an abortion because my life was all planned." However, her family, friends, and boyfriend were all adamantly opposed to either adoption or abortion. As she informed others of her pregnancy and heard their advice to become a wife and mother, Vanessa seemed to enter a dialectic in which her pregnant body corresponded with a woman almost silenced as self. She took care of herself and ate well, yet of that taking care, she said, "I did all the right things, but I didn't feel to do them [*sic*]." She found the fetus's movements within her merely "interesting," and she made no efforts to prepare for the arrival of an infant. Most of all, she "hated what pregnancy did" to her body: the stretch marks and even the "pregnant glow. . . . Isn't that the worst, I mean when you are not happy being pregnant and they say you have the glow . . . you just feel gross."

Vanessa recalled that in the midst of family and friends who celebrated her marriage and impending motherhood, she could not even remember her husband proposing to her. She felt that she had not chosen pregnancy, had not chosen a child, and had not chosen marriage or motherhood. To keep some hold of herself and some sense that she still could choose, she went on reminding herself that despite everyone else's plans for her future, adoption remained an option for her after birth. She differentiated the feelings she experienced at her son's birth from those she searches for within herself now, to find what is best for both him and her:

> When he was on the table there . . . you have a feeling of, this is mine, you know, no one can take him away. But I think it is more of an emotional thing than real true feelings. . . . then you don't feel that emotion any-more. . . . You are starting to feel the realities, they are setting in. . . . [Those] feelings are more what you develop. It's more genuine than an emotion . . . and I think those feelings you have to respond to, you have to.

Vanessa's words, bound up in the ambivalence of what she has experienced in the birth and early mothering of her unchosen son, evoke the struggle of her body-self dialectic. Connolly (1987) writes about the first few minutes after birth as one mother looks at her baby, a baby she has decided she will give up for adoption: "The look said 'you're mine forever,' wistfully, from mother to baby but more significantly from baby to mother and it was absolutely correct. I am his forever" (p. 163).

Vanessa nursed her son while we talked, continuing to question the right choice for her child and for herself. She knows what he needs, and it is extremely important to her that his needs are met. She can't bear to listen to him cry or to leave him in a wet diaper. When her husband holds him "way out here" instead of very close or doesn't go pick him up when he's crying, it hurts her. Feeling that she truly sees a weight of responsibility in parenting that her husband doesn't share, she struggles to disengage her voice from the swell of his and others: "By being a mother you will find out that you are a mother. . . . Or being a wife, you will find out that's what you want . . . yet, do they really know me?"

Vanessa hoped that in having her experience listened to, she might find out more about herself, and thus know what to do for both herself and her son: "I need to find myself before I'm ready for it. And even before I know what I want to do with him." Adopted herself, she feels that she can "realistically" assess the potential benefits and risks of placement for her baby. Yet she remains unsure of what it may mean to her. She is scared of losing her husband and family over a choice they could not understand, and also of "losing someone who might even look like me because I have never had that before." She's not yet ready to make a choice for her son and herself; the dialogue between body and self is not complete. She waits to know the difference between "emotions and truth."

Gadow (1980) suggests that at such a point, a renewed unity of self can be achieved only when a third relation between body and self is achieved: that of "cultivated immediacy" (p. 177). In this relation, she argues, the development of self is achieved *through* this changed body as opposed to in spite of it. Harmony with, not mastery of, this changed physical way of being in the world is sought; self and body transcend their previous struggle and mutually enable the person as a whole. New ability to act unself-consciously, within the context of this renewed body-self, evolves and informs one's way of being in the world. For Vanessa, the outcome remains suspended. The talk goes on and widens, however, as she finds her husband now listening to her concerns and finds herself responding to him and her son differently.

In contrast, Katherine's experience may provide one exemplar of Gadow's (1980) fourth mode of immediacy, "aesthetic relation" (p. 182). In this way of being, there is a relation between self and body that reciprocally informs and creates self-knowledge, knowledge embedded in a rich context of bodily experience. From this understanding of knowing, the body becomes a text that must be interpreted (Gogel & Terry, 1987). The body's text, within the context of pregnancy, may be read for the knowledge that it offers.

Katherine's account of her evolving realization of her body-as-pregnant offers us that text. Three previous pregnancies left her with little doubt about the reason for her absent menses when she took a pregnancy test a few days before entering the study: "I sort of had an idea, well, I must be, and I was hoping that I wasn't . . . and when the clinic phoned me I just hung up the phone and started laughing." Within two days, she had swollen breasts and she had looked at baby furniture—something she had never done with any of her previous pregnancies. She caught herself looking at children in the street with curiosity, noticing their presence in the world differently than she had before. She could imagine being with a child, "on the couch with a blanket and I was just picturing a baby there with me . . . sort of envisioning teaching it how to read 'cause I always thought . . . I will definitely do that with my children." The presence of a possible child seemed to be finding a place within Katherine that did not take away from her-as-self, as Vanessa seemed to experience. Rather, her growing experience of this presence seemed to help her find her own voice and allowed her to imagine herself-as-mother.

In a discussion of Gadow's (1980) definition of the aesthetic relation between body and self, Young (1984) addresses the experience of pregnant embodiment for women who have "been able to take up their situation as their own" (p. 47). Although acknowledging that pregnancy could be seen as a state of physical self-awareness that estranges a woman from herself, Young suggests that for women who welcome pregnancy, a self-attunement that creates a new attending and thus relationship with their bodies-as-pregnant may be occurring. This mode of attending engenders a realization of the foreign aspect of growing pregnancy as well as a growing sensibility of the other, the fetus:

> Pregnancy challenges the integration of my body experience by rendering fluid the boundary between what is within, myself, and what is outside, separate. I experience my insides as the space of another, yet my own body. . . . The integrity of my body is undermined. (p. 49)

For a woman who welcomes the realization of pregnancy, Young suggests that this growing attunement to a changed body, an uncertain line between self and other, is an unseating that may be discriminating rather than unsettling. Awaiting the changes while not yet knowing them, a woman can apprehend them directly in a manner of self-awareness that does not objectify her but, in fact, expands her experience of herself to beyond herself. Even as her new bodily way of being in the world removes her former understanding of herself, the ongoing exchange between this new body and self creates new meanings for her experience and new possibilities for action.

"The pregnant woman notices that the world is full of pregnant women, mothers, and babies" (Bergum, 1989b, p. 62). For Katherine, this was so even before she realized that she intended to continue this pregnancy. She noticed mothers and children and pregnant women and their bellies. The possibilities of her pregnancy included looking where she had not concerned herself before: at baby things in stores and children on the street. She took out her calculator and estimated her financial needs for a child; she looked at the cost of diapers, strollers, and other fundamental items. She noted her efforts to take care of herself, which had been going on for some time, "my self-improvement." Once a fairly frequent drinker, she was refraining from alcohol, trying to get more exercise, and making an effort to eat well. Just pregnant, she was already beginning to imagine a place for a child, to find a way to be *with child.*

For Katherine, the fruits of this body-self dialogue remained evident, even after her miscarriage. She continued to take better care of herself than she had before pregnancy and she opted to keep her own apartment, declining her boyfriend's invitation to move in with him. Taking care of herself feels good, and she wants to keep exploring the personal changes that accompanied this experience of unexpected pregnancy. Having found her voice and heard its sound, the place she wishes to take in the world is taking shape. She does not wish to close the dialogue with self prematurely after she has finally begun to attend to it.

Gadow's (1980) levels of relation between self and body lead us to the question: How does the bodily experience of pregnancy inform each woman as she considers her situation and searches for her own voice, for herself? These descriptions of unexpected pregnancy suggest that in attending to their bodily experiences of pregnancy, each woman recovered knowledge of herself in an ongoing, dialectical fashion. For each woman, the dialectic between body and self within pregnancy formed a different account of knowing, an account that can never be completed in nature. Each woman had questions about her experience at the close of the research, but they were different from the ones they started with. For instance, Katherine began her pregnancy wondering if she could take responsibility for a child; after her miscarriage, she questioned instead when she would become a mother. There was no longer doubt, for her, that she could be a mother, only uncertainty about the right timing.

Gadow (1980) herself asserts that just such incompleteness connotes the quality of the dialectic throughout all of its phases. It seems that, as with the research method itself, understanding lies more with finding the next question than with arriving at one unassailable answer. What seems important for our understanding of women's experiences of unexpected pregnancy, then, is that we acknowledge the potential significance of each account and ask ourselves to listen to them. As we listen, we affirm the place of such accounts in women's experiences; we affirm a place for women. Each woman can hear her own voice, as she questions the place of her pregnancy in her life and comes to understand what its unexpected arrival means for her, as a "choice embedded" (Sherwin, 1989, p. 67) and an experience embodied in her life. Allowed to hear herself, she can begin to contemplate the meaning, for her, of this unique relation with other.

Pregnancy as Relation: The Unique Self-Other

What does the body-self dialogue expressed in unexpected pregnancy by these women help us to understand about their experiences? What does it feel like, unexpectedly pregnant, to move from a daily communion between self and body that is understood and taken for granted to a changing dialogue that is full of unknown possibilities of self and other? In Bergum's (1989b) research with women choosing pregnancy, there was a growing sense of the presence of the fetus expressed, as well as different feelings of vulnerability. Yet, in their experiences of chosen pregnancy, the loss of control and vulnerability seemed to help them to understand the changes to come; the women became aware of what pregnancy and motherhood asked of them. Each woman, in her own way and own time, determined that she *was* now a mother, however enormous the responsibility seemed at times.

How do women experience the vulnerability and loss of control of pregnancy when it is unexpected and unchosen? As with the women in Bergum's (1989b) study, the body-self dialogue for these women became, at some point, dialogue with the fetus as possible other. That dialogue was welcomed or struggled with, bringing with it a strengthening of self or a threat to self. Space for each woman as herself began to transform, as she considered the notion of making room for the fetus-as-other within.

For Katherine and Mary, that notion seemed to strengthen their sense of themselves as women, and there seemed to be enough space for both self-as-woman and self-with-fetus, the unique relation that is self, yet not oneself (Bergum, 1989b). For Maggie, that same notion seemed full of fear and pain. Struggling to retain a sense of self after her relationship with her lover ended, she could not find a relation within that strengthened her. The pregnancy seemed to lead not toward but away from self in a sense that was full of terror. Learning the sex of her fetus after the abortion, she found a relation with her fetus through a priest who listened without judging. Heard once, she found the resolve to write to her lover and be heard again. In this research, she voices her experience once more and expresses a self that is changed and stronger. She will not offer her love again to a man who cannot share genuine intimacy.

For Vanessa, sharing herself with her son felt like a smothering of her own voice as she searched for others to listen to what this experience meant to her. The "taking over" of self that Vanessa spoke of during pregnancy now changes; the experiences of birthing, mothering, and breast-feeding her son create new questions for her. Nursing, with its bodily rhythms of filling and emptying of the breasts, nurturing and being drained, and holding and connecting to one another, informs Vanessa's understanding of her son's deep need for her and her equally strong need to know that he will be cared for. Even as she questions whether she can mother him, she sees what mothering is and takes it on. But with no one listening, she takes it on with fear of drowning, losing herself. She asks others to hear her needs: to have space for herself as woman and to know that others truly understand what it means to mother.

It seems that with chosen or unchosen pregnancy, a sharing of self is asked for that is unique to the experiences of women: a sharing of self within that alters the very boundaries of self as known. For the women in this research, the sharing of self with other was encountered when each woman imagined or realized a possibility of a child. The voice of every woman began with her body as self, but for Katherine and Mary, continuing the pregnancy brought a developing relationship with other, a unique other within (Bergum, 1989b). For Maggie, the sharing began from the safety of a recovered self, with a priest and in this research. For Vanessa, the struggle in sharing continues as she mothers and tries to choose for her child.

For each woman, being heard was the essential first step in contemplating a sharing of self with a child-as-other. Those who found no place in pregnancy from which to speak out and be heard as themselves found no place for relation-with-other. Listened to as they are, in the first voice of self, women may then be heard in a second one: the voice of woman-in-relation.

The Second Voice: Woman-in-Relation

The fact that such accounts of their pregnancies surfaced only when these women were questioned by a researcher seems to support the assertions of Gilligan (1982) and Noddings (1984) that women take very little time for themselves, time that is separate from others. When they described their lives to me, present relational ties and relational legacies of childhood families suffused the talk of these women. More than any other theme, understandings of themselves in relation to others constructed the contexts from which they designated a place for themselves, if any. Often, the women would begin to talk about themselves separate from others only after repeated questioning.

On one level, this thread of others in women's talk may reflect the fact that their lives are embedded in "ties that bind"; that in the binding of these women to others, they come to choose for their pregnancies. Ties that bind can be viewed as those attachments that secure, fasten, enclose, or cause to cohere (Morris, 1978). Alternately, however, ties can also "hold or restrain . . . compel, obligate, or unite . . . make certain or irrevocable . . . [or be] tight and uncomfortable . . . [or] stiff" (Morris, 1978, p. 132). We often speak of such relational ties in women's lives, but perhaps we ask less often what it is to be *bound up in* something—to "be inseparably connected with [or] wholly dedicated to" something or someone in our lives (Morris, 1978, p. 156).

Yet perhaps it is this experience of being bound up in, more than the binding ties themselves, that informs women's choosing in the experience of unexpected pregnancy. Ties that bind—children waiting for dinner, legal partnerships in life or business, colleagues and friends who want some of our time—are all concrete details of relationships, proof of our connections to one another. They seem to show who is important to us, what matters. But what of the commitments in which we are bound up by being in relation with one another, the foundations that create and sustain those ties—the commitments of love, care, nurturance, trust, and understanding of others? How can an exploration of the commitments underlying women's relational ties help us to understand the nature of unexpected pregnancy for these women? What did choosing in pregnancy become bound up in, for these women?

Bergum (1994) suggests that "understanding the nature of commitment and care of One (the mother) for the Other (the developing child) may give greater understanding of what it means to care and nurture one another" (p. 1). This statement is useful as we question how the women in this research, in unexpected pregnancy, determined the possibilities for nurturance from the contexts of their relationships. We can ask: How does each woman find nurturance for herself and for her pregnancy in her experience of relationship with others? For these women, what was inseparable in connection to their pregnancies, bound up in their choices, if a commitment to nurture a child into being was to be made?

Women and Ties: Negation or Nurturance of Self?

Mary said of her recent night at a friend's empty apartment, "It was nice. I haven't had time by myself, just me, oh, it's been over five years." For Mary, the everyday world is one of constant accompaniment, with daughters, ex-husbands, numerous friends, and relatives: "I don't break ties very well. . . . It's not an 'I'-oriented world, it's an 'us'-oriented world." Yet, although Mary did not question the number of people who seemed to need her in her life, she viewed their responsibilities to her as different from hers to them: "I seem to attract dependent people. Probably by my will as much as theirs." If she could be there for others, she would be. That was what she was used to, from early on in life. When she was 5 years old, her little brother died and her mother took ill. Although she did not have to start staying home from school until several years later, when her mother finally had a heart attack, it is from 5 on that she remembers feeling responsible for the others: "Brad died on August 29th and Dad went out to work, he couldn't stay home very long 'cause he couldn't afford to. . . . I know he wasn't home for my birthday and he came home at Christmas; I think I started being a mother then."

Surrounded by others in her present home, Mary often had up to 8 people over for coffee or 11 children over to bake cinnamon buns on the weekend. A nephew who needed a stable home lived with her for the first year of his life, and a half brother with handicaps interrupted her nursing education for a year after his mother died because his "mom died and I took her place." Her family configuration at any given point might differ, yet in the midst of many relationships entering and exiting her life, for Mary one constant remained throughout: "There's always our core," herself and her two daughters. For Mary, her daughters represent the only relationships in which she is loved and accepted as she truly is: "I don't have to be anything more for the girls except me."

In contrast, Mary spoke of her husband as a man who could not accept her or her daughters. Feeling that "a woman's place is in the home," he is even more upset about her being a nurse than he was about her being a waitress: "Good wives don't." As a teenager, Mary had to turn down university scholarships to stay home with her younger siblings. Now, after a long struggle to enter nursing school and to graduate, Mary says of her first few months of nursing, "You're doing the same kind of stuff, you're taking care of people, waiting on them, but you get a lot more respect and people don't treat you like crap."

Mary's husband thought that she was "filling the girls with too much women's lib nonsense. Well, it's not. It's survival and it's just plain ordinary survival." For Mary, that survival also meant not letting her husband divide her family between "his" baby, her current pregnancy, and her two daughters. His comment that "it would be nice to have his own child" seemed to represent a key difference in values between Mary and her husband:

> I have two kids already and if I have another one, I'll have three kids, not two of this and one of that. . . . It can't be two separate families. It is one family. Or it won't be. . . . There is no special one. They are special or you don't have them. And if I carry through with the pregnancy and he does impose his "my baby," I'll just leave.

For Mary, the initial significance of her husband's reaction to the pregnancy receded as her experience of the pregnancy ensued. As he expressed resentment over the inconvenience of a baby at this point in their lives, her conviction that he was extraneous to her decision grew. The realization of what another child meant to her at this point in her life came more from the welcoming of the possibility she received from her daughters, her core. They let her know that the decision was hers and that they loved her no matter what she chose. Unlike her husband, Mary felt that her daughters sought no ownership of her, of the baby, or of her decision.

Deciding to keep the pregnancy and then losing it hurt Mary in a way that she "was really afraid that she couldn't stand up through. . . . I knew I could be strong for other people but I didn't know. I didn't know that I could be that strong for myself. . . . I'm a lot stronger than I thought I was." For Mary, nurturance came from the pregnancy itself and the response of those closest to her, her daughters, in both its joy and its loss. The acceptance and love she already gave and received from them in their daily lives were reinforced as they chatted around the kitchen table about due dates, did homework with friends, and chose baby things. That was the love that was there for her when they cried together after the miscarriage. They are the core that never changes; she finds contentment and strength in knowing that.

Katherine, too, saw her pregnancy as an experience that gave her strength: "Well, it has been building for a while but I think the pregnancy made it come around a lot faster. 'Cause being pregnant . . . you have to be strong because it is not just for yourself." She avoided her boyfriend while she thought about her pregnancy; she feared that his insistence on another abortion, as with her previous pregnancies, would intimidate her if she let him near. With those pregnancies, she had looked to him for care and found none. This time, she did not expect him to care and found strength in deciding that she would not seek it from him. This time, she expected to care about herself and find out, for the first time, what it was that *she* wanted to do.

For Mary and Katherine, it seemed that the dialogue with self initiated by pregnancy revealed their strength. The dialectic within gave them a place from which to imagine themselves, in these pregnancies, as mothers. Lippitz (1990), in his interpretation of Levinas's discourse on the ethical meaning of the Other, suggests that "there is no symmetry in the ethical experience. I am not an equal partner, but . . . The Other enables me to do more than I can do" (p. 55). Perhaps the dialectic of pregnancy for Katherine and Mary, as one that took them toward rather than away from self, allowed for the existence of other, allowed for the possibility of a child-to-be and a mother-to-be. Sensing the strength to be drawn from their own experiences, they protected their self-communion by distancing themselves from relationships that interfered with their listening to it. They disengaged from partners who could not nurture them and sought affirmation of themselves as worthwhile from other sources: for Mary, her daughters, and for Katherine, her sister and mother. In recognizing where nurturance for them as women was not situated, they turned toward relationships where it was present. Nurtured as women, they found a place within from which to nurture the notion of woman-as-mother.

In contrast, Maggie and Vanessa entered pregnancy enmeshed in their relationships, ones that did not seem to acknowledge their needs. Unlike Katherine and Mary, who created space between themselves and their controlling partners, Maggie recalled how "any free time I had, it was he and I. I didn't see other people." They "never had an unpleasant moment" until their breakup. In retrospect, she felt that the pleasant ambience of their relationship seemed dependent on her meeting certain criteria for him as a mate and reliant on her not having an important past that had involved other people. With both him and her ex-husband, the thread of ownership seemed constant: "They were very much alike. . . . They wanted to own me, they wanted me to fit into them, they wanted me to fit into their lives."

To *own* is "to have or possess, [or] to acknowledge or admit" (Morris, 1978, p. 938). To be admitted into another's life only on that person's terms seemed to Maggie to be her experience of both these relationships. In comparison, to *come into one's own* is to "obtain possession of what belongs to one, [or] to obtain rightful recognition" (Morris, 1978, p. 938). Vanessa talked of her need to find recognition from others that her feelings were real, that her differing knowledge of self from their picture for her was valid. She feared that no one would listen to her, that she would not be able to own that knowledge of herself, and would not come into her own: "As the days go on, I am further away from being in touch with my feelings and closer to being swept into whatever the others want. . . . more and more it's taken over . . . you are giving up you."

Vanessa, like Maggie, questioned who could love her for herself-as-woman. Her husband's refusal to accept her feelings as genuine are crystallized in his statement to her when she first tried, just pregnant, to talk with him about adoption: "You'll change, when the time comes and we see that baby, you will change." Her mother said the same thing. Recollecting her experience of being "kicked out of home" at age 14 when she rebelled, she has a deep fear of being rejected by her husband, family, friends, and her entire community of others should she insist on being heard. That fear of being cast out "makes you hesitant to find out how you really feel. . . . It's a real need to be accepted."

In her experience of giving up herself, Vanessa contemplated giving up her son. She did not see a way, during pregnancy or during the first days after birth, for there to be room for both herself-as-woman and herself-as-mother, a rightful place for both her and her son. Caring for her son and wanting his needs met, she felt an inexorable and escalating loss of self. Everyone continued to offer her "the 'right' decisions" for her situation, just as they had in pregnancy. She recalled how with the first news of her pregnancy, her boyfriend had told her, "If you have an abortion, I will never speak to you again," and her mother had told her that if she wouldn't keep the baby, "I'll take it." She was told that as her belly swelled, she would "fall in love with that baby," but during pregnancy, "not once did I ever feel like I loved it. . . . I never bonded with him." In marriage, however, her feelings remain as unacceptable to her partner as before; her husband watched a television program on postpartum depression and suggested to Vanessa that she must have this illness—it is a neat, tolerable explanation to him for the doubts she is voicing.

Meanwhile, Vanessa feels that a choice for her son, which no one wants to hear her talk about, "needs to be dealt with right now and you don't have time to find out what you can do." The ever-present needs of mothering him had left her feeling unable to locate herself and to find her voice. This research is her first claim to that voice and seems to have initiated further dialogue between herself within and with her husband and son. In the nurturance of being listened to now by her husband, Vanessa feels that she can begin to understand what choosing for her son means to her; only then can she make that choice.

For Maggie, too, the process of reclaiming herself could not begin in pregnancy, and without self she could not find a place for mothering. For her, the experience of her pregnancy and her relationship were "part and parcel because the pregnancy was his and I trusted him." Without the nurturance of that trust and the relationship it held the promise of, there would be no baby; there was barely herself. Physically, she faded away and others questioned her will to live; she questioned it also. Only after the abortion and with the nurturance of a nonjudgmental priest could she find a relation with the child she had once hoped for.

Maggie felt that she had barely escaped with herself from her relationship with her lover. She reflected on how little her voice seemed to count with him, as he went on vacation instead of staying with her through the abortion, as he had promised he would. That discounting of her experience was reinforced for her when he telephoned on his return: "The first thing that he said to me was that he had troubles with his car . . . then he asked me how it was and I said that it hurt like hell, it was painful. . . . Virtually, I did it alone."

Over her lover's objections, Maggie obtained the blessing that she felt she needed for her unborn baby's soul. This was the beginning, for her, of counting herself in again; this was what *she* felt her baby needed. She wrote her lover a letter and told him exactly what she thought of his betrayals, to hand back the discounting of her experience that she felt he had shown her. She feels now that his actions spoke not of her worth but of his inability to handle genuine intimacy and his reluctance to include others in his life in a deeply meaningful way. She has drawn a new line for relationships in her life that will not be violated: "I know who I am and what I am and I'm quite content with that." Others will now have to be content with it as well.

Maggie sees now that her feeling of lacking a rightful place for herself in the relationship with her lover was always there, always a problem, but one that she kept hoping would go away. When she changed from simply fitting in to demanding a more intimate and reciprocal relationship, she felt him start to withdraw. Pregnant, she hoped that he would not act as she feared—promise her emotional support and then bail out on her. But "everything I said he was going to do, he did. . . . What I've learned about myself is that my gut feelings are usually right. And go with them. . . . The voice was always there." Maggie says that the reason she wanted a child with her lover was a good one: "We wanted the responsibility of a child." She would keep that reason should she ever want a child with a man. What has perhaps changed, for Maggie, is the man with whom she would plan a child: "What has come out of it is that in a future relationship, we will talk about what has gone on in my life and either you accept me now or you don't."

In almost losing herself and in losing the possibility of a child she had once hoped for, Maggie has determined that no relationship with a man will take precedence over being herself and having her own voice within the relationship. She feels that no man will ever again tell her what her place as a woman is for him; either there will be a place for her that is genuine or there will be no place at all.

A Woman's Voice, a "Woman's Place"

In the talk of all four women, the experience of unexpected pregnancy brought to the fore a notion that all had grappled with in their relationships with men: their sense of what a "woman's place" was for their partners. Mary said, "I have to do a lot of changing before I can be a good wife." Her husband disapproved of her education, her work, and virtually all of her friends. A good wife and mother belonged at home. Katherine's desire to exclude her boyfriend from her thinking about this pregnancy stemmed from her feeling that in past pregnancies, "he didn't give me any breathing room." For her, this was indicative of her place in his life overall: "It's like if our feelings jibe, mine get considered; if they don't, they don't."

Maggie, recalling the constant feeling that they were "on their first date," felt in retrospect that the smooth functioning of life with her lover meant fitting into his schedule and his friends, even though they had both come to the relationship with busy careers, many friendships, and several interests.

She realized that in their time together, her former life had slowly slipped away in many respects. She felt that their life together was filled up not so much with joint interests as with a continuation of what he had always done. Vanessa, too, spoke repeatedly of the expectations of others. Her husband, family, and friends all told her repeatedly that a good woman, a normal one, would naturally embrace pregnancy and motherhood. Of course, a "really" good woman would also never have sex before marriage, but if she did and became pregnant, she would "live up to" her responsibilities. A normal woman would never dream of aborting her fetus or giving her baby up for adoption. Listening to the advice on a talk show about postpartum depression made more sense to Vanessa's husband than did listening to Vanessa's disturbing doubts and fears.

For all four women, to insist on being heard was to step "out of place," that is, to reject the role assigned to them by the men in their lives. To voice their experiences and feel heard, they had to go to a priest or a counselor or friends or children. None found a place for her voice in her relationship with her partner. To some extent, each woman said that she found a place for her voice in this research, and for some it was the first place. Is a woman who "stays in her place" a woman who is not heard? Where, in these women's relationships with men, was a place for their voices? Where was a place for them?

Women's Place: A Place of Nurturance?

What can we see of nurturance for these women in their experiences of relationships in unexpected pregnancy? For all the women, the acceptance they sought with partners differed in important ways from what they had experienced. Yet both Katherine and Mary spoke of growing through this time and realizing strength of which they had not thought themselves capable. That strength came from themselves and seemed nurtured from the place of self. As they gave voice to their experiences, they valued it. They discarded the place their partners had assigned them, pursuing relationships where regard for their experiences was offered: for Mary, with herself and her daughters; for Katherine, with family and, most important, with herself.

In contrast, Maggie did not speak of nurturance during her pregnancy. It was a time of threat to her very self; she felt emotionally abandoned in a relationship that seemed more entangled than intimate. She described her experience of this tie at its end as one of "strong physical attachment and deep emotional absence." Even as they were breaking up, her lover still wanted to have sex. This just reinforced for Maggie that he was not capable of being there for her in any way that counted for her, and she refused. Nurturance of the other was not a possibility; for Maggie, survival of self took precedence. That self now starts to grow again as she speaks of reclaiming "what is mine." Now, like Mary and Katherine, she speaks of distancing herself from relationships that do not take her as she is. Like them, she seeks others who will nurture her now and, like them, she realizes that search starts from a new relation with self.

Vanessa, nurturing her newborn son even as she seeks nurturance, perhaps most clearly presents the tension between the relationships of woman-as-self and woman-as-mother. Her realization of her son's needs leaves her helpless to ignore him, even at the cost of self:

> I do love him . . . how could you not love him? Because he is so helpless and he is so dependent on me. . . . It's 24 hours a day for me. . . . I have to be there at this stage of the game. . . . And men don't feel that. Like Jim will say, "No I don't want to change him." But yet if he was to say to me, "You want to change him?" I would say, "Yes, because he needs a change." So you have to want to. . . . My husband isn't in touch with it the way I am. Because I want his needs met.

For Vanessa, a child cannot be turned from. Even as her husband asks her how she can think of giving him up, she sees that it is she who cannot leave him wet, leave him hungry, or leave him not held. The week before our initial talk, she had packed a bag and almost left her husband. He asked if she was going to take their son with her. She knew that she would, because repeated efforts to get him to take a bottle had failed and he remains on the breast. "Don't hurt him," her husband told her; that wounded her deeply and angered her "that he would say that to me. . . . His big thing is, 'Don't you love him?' And I do love him but that doesn't mean that I have to want him." Loving him is seeing his needs and responding to them as totally as she can, even at the expense of herself. In contrast, wanting him is accepting the room that he needs in her life and finding from that acceptance sufficient room for both of them: "Wanting is having a place in your life for him. Being able to accept the joy that he gives you and want to give him joy too."

Now, as Vanessa's husband asks her more and more about her experience of responsibility for this child, she finds that she suspends making a choice for her son. As he turns toward her and their child, she does not yet see the right place for her child. She does know, however, that she is finding a place for her feelings. Her husband is listening to her for the first time. She finds herself listening to her child anew; perhaps in this new sharing her son is more truly *their* child and their shared responsibility. She asks her husband to struggle as hard as she does and to join her in finding the right place for their child. To search for the right place for one's child is to speak in the third voice: the voice of woman-as-mother.

The Third Voice: Woman-as-Mother

Returning to the verbal meaning of *to place,* which "always implies care and precision in bringing something to a desired position" (Morris, 1978, p. 1001), we can ask, What is it like to look for a place for a child? Every woman in this research sought to find the right place for a real child or for an imagined child-to-be. Three of the women also spoke of other experiences of pregnancy in which this was not the case. Katherine talked of her previous pregnancies, when any ideas she might begin to form about possibilities other than abortion were swiftly terminated by her boyfriend. He had a way of outarguing her, of saying things that "make me feel like dirt." Maggie, talking of a previous abortion from a different relationship, never questioned the status of that first pregnancy before or after the abortion: "The pregnancy was a fact but it was not real and I think there is a big difference between fact and reality. It was a state of my body and I knew that, but there was no sense of baby there." And Mary, after the devastating loss of her twins, never allowed herself to imagine taking home a baby again: "I didn't think about having a baby. I didn't think about taking a baby home, holding a baby, or nursing a baby. . . . I just wasn't willing to be that hurt again."

Where a child-to-be was imaginable, however, pain in unexpected pregnancy for these women was unavoidable. To enter into relation with a possible child, a place had to be found. To seek that place for a child-to-be was to become bound up in the commitment which that child represented to each woman. That commitment inserted great risk of hurt into their lives, and regardless of the eventual choice in pregnancy for Mary, Maggie, Katherine, and Vanessa, pain was part of seeking a place for a child. Vanessa saw her pain as part of her responsibility for her son: "You can take responsibility for your actions by, you know, giving him up for adoption and running the risk of being an emotional wreck for a little while . . . but I don't know what I can live with."

To search for the right place for one's child, real or imagined, was to search with the voice of a mother. It was to leave behind forever, for each woman, herself as she had been, as woman, as she had understood herself. It was to know the pain of mothering and to keep seeking until a place, carefully chosen, was found for one's child.

Searching for a Place for a Child

Each woman's search for a place for her child began in its own time, the time when relation to a real or imagined child became strong and tangible for her. For Mary and Katherine, that relation began and grew in the early days of pregnancy. As each of them searched for the right place for her pregnancy, a search for self seemed to accompany and assist her choice about her pregnancy. For Maggie, a relation superseded by her break with her lover became very real and important to her after her abortion, when she learned the sex of her aborted fetus. For Vanessa, who fought to retain any sense of herself during pregnancy, that time came when she took her son home, where the realities of caring for him set in. In the hospital, she still felt some hope that she could be "the perfect mom"; the walls of the institution somehow made her feel very safe with her son and able to be "just you and the baby, right there." Then she went home and the fact of 24-hour motherhood, with minimal help from her husband, set in: "You have no choice but to take care of the baby."

As she searched her feelings about relinquishing her son, Vanessa returned to her own experience of being adopted. Adopted when she was 3 months old into a family with three children, she recalled how much it bothered her to grow up around people she felt were very different from herself. Although she feels certain that her adoptive parents love her and that they wanted her, she still speaks of a belonging that she has never felt within her family:

> I knew that I didn't know where I belonged and I hated it, I hated not looking like anybody . . . like you look at my family and you can see that they are all from the same place, you know; they just belong. And me, I'm really different, I have a temper and everybody else is really passive. . . . I'm talking about who you are inside. . . . And I knew that I was welcomed and wanted, but I didn't fit.

After she became pregnant, Vanessa felt a need to find out more about her birth mother. She talked animatedly about her discovery of her mother's career as a dietitian when she looked at the adoption papers: "Ever since I was a little girl I have wanted to be a dietitian, you know, that was my dream. . . . It gave me a sense of belonging . . . it made me feel like there was a place for me but I wasn't in it."

As she searches for understanding from her husband and family about the idea of placing her son for adoption, she feels that her birth mother would have a better sense of what she is undergoing than her adoptive parents have demonstrated. Believing that her birth mother gave her up out of love and not being able to provide for her, she seeks corresponding recognition from her present family of her motives, but "I don't even think that they could even venture into how my mind is going." Noting that her adoptive mother and two brothers all married with pregnancies already under way, she feels a futility in trying to act at variance with their deeply held religious beliefs. She does not want to cause anyone any pain, so she assumes the pain must all be hers alone: "So you just don't want to fight them because you're fighting their values and all that kind of thing and that's how I have been raised, so it's right."

Yet Vanessa does not know that "it's right." She does not know that she shares her family's values and she does not yet know what is right for her and her son. Her greatest hope in keeping him is that "he knows that we love him"; her greatest fear is that he would "know that he wasn't a wanted baby. . . . I think children know." Yet those fears and others are not entirely assuaged by the promise of adoption, either. There, she worries that he might be abused or neglected or that he too might never have the sense of belonging that she feels she has missed. And Vanessa is "scared of losing my husband, losing my family, and losing someone who might even look like me because I have never had that before." Still, if she could assure herself that he was going to a good family, perhaps even stay in touch with them, Vanessa speculates that being loved and wanted "would surpass actual fitting in as far as my dreams and desires. And who you are. It would probably surpass that." For Vanessa, the search for the right place for her child continues. She cannot convince herself of the absolute fit of either keeping or placing her son. A lone voice in a community of relationships that reject her words, she continues to care for her son. She cannot leave him, because he will not take the bottle and needs her breast milk. She thinks of leaving her husband, but when she packs her bags, he exhorts her not to hurt her son and suggests to her that maybe she is suffering from postpartum depression. He wonders if she is ill; she wonders if anyone else will ever understand what it means to love this child. She wonders, if no one hears her voice, if she can nurture this child as she knows he needs to be nurtured: Where will the nourishment she needs to nourish him come from?

Vanessa knows that she is not suffering from illness. She is suffering from love for her child and from her full understanding of the weight of that love, the deep need of such love. She will not suffer those needs to go wanting. At the cost of her relationships, she considers what is truthful about his welfare and how it is best served. She cannot trust the advice of others, others who do not seem to trust her to know herself better than they do, others who are not asking her about her own experience. She keeps seeking out what she can find in herself and what she is able to trust in herself. She will not rest until she finds a place for her child, a place that she can trust is the right one for him, and for her as his mother.

A Place for a Child: A Place of Trust

Baier (1986) asserts that "to understand the moral risks of trust, it is important to see the special sort of vulnerability it introduces" (p. 239). Pointing out that to *trust* entails the handing over of what we care about to someone or something else, Baier entreats us to question: Do we really know what it is that we ask of another when we ask him or her to trust us? And what do we ask of ourselves in entrusting what matters in our world to another?

Citing the innate trust of a parent as a relationship of extreme vulnerability and risk for the infant, Baier suggests that it may be women's understanding of the intensity of commitment to a helpless other that differentiates their experiences of caring for children from those of most men. This different experience begins in pregnancy, where, even if unwanted, the developing other draws nurturance from the woman's body and grows. This nurturance continues after birth as most women maintain the major responsibility for the feeding and care of the infant.

This innate trust, "a necessary element in any surviving creature whose first nourishment . . . comes from another" (Baier, 1986, p. 242), may not just accompany but virtually define the relationship that begins when a woman accepts the unique relation of self-other in early pregnancy. What other situation demands greater trust, both of oneself and on behalf of a becoming other, than entering and giving oneself over to pregnancy? How do women find and nurture that sense of trust within to an experience that leaves them uniquely exposed and vulnerable, as no other can, to the profound commitment of loving a unique other, an other within and of themselves?

For Mary, love and acceptance for a possible child had to be forthcoming from the important people in her life if she was even going to consider continuing the pregnancy. At age 37, with two teenage daughters and an ambivalent husband, Mary declared that this pregnancy could not take precedence over relationships that were "already established. They're concrete, and I mean, what do you throw away?" But acceptance did not equate with the notion of ownership that her husband expressed when he talked about finally having "his own child." For Mary, who had lost important people in her life, "life is not a gift. It's not something somebody owes you for." Nor was creating life a just reason to say that one owns another.

Rothman (1989) contends that the idea of *owning* children is more aligned with "the traditional *rights* of fathers in patriarchy than it is to the ongoing *responsibilities* of raising a child" (p. 81). Ownership seemed to divide the women in this research from their partners. Maggie noted her lover's remark that he would never allow any new husband of his ex-wife to adopt their 3-year-old son, a son he had seen only once since his birth, despite legal access. He sent child support payments, but he also had private detectives check up on his ex-wife from time to time to ensure that she was not getting money from any other source. The purpose of the surveillance, he told Maggie, was so that he could legally break their support agreement if he discovered his ex-wife had other sources of support.

Maggie never once heard him express concern for his child's well-being; for him, she felt the issue at stake seemed to be "his ownership of the child." There was also no discrepancy, for him, in expecting acceptance as a mate who was the father of a son, yet not accepting any woman with a child as a suitable partner. As with Mary's mate, the salient feature of a child was not what one owes any child or what the child deserves; it was, rather, whether the child was "one's own."

Maggie's understanding of the place for women and children in her lover's world did not seem to offer any place of trust for her pregnancy, only ownership. What you owned, you did not have to "trust"; it *belonged* to you. What you no longer owned, you "kept an eye on." In the vulnerability of her pregnancy, Maggie searched for a place of trust within this context of ownership that seemed to pervade her lover's relationships; she saw none.

Ownership, for Katherine's boyfriend, seemed to extend to Katherine herself: He would tell her to have abortions and she would do as he ordered. But the scars of owning his decisions within her body built, with each experience, scars of taking pain that did not seem really to belong to her, pain she did not deserve and seemed helpless to avoid. She talked of her fear of her drunk and abusive father, when, as a child, she heard him come home late at night:

I would lay there and wait for him to come in and start something. Because he would do that every time. Come in, and if I had my nails painted, that was a big thing and I remember getting my ears pierced and I woke up one night and he was pulling on my ears, trying to rip my earrings out. . . . It seems like my mom, she would never do anything about it.

Katherine thought in hindsight that perhaps her mother did not see much choice, as "it was either he hit us or she got beat bad." Eventually, her mother did summon the strength to leave him after she found herself with a knife at his throat one night as he lay in a drunken stupor. She kicked him out and they haven't seen him since. By age 17, Katherine was involved with her current boyfriend, a man she described as always in the past able to "control me, push all my buttons." Katherine had never felt that choices in her other pregnancies were hers to make; he always clearly stated his expectation that she abort, and she never saw that she had an option. She did not think that it mattered what she thought.

Katherine's sense that her own words were inconsequential was reinforced when she sought advice about birth control. She tried to explain to the physician that the pill did not seem to work for her, but that she was sure she could learn how to use another method. She wanted to know more about diaphragms and IUDs. The physician listened briefly and told her that the pill was the only thing for her if she did not want to get pregnant. She did not want to get pregnant, but she explained that she just was not good at remembering to take the pill every day. The physician repeated that the only method suited for her was the pill. Katherine concluded that it did not matter what she thought. She forgot her pill, got pregnant again, and had another abortion. The scars grew and deepened.

The scarring came from many painful memories of those experiences. She recalled the nurses who cuddled and played with a baby while staring at her as she cried alone outside the operating room before her first abortion at age 16. They just kept looking at her as she cried and none of them came over to her. Her boyfriend broke up with her right after intimidating her into her last abortion: "It's like I get out of the hospital, he couldn't even wait for me to go home." During that same abortion, she was kept awake. The humiliation of laying there "with my legs up" with the crowd of people present in the operating room kept the worst pain at bay until afterward, when she got an infection. That pain she has never forgotten: "It just felt like someone had their hands up there and was grabbing my insides and pulling it out."

Scarring was what prompted Katherine's call to a local clinic to inquire about the possible damage that a fourth abortion might cause: "I get scared because I thought, it hurts, it's going to leave marks, like that can't be healthy for you." She was hoping that someone would tell her she could not have another abortion; she wanted someone to say, "You can't do this to yourself anymore." But she already knew that herself; she did not make an appointment. Instead, the nurse read Katherine the information sheet on this unexpected pregnancy research, and Katherine telephoned me.

Katherine talked of how her pain had changed her and her beliefs about others in her life. For her, the main source of nurturance for her possible child was herself, a self both scarred and changed by the previous pregnancies and abortions. She no longer expected her boyfriend to be there in any important way while she faced a choice as important to her as this pregnancy: "I feel like every time I've reached out for support when I really needed it, he's turned me down." She knew that, on the other hand, her mother and her sister would be there for her in an instant should she decide to continue her pregnancy. In fact, she knew that her mother would be hurt deeply if she chose anything but staying pregnant. But, for Katherine, the person she must not hurt this time, whatever she decided, was herself:

> I remember being pregnant and crying because I was going to have an abortion. I never even gave myself a chance to even think about having it. But now I am and it feels better. . . . I have a lot more self-esteem now. I think that now, to me, it does matter what I think.

Even before this pregnancy, Katherine was reviewing her life, deciding what she wanted to change. She felt she was outgrowing her friends, and she knew that she was happy to come home at the end of every weekend she spent with her boyfriend. She was working on her "bad habits" when this pregnancy began. With previous pregnancies, "I always knew that I was going to have an abortion, so I didn't really change my eating habits or stop going out or anything like that." This time, even as she was thinking about what she would do, Katherine started taking care of her health. Already drinking less than she used to, she quit drinking altogether. She became "more aware of my health . . . and it was good. I felt better." She stayed away from her boyfriend and talked of trusting herself this time, not him: "My life is more together now than it was before. And I'm sure it's going to get better. It will take time. . . . I still don't feel like I am completely ready, but do you ever?"

As Katherine nurtured herself, her trust in herself as a place of nurturance for a child grew. She looked at mothers and children, looked at baby things, and imagined a child. She looked within herself and saw a place for a child to grow: a place of nourishment, a place to which she could entrust a child. Trusting herself, she chose to have a child. Trusting herself, she entrusted this child-to-be to her care: "Before, I just couldn't even picture it, but this time I could and I was just looking at myself and I could just picture myself being a mother. Before I couldn't, before when I looked at myself being a mother it looked awkward, it didn't look right. But this time it did."

"Women expect to be different as mothers" (Bergum, 1989b, p. 36). What is it that women realize will be asked of them? What is it that they know they must be ready for? When asked what this difference was for her, Katherine said that it was strength, " 'cause being pregnant was sort of like, you have to be strong because it is not just for yourself." The strength is one that can withstand a loss of control of life as known and of self as understood (Bergum, 1989b). It begins with the bodily changes of pregnancy that tell a woman she is not as she was, and grows with the developing fetus as a unique relation-with-other that a woman who accepts pregnancy experiences.

For Mary, pregnancy was cause for a celebration of that strength. She saw it as a sign that she was living, not dying. It was an uncontrollable event that offered her new possibilities as a mother-to-be; strong enough to put her fears of miscarriage behind her, she looked forward to enjoying her pregnancy in a way she had not dared with either of her daughters. She felt able, in pregnancy now, to experience the presence of her fetus as she had with her first pregnancy, the twins. The experience of pregnancy was once again an experience to which she could entrust herself.

Trust within pregnancy, trust of oneself-as-pregnant and of this relationship with an other within, is hidden and difficult to articulate. As Bergum (1990) points out, it is not easy for our conscious, rational minds to accommodate the "embodied experience of knowing the fetus to be part of oneself and yet not oneself" (p. 17). Yet experiencing the presence of the fetus within, being able to entertain this singularly different relation with "self-other," may be very much bound up in whether that trust is present for each woman. How does a woman experience the mother-fetus relationship in the absence of trust? Vanessa, not trusting others who told her what she did not feel, claims that she never "bonded" with her son before birth. Maggie, seeing nowhere to entrust the risks of pregnancy and motherhood, aborted.

This need for trust in pregnancy, which is very difficult to bring into language, may also be some of what we must acknowledge a woman's need for, some of what a woman is bound up in, as she chooses in unexpected pregnancy. Higgins (1991), a physician who has examined trust as it applies to health care, notes, "Trust is both expectation and commitment, necessitated by risk and uncertainty; it is oriented to the future, predictive of possible behaviours, and bears with it a vulnerability, a yielding of control to another" (p. 15).

Although Higgins (1991) addresses his remarks to caregivers, we can use these observations about trust to ask ourselves what it is that women sense is involved in choosing for an unexpected pregnancy. Particularly, in the vulnerability and loss of control that both these women and those in Bergum's (1989b) study speak about, one must ask: What is the nature of the risk; what is "at stake"? Katherine said that with each abortion, "it was still so hard because I felt like I loved it and everything." Continuing those pregnancies entailed the risk of giving birth to a love she could never turn from but did not feel yet able to give. She would not let such a risk be taken for any child of hers. She would not let there be a child until she could trust herself enough to have a place of love for a child. There could not be a place for a child until she could trust that there was a place for herself-as-mother.

Adoption: A Need to Re-Vision Trust?

Where a place for self-as-mother could not be seen, adoption was not even a consideration, for Mary, Maggie, or Katherine. For all of them, giving away their children would be to give away themselves; each said, "How do you give away yourself?" For Katherine, to give her child up would be to ask herself to give away "everything." She spoke of a friend firmly steered by her mother toward giving away her baby at 16: "Up to this day she gets sort of depressed on its birthday. She thinks about it all the time and this is like eight years ago." That same friend got pregnant again a year after giving up her child and had an abortion. To Katherine, her friend's experiences support her convictions about adoption as loss of self: "Obviously, adoption wasn't something she wanted to go through again."

To give over one's child, in adoption, was for each of these women to give over oneself. Katherine further noted that for her friend, there seemed to be no follow-up: After she delivered at a home for teenage mothers in the city, her mother took her back to their town and it was "life as usual." For Katherine as well as for Maggie and Mary, adoption was a story of loss, pain, and intolerable separation of self from self. Nothing that they knew, either of themselves or adoption, allowed them to entrust a child-to-be to this possibility.

The views expressed by the women in this research are supported in several recent reviews of research on the traditional practice of closed adoption in Western society, where acknowledgment of the nature of birth mothers' grief is repeatedly noted as lacking (Brodzinsky, 1990; Winkler, Brown, van Keppel, & Blanchard, 1988). Researchers have found that the losses of birth mothers in closed adoptions are attended by losses for adoptive parents and children, and all are disconnected from self-knowledge by the obscuring of fundamentally important relationships. Yet Winkler et al. (1988), as well as other researchers, do not question the value of adoption itself, but rather ask how more open ways of giving up and taking on children might change the nature of adoption and leave relationships more intact (see, e.g., Baran & Pannor, 1990; Rothman, 1989).

Vanessa, herself a child of the traditional system of closed adoption, knows that she hated not knowing "where I fit," yet does not know quite how she would give her son up for adoption in a more open way: "I just don't know what I can live with." Yet with closed adoption, she worries about abuse or neglect that she could not know of or prevent. Perhaps Baier (1986) clarifies what is at stake for women who consider the possibility of giving up a child when she talks about the "crucial variable in trust relations . . . the relative power of the truster and the trusted, and the relative costs to each of a breakdown to their trust relationship" (p. 240).

Both Baier (1986) and Higgins (1991) claim it is this inequality of power that characterizes relationships that demand, rather than naturally nurture, trust. What do we ask of women, then, when we ask them first to trust the experience of unexpected pregnancy and then to *entrust* their children to unknown and unknowable others? In her discussion of the need to recognize that we all come from a "network of trust," Baier (1986) points out that "any person's attitude to another in a given trust relationship is constrained by all the other trust and distrust relationships in which she is involved" (p. 258). In a web of relationships not allowed to be acknowledged, as with closed adoption, how do trusting relationships that nurture a birth mother, a given child, or adopting parents take root and grow?

For Vanessa, her own questions are accompanied by a conviction that there is no inherent value to one kind of childhood over another or one kind of parent over another. But Vanessa knows that, like pregnancy itself, adoption entails the taking up of a powerful trust, a trust of the unknown, and a trust on behalf of another. Already, pregnancy and motherhood have not been what others have told her they are, what others have insisted that she trust them to be. Perhaps in recognizing the nature of the trust that women in unexpected pregnancy become bound up in, we might better understand the right place for each woman and for any child who is meant to be born.

This interpretation of the experience of unexpected pregnancy thus becomes one that suggests that pregnancy, as a growing relationship of woman-fetus, asks for and must create a powerful site of trust if a mother and a child are to be born. In mistrust of her experience, Maggie could not see her way to such births and could not entrust herself to the commitment of pregnancy. And in considering the possibility of giving her son to another, who can tell Vanessa whom she should trust? Only she can know what she is able to trust; as she asks to be listened to, she asks: Who can I trust to love my child?

As she wonders what to do with her son, Vanessa mothers him in the way that she can, the best that she can. The milk in her breasts and her son's body curved into hers as he suckles them ground her understanding of his trust in her nurturance in a continuous rhythm of feeding and holding, day and night, day in and day out. Her acute apprehension of her son's needs and his inborn trust of her to meet them makes it impossible for her to leave him at this point. Rather, Vanessa imagines the disappearance of herself as no one around her acknowledges what her child's trust asks of her. Seeing his need and trust as no one else will, she feels that "right now it seems like either it has to be all for him or that there is not enough for him." She cannot see, however hard she tries, room for both herself-as-woman and herself-as-mother. She cannot see her way to a place for woman-as-mother.

A Place for Woman-as-Mother

In these experiences of unexpected pregnancy, each woman tried to see her way to motherhood, to question if she could be a "good mother." *To see one's way clear to something* is "to be willing or find it possible to do" (Morris, 1978, p. 1450). *Way* can also be defined as "a course affording passage from one place to another . . . [or the] room or space to proceed with any action" (Morris, 1978, p. 1450). We seek, in looking for a way, safe passage from what we know and are to what we do not yet know and might or might not be. If we find a way, we gain an understanding of ourselves as we already have become (Bergum, 1989b). Whatever way we find, we are never as we once were. Even in trying to find a way, something in us is changed. We have a new way of being and things are not the same way.

How does a woman find safe passage to the place of motherhood? To mother a child is to know pain, and the pain can never be safe. Bergum (1989b) refers to the "terror that is not in talk" (p. 84), the helpless fear we are faced with when we love a child. We are laid open in our deepest way when we know the experience of loving a child who is threatened by pain, illness, or injury. We are responsible and yet we can never fully ensure the child's safe passage. To love and parent a child is not safe.

Mary and Katherine's experiences of unexpected pregnancy were ones in which the place of nurturance for the child was a place of nurturance for the mother, and that place was the place of pregnancy itself. Their ways to motherhood seemed to be a passage through self and a passage-with-other through a beginning relation with self-other, mother-fetus. In a state of mutual nurturance, woman-as-self and fetus as becoming-self began to nourish each other into a mother-to-be and a child-to-be. But what of unexpected pregnancies in which nurturance for the mother is not present? What then of nurturance for a child? How safe is love where there is no nurturance?

We need to question what the unique unchosen nature of the mutual trust Baier (1986) hopes for between mother and infant asks us to recognize for the infant, for the mother, for us all. In unexpected pregnancy, how does a possible mother assure herself of that place of mutual trust and nurturance, that place for self-as-mother and child-to-be? Whereas Mary and Katherine each developed a growing assurance through dialogue with self-as-pregnant, Vanessa balanced the dialectic of a body that mothered hourly through the corporeal relationship of nursing and a self that felt imprisoned by what motherhood seemed to hold.

Vanessa speaks of her situation as one in which she relies on her husband for "help" with her son when he is home—about 4 hours of the baby's wakeful period on most days—but in which she must trust herself to respond to his needs, 24 hours a day, every day. Furthermore, her freedom to rely on her husband for help varies with the nature of what is on television at the time, whether he feels like it at that moment, or whether he even sees a need; timely diaper changes and cuddling their son close are needs that Vanessa, not her husband, sees: "He needs somebody there all the time, somebody who does his job. And I don't feel like my husband is doing his part." As Kuykendall (1984) points out, "It is a mother's practical experience that presents mothering as a trap for women" (p. 272), an experience of silent, unrecognized, and unsupported nurturance.

What are the corresponding moral risks and intents for a father who *helps* more willingly at one time than another and a mother who *commits to respond* in unfailing steadiness? Who can and must the infant trust? And who must be able to trust that he or she can be trusted? In the ideal case, Baier (1986) suggests, the automatic trust incurred with the responsibility for a child may be "unchosen but mutual" (p. 245). Both parent and infant, as they respond to each other and find each other's actions gratifying, learn that their shared faith in being cared for and in being able to care for is well placed. Parent and child are in desired relation to one another and, with the care and precision required in the learning of each other, find a position, a place with each other that engenders further trust. But who stands in desired relation to Vanessa, nurturing her position as mother, supporting the possibility of that mutual trust?

In Vanessa's world, that place for her child and herself-as-mother is not secured. Others tell her that she is a mother but do not ask her how that is for her. She waits for someone to listen to her experience of this overwhelming commitment, to show her by listening that there is a place for both her and her child. A place for both Vanessa and her son must be one that both can trust and be nurtured from. It must be a place where the nourishment for trust, the "network of trust relationships" Baier (1986, p. 258) speaks of, can be trusted to be. Perhaps, as her husband now asks her to tell him what she feels, how this really is for her, such a place becomes possible.

Maggie's dialogue with self did not nurture a sense of self-as-mother. She talked of her beliefs about motherhood, about what a good mother would do, a mother different from her own and more like her friends, who she called her "surrogate parents":

> I thought about things the way they were . . . could I be a good mother? My parents were there for me physically but I think to be very intimate with your children, to talk to them about things, to have that relationship such that your children can come to you for anything, no matter what they have done . . . I just really felt, could I have given it? . . . I didn't feel that I could do this.

Maggie knew the difference, for her, between physically showing up for a child and really *being there* for the child. The former set of actions metes out a recognition of obligation, as perhaps corresponds with ownership and "taking care of" one's own, of helping as required. In contrast, *being there* connotes a wider notion of commitment to a child: the covenant to respond, to *be with*, to make always, ever after, a place for a child in one's life. Such a place is not incidentally or inconveniently children's for as long as they are dependent, but rather might be seen as a place of "living side-by-side with children" (Bergum, 1989b, p. 112), a place where children and parents grow together for as long as they both need. Such a place promises nurturance for a way of being a mother and a way of being with children. It is a place to which a mother can entrust the being of her child and trust that care will take place.

Maggie's pregnancy did not seem to her to be such a place. She imagined the life of her child-to-be: "Someone will say, 'You don't have a father. Well, how come?' And kids can be very cruel." She thought about her lover's acrimonious, controlling, and neglectful relationship with his ex-wife and son. She fought off the terror that her lover's abandonment filled her with, an apprehension fed by memories of a violent ex-husband and a lonely childhood with distant parents. She shed pounds from her tiny frame, unable to eat to nourish herself. She found no place for nurturance; she found no place for a mother.

Still, Maggie searched for a place for her child-to-be after her abortion. She inadvertently found out from a laboratory technician that she had aborted "a normal baby girl." In naming her and having her blessed and entered into the priest's log and the church record, Maggie saw to it that her baby was spoken for. Writing to her ex-lover was a demand that he recognize their child's existence. But she refused to tell him which church she had gone to, and he became angry. Again, for him, ownership was at stake:

> He said he had the right to know and I said, "No." He said as the father he has the right to know and then I told him that no, he didn't, because he didn't participate in what I did with that pregnancy. . . . He expressed his wishes to fit in with how he felt, how comfortable he was going to be and how it would fit in with his life. That's probably the last time that I had anything to talk to him about.

To Maggie, her baby girl's "soul has a chance." Unable to nurture her here and now, she hopes that the rites she obtained for her will nourish her spirit elsewhere. She "had to do that." She had to entrust the care of her child to God. Now, in this research, she entrusts her child's care again to these words. She seeks another place of care for her child: a place that, like the priest, the counselor, and good friends, will care about her too and her experience of this unexpected pregnancy. In her understanding of the pain of this pregnancy for her, she is as good a mother for her child as she can be. Through her pain and in the way that she can, she mothers her child.

Mothering Pains

> Making the decision to have a child—it's momentous. It is to decide forever to have your heart go walking around outside your body. (Stone, 1991, p. 74)

Bergum (1989b) suggests that the pain of birth teaches a woman who she is in a new way. Birth, as pain, offers an all-powerful experience that brings forth a child, finally separating two who were one body. A woman may learn something of herself, through the pain, that helps her find the way to mothering. Just as surely there were other mothering pains, in unexpected pregnancy, for the women in this study. And, like birth, these other mothering pains left each woman changed.

To imagine a child-to-be and begin to see a way to becoming a mother is to lay oneself open for pain. When Katherine began to miscarry, she found herself crying on the X-ray table after her ultrasound. The pain of this miscarriage was "the exact same pain" as with her previous abortions, "just different circumstances." For Katherine, the only difference was that this pain, the pain of miscarriage, was one she was allowed to acknowledge: "When I had the miscarriage I didn't feel bad about crying. I felt like I had every right to cry. Whereas when I was having an abortion, I felt like I had to hold it in, that I didn't have any right to cry . . . but it was the same."

Looking back, Katherine felt that with each pregnancy, she changed: "With every one, it has made me grow." But this time, allowing herself to have the pain and finding others allowing her to do so, the growth seemed to birth a new self for Katherine. She did not get to bear her child, but she now knows she could be a mother. She feels there is a way for her to be a mother. At the right time, she feels that she will now know her way.

Already a mother, Mary found that the pain of her miscarriage delivered her back to herself in a new, stronger way. The pain of this miscarriage was a lot worse, she said; the other times, she had not allowed herself to hope for a child. But in letting herself hope for what she wanted this time, it seemed that even the pain could not take away the gift of the experience: putting herself and her dreams first for a change. She may or may not try to have another child in the future; there is a new man in her life who is good to her and her daughters. But she intends to continue to put herself and the people who are in her dreams, her daughters, first in her life.

After their miscarriages, both Mary and Katherine still drew strength from their experiences of pregnancy. Both felt that they were stronger people, and both attributed the strength that they felt to their pregnancies. As Katherine said, "Just the pregnancy itself was the most significant thing, the thought of motherhood." For Mary, her strength showed itself in a new way when she allowed herself both to hope for this pregnancy and to cry for its loss. Comparing this time with her other miscarriages, she talked about coming home after her D&C: "I was sitting in the kitchen all wrapped up, I sat down and I cried and cried and I cried a lot this time. And it didn't bother me that I cried. Because before, I wouldn't cry."

Although both Mary and Katherine cried from the pain of losing a child-to-be, an other for whom they had made a place within themselves, the place of nurturance found for the child carries on. They both talk of motherhood again in the future; the nurturant strength of woman-as-mother remains. For Mary and for Katherine, nurturance was mutual between mother-to-be and child-to-be, as it is now between woman-as-self and woman envisioned-as-mother. The place for a child is a place for woman-as-self, for woman-in-relation, and for woman-as-mother: a place of nurturance.

Maggie, too, grew through her pain. She does not have an overriding need to have a child in the future. She has named this child, grieved for this child; can anyone say that she did not have a child? From this experience, she has learned that her need for genuine intimacy is something for which she will not apologize. She will share her life with someone who is willing to risk that intimacy or she will not share it at all. Safe passage to self will come first for Maggie. From a place of nurturance for herself as a woman, she will seek the nurturance of better relationships with others.

For Vanessa, the pain still in reserve is the possible notion of someone else as mother to her son. Since the onset of pregnancy, that pain has competed with the pain of feeling herself discounted and her voice not heard. For Vanessa, the pains of birth and mothering her newborn son have not guaranteed her safe passage to motherhood. Her exploration of self and self-as-mother continues, and both must be listened to. Nurturance of her son, at the cost of herself, cannot continue indefinitely; her experience of being heard, in this research, must continue with her husband and others.

Recently, I returned from a memorial service for the son of a friend. In the eyes of my friend and her husband was pain that is not served up in words; when my friend and I embraced it was not just in friendship—we held together as two mothers. Bergum (1989b) says that "mothers know how mothers are—how mothers need their children" (p. 111). Our bodies know the pain we will not try to speak and give us a way to hold the world together for a minute. The minutes of holding for my friend and her husband will go on forever: Who would say that she is no longer a mother, he not a father? Their son, in death, cannot be with them in the same way as in life, but she mothers him, he fathers him. The pains of mothering and fathering do not stop with the death of one's child. The pains go on, as does the parenting.

How often do we hear someone newly fathering or mothering say, "I never knew. Is this what my parents went through?" Like any kind of love, parental love is surely in the eye of the beholder; do others ever truly know just how we love them? It is not meant to be that our children should ever know just what they are to us; as their parents only we can know, only we can ever carry that pain.

If mothering pains do not cease with the loss of a child, how do we know when they begin? Do they begin at the birth of every child and no sooner? Do they begin much sooner for some children-to-be, gradually after birth for some others, and never at all for some others who are born? What are the mothering pains for a woman who gives birth to and gives over a child to someone else, who trusts someone else to love her child, the child she loves enough to "relinquish" (Winkler et al., 1988, p. 50)? What are the special pains of waiting to mother a child, as in infertility treatment or adoption?

The pain of "having a child on one's mind" (Bergum, 1989b, p. 101) may not start at the same time for all women, for all mothers. For infertile couples or adoptive parents awaiting the long-hoped-for child, or for those who mourn the long-absent child who has been relinquished or who has died, the experience of having a child on one's mind may be very different from that of the women in this research or Bergum's (1989b). Yet the stories of all of these women and that of my friend seem to speak of having the pains of mothering in one's being: the pains of hoping for an other, of being vulnerable to an other, of seeking the right place for an other, of responding to an other. It is the preparedness to do what must be done because of the unique nature of that relationship. For each woman, the pains are different and what must be done is different; years with a loved child do not correspond in meaning to a time of pregnancy with a developing other. Yet, for every woman who has had a child or has lost one in pregnancy, mothering pains began and the call to respond in some way to a child was felt.

Even after a child is gone, the mother and father continue to prepare, unconsciously, to respond to their child. And in the choice being made in each of these unexpected pregnancies, the woman made the preparations to respond to a developing other at a time when, for her, the mothering pains began. For Katherine and Mary, that preparation evolved as they determined that they would continue being pregnant and found themselves opening to the experience. For Maggie, mothering pains did not begin until after her abortion, when she learned the sex of her child-to-be and obtained the name and blessing that she had to have for her. The pains continue as she moves toward the anniversary of her abortion, knits socks for a friend's baby, and cannot bring herself to go visit her friend after the birth. For Vanessa, the pains ensue as she mothers, as she responds to and prepares for the needs of her child.

Kristeva (1986) speaks of the pain of loving a child, the pain that "comes from inside, never remains apart, other, it inflames me at once, without a second's respite" (p. 167). Although her words speak of her own experience of motherhood, they shed an understanding and healing light of acknowledgment on many kinds of mothering pains: "One does not give birth in pain, one gives birth to pain: the child henceforth represents it and henceforth settles in, it is continuous. . . . a mother is always branded by pain, she yields to it" (p. 167).

For each woman in this research, making a choice about her pregnancy was bound up in experiences of loss of control and vulnerability, changing boundaries of self and other, searching for trust and nurturance, and submitting to the pain of finding the right place for her child or child-to-be: a place where each woman could commit to responding to her child or child-to-be, a place from which she could mother. As caregivers, we need to ask of these women and others what they can tell us about their pain. We need to seek better understanding of their mothering pains and of our own roles in caring for them.

Voices of "Care":
What Do Women Hear?

The stories of unexpected pregnancy shared by the women in this research included both caregivers who gave pain and caregivers who eased it: nurses and physicians who acknowledged the pain of these women's experiences and those who did not, men and women who took away from a woman's sense of self and those who nurtured it. From the stories of the women in this research, some questions follow: In the voices that we allow women under our care, what do we enable them to say?

What do we hear? In the voices of caregivers, what do women with unexpected pregnancy hear?

Understanding Women's Pain

In an analysis of ancient and contemporary cultural treatments of women, Spelman (1982), like Bergum (1989b) and Rich (1976), notes the failure of Cartesian mind/body dualism to account for the fact that "pain itself is not usefully catalogued as something just our minds or our bodies experience" (p. 126). To recognize the "integrity" of women's experiences of pain, Spelman (1982) suggests, is to understand the embodied nature of that pain and its connections to women's sexuality (pp. 126-128). Katherine's experiences of caregivers, over several unexpected pregnancies, are a narrative of a woman seeking to find the integrity of her experiences of pain in order to begin to find a sense of self that could take her away from more scars and toward long-awaited healing.

For Katherine, the way to understanding her pain began when she telephoned a local reproductive health clinic. She really wanted someone to tell her that she could not have another abortion, but what she asked was how long a waiting list they had to see a doctor. The nurse began to ask her a few questions, and Katherine started to test the waters with her real fears: Would she be scarred by another abortion? What happened to women who had abortions over and over? The nurse wondered if she would like to know about this research on unexpected pregnancy; Katherine said that she would. She listened to the information, hung up the telephone, and, shortly afterward, called me.

What had intrigued her, Katherine said at the outset, was that anyone cared to know what this unexpected pregnancy meant to *her*. That had not been her experience in her other pregnancies. Recalling a time just prior to having an abortion, she said, "I'd been in the waiting room and I wanted counseling but I didn't because I didn't think I could." Katherine's powerlessness in childhood against an abusive father and negation in adulthood with a domineering boyfriend translated easily into her dehumanizing experiences of hospital abortions. There, as in life, she found no shortage of people to disapprove of her: nurses who played with a baby and stared at her while she cried before a first abortion, and a nurse after her third abortion who said, "You've had one in '88, '89, and '90; don't bother coming back in '91."

Katherine recalled seeing a film on birth control with a group before one abortion and a doctor she visited another time to discuss alternate birth control methods. She did not remember anyone ever asking her what she thought was feasible birth control for her and what was not. When, after her third abortion, her repeated attempts to convince the doctor that she needed an alternative to the pill failed, she acquiesced to what she saw and heard all around her: what she thought did not matter. She dutifully bought her pills again, forgot to take them again, and got pregnant again.

Coming into this fourth pregnancy, Katherine did not know what scared her most about another abortion. She talked of scars, but she also was not sure where all the pain of her experiences was; she could not locate her feelings about her experiences easily:

> Like I know the way people block things out and I have thought to myself, I wonder if there is anything that has happened to me that I have absolutely no recall of because I completely blocked it out. I wouldn't be surprised to find out that there was. Maybe there was.

Katherine knew that her last abortion, for which she was awake and surrounded by strangers, with her "legs up," remained an indelible memory, one she was still trying to make sense of and put to rest. As a girl, she lay in bed waiting for her father to come home and beat her; now as a woman she lay on a cold operating table while strangers entered her body without adequate anesthesia. She knew that they had not given her enough anesthetic, but when she asked the doctors, "they said, 'This'll take the edge off' . . . but it didn't." She talked about physical pain—grabbing, pulling, taking her insides out. And she talked of humiliation and embarrassment, shame strong enough to keep the full nature of the pain from her consciousness until after she left the operating room, the room full of strangers looking at her with her legs up in the air, her most private body exposed. Katherine knew she could not undergo such an experience again. Many nurses and physicians have heard more than one colleague express the notion that being forced to undergo an abortion without adequate anesthesia ensured that a woman would "learn her lesson." Katherine has experienced this belief that "bad" women need to be "taught a lesson" all of her life, starting with her own father. Epstein (1987) points to this connection between women's pain and their sexuality when she states, "We have come to understand that the body represents a locus of power, a canvas on which power relations may be drawn" (p. 25).

For Katherine, the "stripping procedures" (Hartmann, 1984, p. 65) of her medicalized experiences of abortion in a hospital reinforced to her that she, as woman, was powerless. Stripped of her clothes, her voice, and even the freedom to move, she was powerless as she had been in her childhood, powerless as she had been in her relationship with her boyfriend, and powerless as she had been in her failure to convince any doctor or nurse that she was intelligent enough to learn about birth control. The objectifying look of Other (Leder, 1984; Sartre, 1956), as stranger-doctor, stranger-nurse, confirmed her interpretation of herself as a woman who did not matter and as a woman whose body was the object of shame, pain, and infinite loss of power.

If the lesson intended for Katherine was that she was powerless and unimportant, she incorporated it well; she got pregnant again. The nurse at the clinic she telephoned who finally listened and asked, "Are you wondering about what you want to do?" may have been the only difference between yet more "lessons" of the same kind and finally coming across someone who asked Katherine, "What is this like for you?"

Katherine reflected on those experiences of hospital care again after her hospitalization with her miscarriage. Remembering the caring that she felt from both the physician and the nurse in ultrasound with her miscarriage, she said, "It helped, it helped a lot. . . . You were allowed to feel bad." With her abortions, which she described as "the exact same pain, just different circumstances," she "never, ever, felt that." She never felt allowed to cry, although she wanted to. The "good" pain of miscarrying a child-to-be was allowed; the "bad" pain of aborting a child-to-be, a self-other not tenable or trustworthy, was not allowed.

Vanessa also remembered only *strangerness,* the objectifying experience of being anonymous, in all her recollections of seeking advice from caregivers on both this unexpected pregnancy and a past "scare" at age 16. Then, she had gone to a pregnancy crisis center to get a test and find out what she could do:

> I just know it was a bad experience. They made me watch this movie about the baby and what it looked like in its development and everything while they were checking me to see if I was pregnant. . . . I walked out of there very angry because it was like, "You stupid girl! What are you doing playing with fire? You are going to get burned."

The thing Vanessa remembered most about the volunteer counselor, six years later, was that he smelled. She found him "very unprofessional" and she ran out of there as fast as she could. She went to her own physician, who was "okay. . . . It was fine me talking to him" and went on the pill.

Because it always took at least a week to see her own physician, Vanessa again sought strangers when she suspected this pregnancy. At the medical clinic where she went to get tested, she recalled how the physician gave her the news of the positive results:

> She goes, "It's positive." I just started bawling right there. She goes, "Do you know what you are going to do?" And I said, "No." And she says, "Well, you should get in touch with somebody and find out what you want to do." . . . It was almost cold . . . but I didn't know if I was just taking it too personally or not. . . . I was thinking that this is her job and what does she care?

Things did not improve much when Vanessa saw her own physician a few weeks later, however:

> She asked if I was married and I told her we were not married and she goes, "Well, we'll just call him your husband to make it simpler for me." . . . She never asked me what I wanted. . . . Everyone just told me what to do.

Her physician did not raise any discussion about either adoption or abortion. Like her boyfriend, her family, and her friends, her doctor let her know, with what she asked (Are you married?) and what she did not ask (What is this like for you?), that what Vanessa was experiencing did not matter and would not make any difference. Silent, she would stay pregnant and muted, she would give birth to a child. She could fight back only with a refusal to give birth to a mother.

What happens to all the pain that women do not feel allowed to voice? Where does it go? What becomes of pain that stays unspoken, hides in shame, and remains not listened to? How do we, as caregivers, negate women's pain and take them away from their understanding of their experiences? How do "options" coolly listed by a stranger meet the tears of a devastated Vanessa? Where, in Katherine's story, does nurturance for her pain begin? In our care, when do we nurture women in their pain and when do we add to it?

Pain and Nurturance

Maggie, too, was traumatized by her experience of hospital abortion with her first pregnancy, enough to vow that she would not have a second abortion in a hospital. She remembered her fear, when she woke up from the surgery, that the abortion had not happened. She went to the bathroom and "there was no blood, I wasn't bleeding and I was frantic. I thought, they didn't do it. I kept asking the nurse why there wasn't any blood but she just said, 'It's okay, you had it, don't worry.' " Maggie asked a few more times, but no one wanted to talk with her about her concern over "the blood, there being no blood." She felt stupid and embarrassed, and she stopped asking.

Pregnant again and recalling that experience, she looked for another option. A close friend in law practice was going out with a female resident in obstetrics and gynecology. As a woman, this doctor questioned much of what she was seeing in her residency of women's treatment during childbirth and other procedures. She and Maggie had become friends over the previous year, and Maggie decided to approach her for help; Maggie wanted to know if she could "take something" and avoid a surgical abortion. Her physician friend agreed to meet Maggie and discuss the use of an antiprogesterone to induce abortion at home. They went over the details together carefully; her friend told Maggie what to expect, that it would be much like labor and that she should have someone available to be with her in the apartment. She gave Maggie her telephone number, to call "day or night" if she needed her during or afterward. Maggie asked another friend who lived in the apartment above hers to stay home while she took the medication, and she passed the fetus at home, alone, three nights later, with her friend keeping vigil upstairs.

The pain was awful, Maggie recalled, but there was no embarrassment and no shame. She took up her pain as her own, chosen by her and not by a stranger-as-other, and began her healing with a priest. Like the choice itself, the pain, for Maggie, was hers. Owning her pain made it bearable, knowable, and able to give her, over time, a different understanding of this unexpected pregnancy, of herself, and of what she intended to seek in her life. Her pain, listened to by others, became an experience that could nurture an understanding of self that could begin to heal.

Mary also found a way to nurture herself, in the pain of miscarriage, by taking her pain up as her own and getting back to her home and daughters as quickly as she could after her operation. A nurse herself, she did not want to cry too much in the hospital "because the nurses are so busy and I didn't want them to think that they had to sit and hold my hand. You know, they're as understaffed there as they are any place else." She felt doubly protective of the nurses because she felt that they, along with her physician, advocated for her in the emergency room. There, a resident unleashed her grief when he crudely informed her that the miscarriage was a good thing because with her medical history, she should have known better than to get pregnant. He then returned with two student interns who said that they wanted to do another vaginal exam, to feel her retroverted uterus. Mary flatly refused the exam; she recalled the conversation that ensued with the intern: "He said, 'You're in here and you signed papers, you have to.' . . . I told him I didn't have to, I don't have to do anything." Her tears increased and the nurses, enraged, told the intern to get out of her room and called her physician immediately. He came down and sat with her for half an hour, "just holding my hand and stroking my hair." There was not much talk, but she found his presence comforting and calming. He stayed until her friend came back from her house, where he had gone to get toiletries for her stay in hospital.

Mary's physician did not really want to release her the next day because she had lost quite a bit of blood. Assured that she had her daughters at home to care for her and that she would return immediately if the bleeding picked up again, he let her go. She went home, wrapped herself up in a big blanket, had milkshakes with her daughters, watched television, and "cried a lot." It was safe and familiar at home; surrounded by her baby things and her "core," she felt free to grieve, free to begin to heal.

In these stories, there may be "good" physicians and "bad" ones, "nice" nurses and "nasty" ones—or are there? In a mode of knowing either the women or the caregivers as "good" or "bad," what understanding of their shared experiences of being cared for and caring for do we gain? Katherine talked about the comfort of the nurse who held her hand in ultrasound after her miscarriage, about how much it helped. We do not know if this same nurse would have held the hand of Katherine at age 16 waiting for an abortion; she was not there. We cannot ever say what any of these nurses or physicians would do another time. Our interpretation of what they did this time is limited more by what we do not know about them than by what we might imagine about their motives. Labeling caregivers or patients helps us understand neither.

A more helpful manner of seeking knowledge about these women and their caregivers may be to return to the pedagogic value of tactful action. What we may be able to see, in these stories, is where tact was present and where it did not seem to be. We may be able to see beyond the stereotypes of both the caregivers in the women's eyes and the women in the caregivers' eyes. We might, by searching less for explanations of apparent "goodness" or "badness," ask more about what the shared pain or nurturance of their experiences together can tell us. Pain for these women, like unexpected pregnancy, turned out to be unavoidable; pain claimed them, as Kristeva's (1986) child claims her. Pain, then, may be the *problem* we leave each other when the stranger-making environment of an entrenched hospital system lends caregivers and women anonymous to one another, so that they never really touch each other and never share understandings of their experiences that are attentive to concrete particulars.

That we leave pain as a problem to each other may be very important to recognize; caregivers struggle to deal with their own feelings about women's choices in unexpected pregnancy, just as the women experiencing the pregnancies do. Perhaps we move beyond our separate struggles, as "caregivers" and "patients," only when we recognize the mutual nature of the experience of health care for both the givers and receivers of care (Gadow, 1990; Marck, 1990). To move toward that mutual understanding of these women and their caregivers, we need to consider other possible ways of envisioning pain, ways that recognize what pain may mean to each of us.

Just as possible as viewing pain as a problem that patients present to us, we as caregivers may choose to envision pain as an *experience*, embodied and available for our understanding. Caregivers who view pain as experience do not try to remain strangers. They do not refrain from tactful touch and connection with patients. They thoughtfully attend, for however long or short a time they have, to the real details of each person under their care. Perhaps it is possible that, just as there are no actual good or bad caregivers or patients, there are no good or bad ways to ignore pain, because it should not be ignored. There is only hope in letting women have their own pain in their own way, letting them voice their pain, and asking ourselves to listen to them and to share their pain.

The Nurturance of Listening

What does the narrative of unexpected pregnancy for these women tell us of our roles as caregivers? How do we ensure that, regardless of what we believe to be true at a certain moment about any woman under our care, we are tactful in our actions toward her? There are clues, in their words, of very simple gestures that made all the difference for some of them. The physician who held Mary's hand, like the nurse in ultrasound with Katherine, left a lasting impression not only that he cared but that the pain was real, it was permissible; it was "an admissible concern" (Walker, 1989, p. 19). With the admission of each woman's pain to their time together, these caregivers transmitted healing. Being held through their tears gave each woman a place to voice her pain: a place of nurturance.

Mary's physician stayed for half an hour, but Katherine's nurse could stay only a minute. Yet both women vividly remembered being touched; both said that it made a difference. After three abortions during which she felt "ridiculed and humiliated," Katherine found in one minute from a kind nurse a brief connection that "helped, it helped a lot." She wondered what it would have felt like, with any of her abortions, if anyone had even once shown her regard as a person instead of giving her "dirty looks." She never expected others necessarily to agree with what she was doing. Still, she wonders if there was not some way in which at least one person, somewhere in her life, could have just said to her, "What you are going through, it's hard and somewhat painful." She asks only for "somewhat"; perhaps she does not think to ask for more than that. On the other hand, it is only in this research that she has ever asked for it at all. One nurse who asked her if she was "okay" and this research are Katherine's first recollections of ever being asked for her own experience in her own words.

In response to Kristeva's (1981) question, "What will women write that is new?" (p. 32), Goldenberg (1990) suggests that "it is most likely that women will actually write things that are very old" (p. 186). Perhaps, in attending to the words of these women in unexpected pregnancy, the healing powers of a touch or a regarding look that does not objectify or a posture that says, "I want to hear you" should not surprise us in either their simplicity or their timelessness. Rather, do we need to reexamine our own practices and ensure that we have not "written off" the value of such acts to those who look to us for care?

Summary: One Pedagogy of Unexpected Pregnancy

This research represents an attempt to learn from women's experiences and bring back to our discourse of care what is and what is not ethical comportment (Benner, 1990) for caregivers toward women with unexpected pregnancies. The experiences of unexpected pregnancy spoken of by the women in this research, as well as those available to us in our daily practice, offer a beginning pedagogy for caregivers in practice, research, moral theorizing, and education. That pedagogy teaches us that tact toward each other and those we care for is integral to ethical practice, research, and dialogue with each other. It suggests that we have seldom asked women in either our research or our practice, "What is this like for you?" and therefore we have seldom encountered women as they truly are. In order to add either their voices or our own to our thinking about unexpected pregnancy, we must begin by allowing their experiences into our language.

Perhaps we can enlarge our allowance for the experience of women in unexpected pregnancy by asking, as Lippitz (1990) does, what the Other can teach us about our own moral capacities: "My responsibility springs from an obligation brought about by the Other, who acts as my master (maitre). He or she enables me to do what I am not able to do myself: to discover *myself* as an *I* in my responsibility for the Other" (p. 59). What does the giving of nurturance, trust, listening, and respect to women in unexpected pregnancy offer us, regardless of our personal values about choice in pregnancy? Is it the reward of giving itself, of knowing that a need was responded to? Lippitz (1990) suggests, as do the stories of the women in this research, that where a response to an Other is made, there is something more at work, something more at stake (Bergum, 1989b). Is that "something more" the ethical relation *between* one and another that asks us to hear the Other and shows us how we have responded? Is it the revelation of what we see of both ourselves *and* the Other in our act of responding?

The purpose of this research was to ask women in unexpected pregnancy, "What is this like for you?" That purpose now extends itself, as the voices of these women seek to understand, with us, what we are bound up in together, as they make choices in unexpected pregnancy. The purpose that their voices give this research is one of commitment and connection to each woman who comes to us for care in unexpected pregnancy. It is my hope that all caregivers, regardless of personal values about choice in unexpected pregnancy, will come to value the voices of the women who seek their care.

References

Baier, A. (1986). Trust and antitrust. *Ethics, 96,* 231-260.
Baran, A., & Pannor, R. (1990). Open adoption. In D. M. Brodzinsky & M. D. Schechter (Eds.), *The psychology of adoption* (pp. 316-331). New York: Oxford University Press.
Benner, P. (1990, September). *Caring.* Paper presented at Celebration 1990, Winnipeg, Manitoba.
Benner, P., & Wrubel, J. (1989). *The primacy of caring: Stress and coping in health and illness.* Don Mills, Ontario: Addison-Wesley.
Bergum, V. (1989a). Being a phenomenological researcher. In J. M. Morse (Ed.), *Qualitative nursing research: A contemporary dialogue* (pp. 43-57). Rockville, MD: Aspen.
Bergum, V. (1989b). *Woman to mother: A transformation.* South Hadley, MA: Bergin & Garvey.
Bergum, V. (1990). Abortion revisited: Toward an understanding of the nature of the woman-fetus relationship. *Phenomenology & Pedagogy, 8*(3), 14-21.
Bergum, V. (1994). *Toward an ethic of nurturance: Responsibility to self and other.* Research in progress, Faculty of Nursing and Division of Bioethics, Faculty of Medicine, University of Alberta, funded by the Social Science and Humanities Research Council of Canada.

Brodzinsky, A. B. (1990). Surrendering an infant for adoption: The birthmother experience. In D. M. Brodzinsky & M. D. Schechter (Eds.), *The psychology of adoption* (pp. 295-315). New York: Oxford University Press.

Callahan, D. (1981). Abortion: Some ethical issues. In T. A. Shannon (Ed.), *Bioethics* (2nd ed., pp. 13-24). New York: Paulist Press.

Condit, C. M. (1990). *Decoding abortion rhetoric: Communicating social change.* Urbana: University of Illinois Press.

Connolly, M. (1987). The experience of living with the absent child. *Phenomenology & Pedagogy, 5*(2), 157-174.

Drew, N. (1989). The interviewer's experience as data in phenomenological research. *Western Journal of Nursing Research, 11,* 431-439.

Epstein, J. (1987). Reading the female body [Review of *The female body in Western culture: Contemporary perspectives*]. *Medical Humanities Review, 1*(2), 25-28.

Etches, B. (1990). [Review of *The body in the mind: The bodily basis of meaning, imagination, and reason*]. *Phenomenology & Pedagogy, 8,* 256-260.

Gadow, S. (1980). Body and self: A dialectic. *Journal of Medicine and Philosophy, 5,* 172-185.

Gadow, S. (1990, October). *Beyond dualism: The dialectic of caring and knowing.* Paper presented at the conference "The care-justice puzzle: Education for ethical nursing practice," University of Minnesota, Minneapolis.

Gilligan, C. (1982). *In a different voice: Psychological theory and women's development.* Cambridge, MA: Harvard University Press.

Gogel, E. L., & Terry, J. S. (1987). Medicine as interpretation: The uses of literary metaphors and methods. *Journal of Medicine and Philosophy, 12,* 205-217.

Goldenberg, N. R. (1990). *Returning words to flesh: Feminism, psychoanalysis, and the resurrection of the body.* Boston: Beacon.

Hartmann, F. (1984). The corporeality of shame. *Journal of Medicine and Philosophy, 9,* 63-74.

Heidegger, M. (1962). *Being and time.* New York: Harper & Row.

Higgins, G. L. (1991). *Trust in medicine.* Unpublished manuscript, McGill University, McGill Centre for Medicine, Ethics, and Law.

Johnson, M. (1987). *The body in the mind: The bodily basis of meaning, imagination, and reason.* Chicago: University of Chicago Press.

Kristeva, J. (1981). Women's time (A. Jardine & H. Bicke, Trans.). *Signs: Journal of Women in Culture and Society, 7,* 13-35.

Kristeva, J. (1986). Stabat mater. In T. Moi (Ed. and Trans.), *The Kristeva reader* (pp. 160-186). New York: Columbia University Press.

Kuykendall, E. H. (1984). Toward an ethic of nurturance: Luce Irigaray on mothering and power. In J. Trebilcot (Ed.), *Mothering: Essays in feminist theory* (pp. 263-274). Totowa, NJ: Rowman & Allanheld.

Leder, D. (1984). Medicine and paradigms of embodiment. *Journal of Medicine and Philosophy, 9,* 29-44.

Lippitz, W. (1990). Ethics as limits of pedagogical reflection. *Phenomenology & Pedagogy, 8,* 49-60.

MacKay, C., & Marck, P. B. (1990, September). *Promoting women's health: Nursing practice in a reproductive health clinic.* Paper presented at Celebration 1990, Winnipeg, Manitoba.

Marck, P. B. (1990). Therapeutic reciprocity: A caring phenomenon. *Advances in Nursing Science, 13*(1), 49-59.

Merleau-Ponty, M. (1962). *Phenomenology of perception.* London: Routledge & Kegan Paul.

Morris, W. (Ed.). (1978). *The American heritage dictionary of the English language.* Boston: Houghton Mifflin.

Noddings, N. (1984). *Caring: A feminine approach to ethics and moral education.* Berkeley: University of California Press.

Rich, A. (1976). *Of woman born: Motherhood as experience and institution.* New York: W. W. Norton.

Rothman, B. K. (1989). *Recreating motherhood: Ideology and technology in a patriarchal society.* New York: W. W. Norton.

Sacks, O. (1985). *The man who mistook his wife for a hat and other clinical tales.* New York: Simon & Schuster.

Sartre, J. P. (1956). *Being and nothingness.* New York: Philosophical Library.

Sherwin, S. (1989). Feminist and medical ethics: Two different approaches to contextual ethics. *Hypatia, 4*(2), 57-72.

Spelman, E. V. (1982). Woman as body: Ancient and contemporary views. *Feminist Studies, 1,* 109-131.

Stone, E. (1991). Making the decision to have a child. In *The quotable woman* (p. 74). Philadelphia: Running.

van Manen, M. (1990). *Researching lived experience. Human science for an action sensitive pedagogy.* London, Ontario: Althouse.

Walker, M. U. (1989). Moral understandings: Alternative "epistemology" for a feminist ethics. *Hypatia, 4*(2), 15-28.

Winkler, R. C., Brown, D. W., van Keppel, M., & Blanchard, A. (1988). *Clinical practice in adoption.* Toronto: Pergamon.

Young, I. M. (1984). Pregnant embodiment: Subjectivity and alienation. *Journal of Medicine and Philosophy, 9,* 45-62.

4

The Influence of Guarding on the Developing Mother-Unborn Child Relationship

Karen McGeary

Medical science is making great strides in the management and treatment of high-risk pregnancies. The result is often medicalized pregnancy, with the fetus being treated objectively, separate from the pregnant woman. The research reported in this chapter represents an attempt to address the subjective experience of high-risk pregnant women as they moved toward developing relationships with their unborn children.

Women in this study described themselves as being at risk, feeling uncertain that there would indeed be children to mother. It is within this context of uncertainty that the women guarded both themselves and their unborn babies. The findings presented in this chapter demonstrate a unique and variable prebirth relationship. For some women the need to guard themselves by holding back from emotional relationships with their unborn babies is not abnormal but rather a healthy means of coping with uncertain pregnancy.

Eight women currently experiencing diagnosed high-risk pregnancies were recruited for this study when their pregnancies were between 20 and 23 gestational weeks. All were attending the private practice of an obstetrician

AUTHOR'S NOTE: This research was supported in part by the Alberta Foundation for Nursing Research and the Alberta Association of Registered Nurses.

specializing in high-risk obstetrics. Five of the eight women were primary informants who were interviewed three times, at five, seven, and nine gestational months. Three additional informants were recruited after data analysis began. One woman was purposefully sampled at 28 weeks' gestation. This woman had a complicated medical condition, and the pregnancy could threaten both the child's life and the woman's life. A second woman was purposefully sampled in the first trimester of pregnancy because during analysis it became evident that the first trimester of pregnancy was related to when women guarded. A third woman was interviewed at 37 gestational weeks to validate the developing theoretical model.

The majority of the women were married and living with their spouses; one lived in an ongoing relationship with a partner, and one was single. The women ranged in age from 23 to 42 years; four were primiparous and four were multiparous. The pregnancy risks among the women included gestational diabetes, premature labor, twin pregnancy, and renal disease. Two women delivered during the course of the research, one at 35 and one at 36 weeks. One postpartum interview was also conducted with each of these women to provide an opportunity for reflection and closure. Three secondary informants were interviewed one or two times to enrich the data.

Guarding

Guarding is a protective process mobilized in response to perceived uncertainty, based on self-definition of risk status, that enables pregnant women to guard self and baby. Guarding has several properties. First, it is not a passive process, but rather an active process whereby women take action in response to uncertain pregnancy. Second, it has a course that can be conceptualized as raising and lowering one's guard. *Raising one's guard* occurs when uncertainty is perceived as threatening; there is a focus on possible harm or loss in terms of either the self or the baby. When the mother perceives a threat, she attempts to do things right and/or to seek reassurance that all is well. She also holds back from connecting. *Lowering one's guard* occurs when the uncertainty becomes reframed positively as a challenge; the focus changes to hope that the pregnancy will progress normally and conclude with a healthy baby. This allows the woman to move toward connecting. A third property of guarding is that its course tends to be circular and ongoing, rather than linear.

Among the women in this study, the course of guarding was determined by positive turning points, or critical incidents that enabled the women to lower their guard. It should be noted that the pregnancies of the women in this sample were considered to be on course; that is, there were no complications, thus the critical incidents were positive and progression was forward. It is probable that if a pregnancy were to go off course—that is, because of a negative critical incident—the woman would raise her guard again. Another possible scenario is that there would be no turning points of enough magnitude or critical enough to alter a pregnancy's course. It is the course of guarding that sets perimeters around the nature of the inner mother-child relationship, which will be referred to here as *connecting*.

Guarding, a basic social psychological process, is depicted in Figure 4.1. As applied to this context, guarding was an attempt by the women to guard themselves while simultaneously guarding their babies within in response to perceived uncertainty. Guarding the baby comprised two strategies: doing things right and seeking reassurance. *Doing things right* involved the perception that there was something one could do to influence the outcome. The aim of doing things right was twofold: first, to maximize the chances of having a healthy baby, and second, if something did go wrong, to minimize the feelings of guilt. In *seeking reassurance,* the women attempted to convince themselves that everything was progressing normally. Guarding the self involved the strategy of connecting, which had two dimensions. Initially, when feeling threatened, the women made conscious efforts to hold back from connecting with their unborn babies because of fear of loss or harm. Then, when they felt safe and that everything was going to be all right (when they reached a positive turning point), they made conscious choices to move toward connecting. For the purposes of this study, *connecting* refers to the inner mother-child relationship.

Due to variations in the course of guarding, the women progressed toward connecting at different rates. Two differing patterns of movement were identified among the five primary women. Two of the women were relatively slow in their progress toward connecting. In this slow pattern, the women's guards remained raised, and they continued to hold back from connecting during their pregnancies. Movement toward connecting occurred only once these women were able to lower their guards following the births of their healthy babies. In contrast, three of the women made relatively faster progress toward connecting. The women in this fast pattern were able to lower their guards and move toward connecting during pregnancy. There was some variation among the rates of progress made by these women, related to the timing of their turning points. The two patterns found among the women in this study clearly show that not all women go through the process in the same manner; of course, it would be impossible to ever

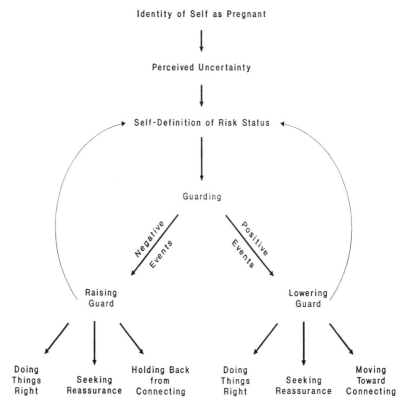

Figure 4.1. The Process of Guarding in an At-Risk Pregnancy

capture all the variations in change and movement that can take place. Figure 4.2 depicts the two basic potential paths: slow and fast.

In the following sections, I present discussion of the conditions that gave rise to the variations found in the movement toward connecting, as well as the turning points that moved the process forward for these women. The women's own words illustrate their experience with guarding and high-risk pregnancy.

Perceived Uncertainty

The women in this study were faced with two types of uncertainty: conception ambiguity and unpredictable pregnancy. The women who

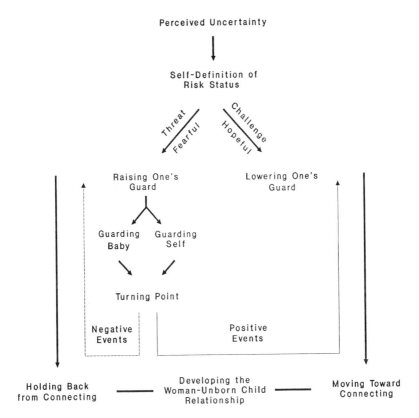

Figure 4.2. Potential Paths to Connecting: Slow and Fast

were slower to move toward connecting had also been faced with the additional uncertainty of conception ambiguity—that is, whether they would get pregnant. These women talked about laboring to conceive:

> We had tried a year on our own and then we went to our family doctor and he did tests for about six months. And then we were referred to a gynecologist, a specialist, Dr. M, so we went with Dr. M for about six, eight months and then we were referred to the infertility clinic and that took about five months to get in there.

One aspect of the conception ambiguity these women had to deal with was not knowing the reasons for their infertility. No medical dysfunctions were discovered, and so the infertility remained unexplained. All but one of the three women had stopped seeking medical assistance:

> We were playing out all the options and there was that one option about going to Hamilton where you can get the white blood cells injected from the husband, I guess it's the allergy one. We were even, if necessary, going to go through that but we had talked—I talked to him actually about an adoption a year ago. Because I didn't want to go through life without kids. One of the last things before this trip was to do the operation on the uterus. They didn't figure that was the problem but just to eliminate it as a factor they would do it.

Once conception occurred, these women first had to identify themselves as being pregnant; they then had to address the second part of the conception ambiguity, which was related to what kind of pregnancy they had achieved:

> Well, I was really happy but I was a little apprehensive because I knew that there was a risk of miscarriage. Then we went for an ultrasound at seven weeks and they could see the sac but not the baby, so we had to wait two more weeks to see if there was a baby. So that was a tense time because we were pregnant but we may not be, kind of. That was a little difficult for us, then at nine weeks we saw the baby and the heartbeat and that was wonderful.

For the women who were slow to progress toward connecting, prior conception loss determined the need to resolve the ambiguity over what kinds of pregnancies they had achieved. Once assured of their pregnant status, they were then able to assume an identity of self as pregnant.

Common to women in both the slow and fast patterns was the wanting and achieving of pregnancy; the difference for the women who were slow to progress was that they had labored to conceive. Women in both patterns described their babies as special, something they thought would never happen to them:

> We were just both really happy. Yeah. Elated, and that was right from the beginning. When we found it was twins, it was even more so, like we were just thrilled. I don't think once I've ever felt, oh my goodness, it's twins, how will I ever manage? I've never felt that. I almost feel that it's kind of like a double blessing or more special.

The women in the slow-to-progress pattern were characterized by holding back from connecting throughout their pregnancies. A common influencing condition was a sense of caution:

Even in my normal everyday life, whatever that is, I'm not sure what it is anymore, I don't like to talk about things until they happen. There's an old cliché, [don't] count your chickens before they hatch, or something, and I don't like doing that. I've kind of always been like that. I would never tell anyone I was up for a job interview until I had the job and I've never phoned anyone with any good news until I knew for sure that it was good news. So it's kind of the same thing.

The women's caution could be attributed to several factors. Initially, it was related to their feeling more at risk because of the experience of infertility. Although this factor is not scored on the prenatal risk form, pregnancy after infertility often increases the perception of risk just because there may not be another chance for a pregnancy. A second factor contributing to cautiousness was prior reproductive loss; these women had not been able to take their reproductive health for granted and were now unable to trust their bodies to carry their babies to term.

The second type of uncertainty facing the women in both patterns of progression stemmed from unpredictable pregnancy. In a normal pregnancy there is an expected trajectory, a normal course of events that ends with the birth of a healthy baby and the assumption of the motherhood role. For the women in this study the normal trajectory was altered, leaving them unable to project what would happen. They were uncertain about how their pregnancies would end.

Self-Definition of Risk Status

Although the women were diagnosed as medically high risk based on a scoring system developed by the Alberta Medical Association, they did not define themselves as high risk:

I think of high-risk pregnancy as being someone with really high blood pressure or some known problem that they're working on. For example, an acquaintance, when she carries around her twenty-fifth week, her placenta tends to die for some reason and she has lost a couple of babies. That's high risk to me because it's diagnosed and then she loses. Like this was sort of, "Maybe, maybe you'll deliver early or maybe you'll have a C-section or maybe you'll deliver vaginally," but it's just maybes. It's not, "Okay, you have this problem and this is what we're going to do." So I think that's why I didn't really see myself as high risk.

Although they did not think of themselves as high risk, the women did define themselves as being at risk for possible complications. A common meaning of being *at risk* for these women was the expression of differentness:

> The people that I've talked to that were in a normal pregnancy, they just never thought. I've told them some of the things that I've been feeling and they just never felt that. Like they never worried, [never] had that sense of worry that I do.

For the women in the slow-to-progress pattern a sense of differentness occurred in association with the infertility:

> I think I appreciate my pregnancy a lot more than some people do. I have a girlfriend right now who's pregnant and this is their third, and with each one they've sort of just said, "Well, I think it's time." So to her it's all kind of natural and it's just, "Yeah, okay, now I'm pregnant again," and it kind of just rolls, whereas I think I've really appreciated this, the two and half years of tests and surgery and whatnot, I think I appreciate it more.

Several women experienced differentness because of their ages:

> Well, I think my body isn't holding up very well this time around. Surely when you're younger, maybe you can handle it better. I don't know. I don't think pregnancy is nice, like I don't enjoy pregnancy and I don't think it gets any nicer the older you get.

Thus uncertainty arose for these women from defining themselves as at risk and resulted in their expression of differentness. For all the women, raising their guards occurred when the uncertainty was perceived as a threat.

Raising One's Guard

For the women whose movement toward connecting was faster, raising their guards occurred when their pregnancies were diagnosed. This differed from the women in the slow-to-progress pattern, who did not raise their guards until they were assured that they were pregnant:

> I was just so unsure in the beginning. Like there were so many questions and it seemed so long to go. Because we knew at six weeks and then had the ultrasound at seven that showed the sac and not the baby and so then

we had to wait until nine to find out that everything was okay. Well, okay to that point and so I didn't even bother to distance myself. It was just that this was happening and it was all very neutral.

Once assured that they were pregnant, these women raised their guards in response to being at risk:

> Finding out that this pregnancy was still okay, I felt protective. I don't know how to explain protective, it's just you read everything you can and then you try to make sure that you're following everything that is supposed to happen. You wonder if things are going the way that they're supposed to.

Guarding takes the form of the woman's protecting the baby while paradoxically protecting herself in case something goes wrong: "I suppose part of you doesn't get as attached to the baby until you know, so you still maintain some kind of distance until you know that things are going to be okay."

For the women in both patterns, raising their guards occurred when the uncertainty was perceived as a threat, so that they felt fearful of loss or harm to their unborn children:

> At first I could only feel movement on the one side. So my first concern was, one's okay, one isn't. For the longest time I did feel that something was wrong with the baby on this side of me. And I felt, too, that the baby on this side was smaller. But for some reason, I guess, maybe because I couldn't feel as strong movements, I figured a smaller, weaker baby over there.

For the majority of the women, raising their guards occurred when the perceived threat was directed at the child within. For one woman, however, the perceived threat was directed at herself; she was fearful that the pregnancy would threaten her kidney transplant, which would mean she would have to go on dialysis again. Raising one's guard involved three strategies: doing things right, seeking reassurance, and holding back from connecting.

Doing Things Right

The women all consciously imposed additional limitations upon themselves to protect themselves and their babies. The focus of these limitations was on doing everything right to ensure the possibility of a healthy baby and to allow freedom from feelings of guilt if complications arose: "I don't want to take any chances. You don't want to cause any problems that you may have prevented otherwise. I've canceled two trips this summer because I didn't think that I should be traveling or anything at this point."

Doing everything right involved making changes in four areas: occupational, household, and recreational activities, and self-care. Two underlying themes in changing activities were pacing and sacrificing:

> Once I found out it was twins, I automatically started being more careful and again at work, you know, I thought I was just being wimpy at first because I was getting so tired. Well, then, when I found out it was twins, I thought, no, I'm not, now I'm just not going to push that extra little mile that I should've, you know, like if a patient would phone, I would say, "Okay. Well, let's book it for tomorrow." Normally I would've said, "Okay, I'll be right there," and when I found out it was twins, I think I just started being a little more careful.

For four of the primary women, pacing themselves meant not only slowing down but, in fact, quitting work:

> I had opportunities to work for the last two months and I've declined those, partly because I was feeling unwell but also because of the risk, like in the first trimester, you just don't want to be exposed to a lot of X rays and halothane. So I think, to me, that's a big sacrifice, because I really enjoy my career.

Some women not only changed their occupational activities, they also changed their household activities:

> Now I'm more conscious of taking it easy; working a bit, taking a break. Whereas at the beginning I would just try and get it all done. Like it's frustrating for me because usually in a day I would have the house and my garden back in order.

Another common theme was that of sacrificing the things one enjoys, such as quitting work and giving up golf. These sacrifices were willingly made to increase the odds of having healthy babies.

Many changes in self-care centered on nutrition:

> I would like to be eating more balanced than I am and I've been on folic acid, I haven't been on a multivitamin probably because of my nausea, heartburn, and constipation. I am eating as well as I think I can but I guess you could get down to the molecular level and think of all the cells that are replicating,

you know, and that's a pretty fine process and you think, gosh, what if there wasn't the amount of protein or something available for whatever?

Even though the women reported eating healthier diets than ever before, they still sought confirmation regarding their nutritional status. By seeking information about weight gain and fetal growth, the women felt reassured that they were doing things right. This led to a degree of hopefulness that, in turn, could lead to reappraisal of the perceived risks and hence to a lowering of a woman's guard.

Seeking Reassurance

The second strategy utilized in guarding was that of seeking reassurance. The women's uncertainties resulted in worries that were, for the most part, specifically related to their being at risk and that were directed at their unborn children's welfare. Three of the women were worried about prematurity. One worried about the normality of her unborn child because of medication she had to take during pregnancy. Two of the women perceived their age to be a risk factor. All of the women worried about all the possible things that could go wrong during pregnancy, labor, and delivery.

Worrying led the women to seek reassurance. They employed various strategies in trying to reassure themselves that everything was fine. As the worry intensified, the women responded by increasing the degree and variety of reassurance strategies they used. To gain reassurance, the women used five strategies: (a) monitoring, (b) getting information, (c) choosing the best, (d) getting their husbands involved, and (e) comparing. For short periods these strategies enabled the women to feel reassured, but the worries would eventually resurface and the cycle would begin anew. They were able to get out of this cycle only by reaching significant turning points; these will be discussed below.

On occasion, the strategies used to gain reassurance backfired, as one woman described during the interview at five gestational months:

I made the mistake of reading [about] complications that occur during the second half of the pregnancy, which was a really stupid thing to do because then, of course, I panicked for the first few days after that, wondering if this was happening and that was happening.

Later, during the interview at seven gestational months, the same woman described the change: "No, I haven't touched a book in a long time actually. Not for a couple of months, not since I read too much and was getting really uptight about everything." When the women were not reassured by their strategies they stopped seeking reassurance, as one woman said, "so I don't put too much pressure on myself":

> I could have a stethoscope. I could listen, I know what I'm listening for. I could listen all the time. I guess the other side of it would be paranoia about it, you're so concerned about every little twitch and not having a movement, you could drive yourself nuts to know. Oh, I haven't had a movement every hour and a half today, or something like that.

Monitoring

The most common reassurance strategy employed was monitoring, which involved both self and doctor. Fetal movements were by far the most common form of self-monitoring:

> Feeling movement every day, it's wonderful, you know. When I feel movement, I kind of sit back and let them move for a while, just so I know everything is okay, it reassures me and I kind of revel in it almost. But there are times when I will purposefully look for it, I think I'd better see if I can feel them and I'll lay down and get into a position where they'll move. If I'm sitting and relaxing and if I don't feel any movement right away, sometimes I give them a little push or a poke and I'll get a kick back.

Keeping track of movement did not require much effort at seven gestational months, because the movements were more obvious and formed a kind of continual reassurance. Irrespective of the obvious movement, all the women talked about making mental notes of the movement each and every day.

Appointments with the doctor were also very reassuring, for he played a role in monitoring for premature labor and in checking the baby's well-being, which was a necessary addition to the self-monitoring:

> They're very important, the doctor's visits. I really look forward to them actually. Once I have one and then, I won't have one Monday but next Monday I have one—so the week in between I can't wait till the next one comes.

The nature of the doctor's visit could also be taken as a reassuring sign. As one woman noted, "He just checked me over so fast, that obviously there was nothing wrong."

Getting Information

The women sought information for reassurance from a variety of sources, including books, technology, and the doctor. Getting information could confirm that things were going as they should and thus could cut down on the need to guess. Ultrasounds were the most important source of information. One woman said: "I went for so many ultrasounds that I had the reassurance, I went for I think six or seven ultrasounds. I don't think I even had a chance to worry because I was always seeing the baby move on the screen." For this woman, seeing the baby move so frequently on ultrasound meant she did not have to spend the time and energy in self-monitoring that the other women did. On average, the women had four ultrasounds. One was at the time of pregnancy diagnosis and one was during the third trimester of pregnancy to assess growth and development of the child. The remaining two were to assess cardiac function, which was part of another study in which the women had volunteered to participate. Ultrasound examinations had a profound influence; one woman stated, "I'd like to have an ultrasound every week, it makes you feel so good."

The women also sought information for reassurance through reading and from the doctor:

> I remember specifically asking the doctor about weight gain and how much I should be gaining because I had read in one book that they recommended 80 pounds for twins and I thought that was a ridiculous amount. And he was good too, he said, "No. No. No. You don't have to gain that much." He thought 40, 45, somewhere in there. And if I got as high as 60 he still wouldn't be worried.

A component of seeking information was the doctor's giving information. Not only did the women set their own limits, but the doctor also set limits to which the women adhered:

> The doctor said I won't be doing any traveling, I'll have to stick close to home after the end of July. So that is good to know because now I know where my limits are. Because at first, we were like, should I go up to the lake? And something as simple as three hours in a car, I thought, well, maybe I'm bouncing around too much.

Choosing the Best

The women described seeking reassurance by going to credible authorities:

I feel very reassured that I was under the specialist's care. Because that was also a concern for me. When I was in [Steinbach], first of all, knowing that we were moving and I had to find a new doctor. And then finding out I was having twins and thinking, I don't just have to find a doctor, I have to find somebody who specializes in this, who knows what they're doing. And it worked out very well.

Having confidence in the doctor and the hospital was reassuring:

People have said to me, "Oh, you're delivering in the big hospital. Do you like it there?" Like I think, who cares if you like it there? You don't pick a place because you like it or I'm going to have a wonderful time when I'm there. Rather I picked a hospital that had everything. I mean everything. It really doesn't matter to me how much or how many instruments or people or anything, the more you're followed, I think, the better. I read these articles on home birth and that's not for me because I could anticipate a problem that would need some sort of intervention.

Getting Husbands Involved

Another strategy that helped to buffer the worry was getting support or affirmation from a husband or partner; support also came sometimes from relationships with other at-risk pregnant women:

The girl that had the twins, we were joking, we decided that we were made to have babies, we're not made to be ballerinas or anything. She said, "No, I'm definitely made to have kids" because she didn't have any problems. She carried right till 37 weeks I think and then had a cesarean section, for whatever reason, there were other complications. I think the babies were getting too big. Which I think, wonderful if they get too big.

For the majority of the women, the experience of differentness made it difficult for them to get affirmation and support:

You talk a lot to other women and they may let you know about their experiences and then you just kind of compare them, not so much verbally as to yourself. It's pretty hard to admit to someone that you're really worried about it when they figure that you should just be taking it easy and everything will be fine.

Because of the lack of support from others, there was an even greater need to get partners involved. One woman described her partner, who was not involved, as follows:

He was so hesitant. I mean they don't carry it, they don't get kicked and he was so hesitant even to touch sometimes. Like he would touch for a couple of days and then he wouldn't. He feels like an outsider, he'll cuddle with me but not touch the baby. And he says that he kind of feels like he's almost infringing on my privacy 'cause we've talked about it and I'll say, "I tell you the kid's kicking and you don't want to touch." But he's also not a very emotional guy, it's just the way he is.

Although the doctor did provide support, contact with him was not frequent enough, and the women described working to get their partners involved:

This ultrasound that I went to, I felt it was very important for my husband to be there. Actually he did manage to get the time off work to come. I didn't know he'd be there until he sort of walked in the door. That's when I was waiting in the waiting room, which was kind of nice because I thought it was very important that he see them. So he feels, I guess, what I'm feeling. I know he can't feel them move the way I feel them move, however, I thought if he just saw them on screen and saw them, you know, the real-life, so to speak, version of them, that he'd start to feel that, yeah, they're real.

Often the husband became involved after seeing the baby on ultrasound:

Then at 14 weeks the ultrasound was really nice because then S could pick it out, he could see it and that was important for him because up until that time, it wasn't real for him. When he saw it, that made a big difference in his attitude and in how he viewed the pregnancy. Now he comes home and talks to my stomach a lot and says, you know, "How're you doing today?" or they'll be moving around a lot at night and he'll say, "Time to settle down and go to sleep." Like he'll talk right to them which makes me feel really good because I feel he's already interacting with them somehow, which again, not being a very emotional guy, outwardly, I see that he is because he's doing emotional things whether he would admit it or not.

Once involved, husbands could take on a supportive role; they were sought out for their opinions and their listening ear to help buffer the worry and affirm that the babies were indeed okay. The husbands played a relatively constant role in affirmation and support, whereas the doctor played a role as an official affirmer during the biweekly appointments.

Comparing

The last strategy for gaining reassurance mentioned by the women, and the one that had the least value, was that of comparing themselves to other pregnant women. They talked about comparing themselves to other at-risk pregnant women with similar complications and being reassured, but comparing themselves to pregnant women who were not at risk was not as helpful, because, as one woman described it, "they have not gone through what I have." It was of some value to compare notes with others on the normal discomforts of pregnancy, but even then there was an experience of differentness; as one woman said, "Anything I get that I know I'm supposed to get, I feel better when I do get it. Even if they're things like constipation, nausea, or heartburn."

Holding Back

The third strategy in guarding, holding back from connecting, was employed by the women to guard themselves in case something was wrong with their babies. Holding back had two characteristics: expression or recognition of feelings, and conscious effort to hold back those feelings.

The women talked about not getting emotionally involved:

> I feel attached to this baby but I don't know if at this point I'd say I'm really close to the baby that way, emotionally tied to the baby in that way. That's been part of the detachment, I think. Wondering if things are going all right in the event that something didn't go the way it was supposed to.

The worry that something would go wrong resulted in the women's holding back from connecting. For example, one mother spoke of her fear that if she became too attached to the baby she would not be able to handle the loss if it occurred: "It's difficult enough to handle the loss let alone if you build yourself up for it. I like the baby now and I think I'll love it. Well, I know I'll love it once it's born."

The women went to great lengths to explain that they had some feelings toward their unborn babies; some used the word *attachment* to represent those feelings. However, they could not yet feel close to their babies. Other women used the term *bonded* to refer to emotional feelings toward their unborn children. Some used the terms *attachment* and *bonding* interchangeably.

One woman talked about holding back feelings in relation to one twin: "Am I going to be really close to one and not close to the other?" This woman was worried about something being wrong with one twin because she had felt movement initially from only one side of the uterus (the healthy, strong twin) and then two weeks later felt movement on the other side (the smaller, weaker twin). Holding back from connecting to the one twin was related to her fears about the baby's well-being.

A second characteristic of the strategy of holding back was that it was conscious:

Because I think [with] distancing, you still have an attachment but you're working not to let the attachment affect you too much in case something goes wrong, whereas [with] the feeling[s] [of] closeness and attachment, you're all caught up in it.

The women talked about not getting to know their babies, which facilitated their holding back from connecting. There was an awareness of the baby as an idea, as evidenced by the focus on the baby, yet at the same time there was a need to keep the baby "sexless": "I think of having a baby but it's sort of a sexless baby. Right now it's not a male, it's not a female, it's just the baby." One woman talked about not wanting to assign a sex to her baby; she went to great lengths to ask the different radiologists at each of her six or so ultrasounds not to tell her the baby's sex:

If I just lost a baby and it was a boy or if I lost a baby and it was a girl, then it's still the baby that I've lost, but when you put a sex to it, it becomes much more personal. And I didn't want to do that.

The baby for this woman did not yet have a personhood:

If I lost the baby . . . I would feel really bad but mainly because of all the other circumstances of the infertility and because of the hopes but not so much because it's an actual person. Like when you lose a friend, you have that rapport, but if I lost the baby I would feel bad because I lost it but not so much because it doesn't have an identity to it really. It wouldn't be like losing a child or losing a friend, someone I knew.

The women described being aware of the presence of the child within by the seventh gestational month, when the fetal movements were more obvious, but at the same time not wanting to acknowledge the meaning behind that movement:

I've felt movement more recently in the last week or two. You know, I feel something sporadic once in a while but then I wasn't sure if that was it and I didn't want to make up my mind as to that being the movement until I was sure.

In not acknowledging the fetal movement, this woman was able to hold back from affirming the reality of the child and thus delay connecting until she could be certain that it was indeed movement that she felt. The women described in detail both the types and timing of their unborn children's movements and referred to the babies' behaviors in terms of the movement, using expressions such as "being active" and "laid back":

Just more, stronger movements, I guess and I'll watch my stomach sometimes and you can actually see the baby move, which is something. But, as I said, the movements are more pronounced than they ever were before. But then as they say, I'm lying around and there may be nothing and then all of a sudden it's like trying to change position or something.

I get up and I read the paper and I do the crosswords, so during that time it's kind of active. And then it settles down for most of the day. There's, you know, kicks and twinges throughout and then about 10 to 11 at night is an active time for it.

One can only wonder if these women's depth of knowledge about their babies' presence indicates the importance of the babies' movement in reassuring the women of the healthy development of their babies.

None of the women talked about communicating with her child. Rather, there was a sense of the child as separate, that he or she had his or her own rhythms: "People have told me [that] I should be reading to the baby and things. I just feel uncomfortable doing that at this time"; "This is why I don't think I'm very good in a study like this because we don't talk a lot and I don't play music to him." "Keeping their babies sexless" and not communicating with them helped the women to hold back from connecting to those children within. Although the women held back because they needed to, in an effort to guard themselves, they also felt guilty about it:

I feel terrible, I feel like I should but I don't feel close at all to it. And I read all this in these books about bonding with the baby and I'm thinking, oh, I hope . . . I mean I'm sure that it will be really easy to do once it's born.

I should go for counseling, shouldn't I? I need to go to a shrink: "Hi, I'm emotionally unattached to this critter."

In response to perceived threat, the women employed three strategies to guard themselves and their babies. By doing things right, seeking reassurance, and holding back from connecting, the women tried to protect themselves and to be protective. Then some events took place that enabled some of the women to feel less uncertain, and they were able to lower their guards.

Lowering One's Guard

All but two of the women were able to lower their guards during pregnancy. In each case this occurred after a significant positive turning point, the timing of which varied for each woman. All of these women described *reaching a safe stage* at which they perceived uncertainty not as a threat any longer, but as a challenge. This resulted in their feeling hopeful rather than fearful, as they had felt when their guards were raised.

For two of the women whose movement toward connecting was faster, the turning point occurred relatively early in pregnancy. A discussion with the doctor at six weeks of pregnancy was a significant turning point for one of the women:

> I had to talk to the specialist who had handled transplant patients. The normal doctors weren't really all that familiar, they had patients who had children before a kidney transplant but they didn't have a lot of information to give me on what could be expected. What were the normal problems that could arise from the transplant as well as what kind of complications would it add? After talking to the specialist, I felt a lot more at ease. He answered the questions that we were concerned about.

Once her health status was no longer threatened, the woman was able to lower her guard: "The odds are now in my favor that things will go well." Rather than feeling fear, she now felt hope, both because of having a baby, which she had thought would never happen, and because she felt healthier than ever before:

> When I was on dialysis I was very weak and it didn't really agree with me. There were lots of times that I never got a period, so I wasn't very fertile then. I just wasn't healthy enough to even conceive. But I think with this second transplant, I've taken a long time to get back to being healthy and I guess it just tells me that my body is working much better than it ever had been before.

The second woman who made fast progress toward connecting described two critical incidents that enabled her to feel that she had reached a safe stage:

Having this last ultrasound done on Thursday made a big difference to me because now I know [the twins are] the same size, but I would say up until Thursday, yes I still thought weaker, stronger but now I know they're the same size and I had the radiologist's confirmation that, yes, everything looks fine.

Five months to me was a big hurdle. I think in part because I can remember babies being born at five months and sure, they're pretty weak then and their chances of survival aren't very good, but for me it was like, well, at least then after five months, it's no longer a miscarriage, there's a chance of saving them. I don't know that much about twins as far as having a very good success rate but, to me, five months was sort of just a real big hurdle for me.

This woman's feeling equal fetal movements on both sides was the third critical incident in the turning point that resulted in her feeling more at ease and willing to lower her guard. Both of the women just described still had uncertainties, but their intensity was lower. Now they perceived their uncertainties as challenges; they acknowledged their risks as minimal and framed them as positive, in the sense that there was hope:

I have a lot of confidence in the fact that I am doing a lot of things right. Like I'm doing a lot of resting and I'm not working. I have a lot of confidence that I'll make it to term.

Well, I just really hope that she's perfect, that there's no problem because you know you do have concerns. I read a little bit in some of L's books as well about the effects of the drugs I'm taking and although there is some risk there, they've not exactly determined how much and there's no documented cases of them actually having a bad effect, but nonetheless it's still there. So I guess that's my concern, I'm just really praying that it hasn't harmed her in any way.

Two other women who progressed toward connecting during pregnancy experienced turning points later in their pregnancies. For these women, the major concern was taking their babies to term. Both had charted their own trajectories in terms of when they would feel they had reached a safe stage. For one woman, the safe stage was at 38 gestational weeks, but she felt anything after 32 weeks was okay "because you don't have to worry that the lungs won't be ready or as mature as they need to be." For the other, the safe stage was at 37 gestational weeks, but anything after 28 weeks was okay "because there would be a good chance that the baby could survive outside the womb." For both women, the passage of time itself was the major positive turning point. Making it past what they considered the critical period changed the uncertainty from a perceived threat to a reason for hope. As one woman noted: "I'm sort of on the home stretch now. Even if I did go into labor, the chances are more in my favor that the baby will be okay is how I'm feeling now." These two women based their understanding of when they could feel safe on their own personal beliefs about gestation; the trajectories they plotted for themselves were not necessarily grounded in medical knowledge.

For the women who were slow to progress toward connecting, the turning point did not come until they had borne healthy babies; only then were they able to lower their guards and move toward connecting:

> I think my turning point will definitely be after and actually I'll probably even think there's got to be something wrong, knowing me. I guess I'm pretty negative about it just because it did take so long. After, I'll probably pinch myself and the baby, "Are you still there?" I'm sure I will.

The women in the slow pattern continued to feel highly uncertain, threatened rather than hopeful, throughout their pregnancies. Because of risks associated with their ages, it was impossible for them to chart courses for themselves during pregnancy, and so their trajectories remained uncertain until delivery. Despite reassuring amniocentesis results and one of the women's prior successful delivery of a healthy term infant, these women remained highly uncertain, a state they attributed to their wary personalities. It seems that the risks associated with age plus infertility may have made their pregnancies so special to them that they felt the need to guard themselves right up until delivery:

> Just because your amnio comes back and what few things they can determine on your amnio that are okay and negative or whatever doesn't mean there still aren't other things; there still could be some major birth defects and that sort of thing that you don't know of until delivery and I think there's those things that happen at delivery too. I just had it reinforced when, on the weekend, there was a stat section for fetal distress. At this point you can't predict it.

Women in the slow-to-progress pattern were unable to get excited in anticipation of birth; rather, they held off preparing rooms and/or clothes for their babies in case something went wrong.

As is evident, the women in this study lowered their guards at differing times, based on trajectories they had plotted for their pregnancies individually.

That is, each woman had to reach a turning point in her pregnancy, a time when she felt she had reached a safe stage and could relax a little, let down her guard. Once the women's guards were lowered, the three strategies they had employed in guarding themselves and their babies—doing things right, seeking reassurance, and connecting—changed in intensity and focus.

Doing Things Right

In addition to trying to do things right as they had all along, the women had to take into account some limitations imposed by themselves, the doctor, and the growing unborn children. Getting ready for the reality of a baby after birth was also important:

> Just setting things up for the actual baby to be out there in that room versus just taking care of yourself and making sure you're eating right. That is a priority now too, but now you're actively setting up a facility for the baby. So that's kind of initiated a change in focus.

Seeking Reassurance

Once the women had lowered their guards, worries were less prominent. Thus the strategy of seeking reassurance, although still present, lessened in degree: "I do feel better about things. It's just I won't feel completely assured until the baby's actually born and everything is all right, but I mean it's as good as it probably can get."

Moving Toward Connecting

Holding back from connecting changed to moving toward connecting, which heralded changes in feelings, a desire to get to know, and a readiness to prepare. Moving toward connecting occurred once the women lowered their guards, feeling more at ease and hopeful that their babies were going to be healthy. Whereas before their feelings were held back, the women now described themselves as feeling close to the children within. Before, the women perceived their unborn children as separate from themselves, but now the women expressed feelings of "oneness." As one woman said, "It's part of me, it's a little half of me, it's like we are in our own little world together."

Women who were slow to progress toward connecting exhibited more subtle changes, with uncertainty still present as an inhibitor:

My feelings have changed a little bit. As I say, I'm getting more attached to the baby emotionally but not 100% yet. Certainly nothing like if it was a normal pregnancy. Because I was talking to my sister-in-law and she never gave it a thought that things wouldn't go well. So the preoccupation that I've had wondering if things are still going to go all right has probably taken away a little bit from getting as attached to the baby as someone else might.

A noticeable change in knowing the baby was a sense that the baby was real, that is, taking on an identity, no longer an "it" or "just the baby." The baby, as real, was associated with the strong, obvious movements in the last trimester of pregnancy: "I think loving them you have to have some kind of feedback from something to love it. And I feel like I'm getting that now from the movement." Feeling both the reality of the child within and more at ease, the majority of women now wanted to know the sex of their unborn babies. Several women still wanted the *surprise* at the end, but did imagine a particular sex: "For some reason I keep thinking it's a boy but, you know, I really don't know. I guess that's the way I seem to think of it right now, as a boy." Knowing the sex permitted the baby to become a person with an identity of his or her own. Now fetal movements were interpreted more in terms of individual personality:

With D's voice they'll move and stuff but with too many voices they'll never move. If you're at a social function or at a supper or whatever, they stay pretty quiet. All along I've been saying, they don't like crowds.

Finally, the women began to communicate with their babies:

I would wake up in the morning and sort of ask them how they're doing. So I would say, "Good morning" or "It's time to get up" or something, and it's not like I would talk to them all day long but, you know, just kind of acknowledging that they're there.

One woman described her talk as "soft talk": "It's like you sort of talk to yourself as if she were listening and must be listening." For several of the women, communication seemed to be two-way: "Sometimes too, if I really think about them or I'll say, 'Hey, like what are you guys up to?' then they'll move. I don't know if it is just a coincidence." Another woman, whose size made it difficult for her to move anymore at night, felt that the baby kicked her more at night because he was uncomfortable.

In addition to knowing the sex and communicating with the baby, another factor that indicated a woman was moving toward connecting was a readiness to prepare for her baby's arrival, accented by an eagerness to hold the baby in her arms:

> The fact that it's coming closer, you know, scares me in one way because with them I'm going to have a big responsibility on my hands, so there's a little bit of fear there but more excitement and more anticipation, finally getting to see them. I guess, you know, meet them and see what they look like, meet[ing] them is kind of a strange word because I feel like I already know them in a way but yet that's what it will be that day, sort of an introduction.

The women began to get ready for more direct relations with their unborn babies by preparing nurseries and fantasizing about the postbirth relationship:

> I hope to breast-feed. I imagine, first of all, how I'm gonna do it, holding two little footballs. But I imagine that a lot. And I imagine it being very special. I mean I've been told that breast-feeding one is very special and I just think two is going to be very, very special. I imagine them a lot interacting with other kids too when they're older. I found myself a girlfriend up the road and she has twins and I can picture us going on outings together when they're older.

A final component in the women's getting ready for their babies was preparing themselves for labor and delivery. They started reading and asking questions about childbirth. For the women in the slow pattern, whose guards remained raised throughout their pregnancies, moving toward connecting occurred after delivery. During the postbirth interview, one of these women described her feelings:

> Well, I was probably more infatuated when I first saw him. Then, obviously the more time I spent with him, I think the love gets stronger over time, especially when he's finally looking at you and responding to things that you do and say and it just makes him more of his own person I guess than anything.

For the women in the slower pattern, the sense of their babies as unique persons began after birth, whereas for the women in the faster pattern, who were able to lower their guards during pregnancy, the process of getting to know their babies and developing emotional ties with them began during pregnancy. The end result was the same, however: All of the women connected with their babies; the process of making that connection was simply slower to develop in some of the women.

5

Livebirth Following Stillbirth

Ann Lever Hense

For a woman who experiences a stillbirth, the loss of the child can be devastating. Although the reaction of women to stillbirth has been well documented in the literature (Bourne, 1983; Clark & Williams, 1979; Dunlop, 1979; Furlong & Hobbins, 1983; Kirk, 1984; Kowalski & Bowes, 1976; Stringham, Riley, & Ross, 1982; Wolff, Nielson, & Schiller, 1970), little research has addressed the effect that having a stillbirth has on a subsequent pregnancy. What is it like to carry a child when a previous pregnancy has ended in tragedy? What is it like to find oneself pregnant again and to relive the experience of pregnancy and birth? What is it like to care for a child when another child was lost? Bergum (1989) describes the transition to motherhood that occurs during pregnancy. When the joyful anticipation of impending motherhood is shattered by the experience of stillbirth, the transition to motherhood in a subsequent pregnancy is indeed uncertain.

The purpose of the research reported in this chapter was to document a beginning understanding of the experiences of women in subsequent pregnancy following stillbirth by listening to the stories of 10 women as they lived through the experience and by analyzing their stories to identify a shared experience. It is this shared experience that is presented. The women in this study willingly shared their most intimate thoughts and feelings in

AUTHOR'S NOTE: This research was supported in part by a Province of Alberta Graduate Scholarship and a bursary from the government of Newfoundland and Labrador.

hopes that they might help other women who have experienced the tragedy of stillbirth and who embark on the journey of having another child.

Eleven women participated in this research. The four who participated as primary informants (Grace, Tina, Helen, and Sally) were pregnant for the second time, having had stillbirths in previous pregnancies. These primary informants, therefore, had no experience in mothering live children. The criteria for selection of the primary informants were as follows: (a) ability to speak and read English, (b) married or in a stable relationship with the father, (c) in the last trimester of pregnancy, (d) stillbirth in the previous pregnancy, (e) 21 years of age or older, (f) resident of the metropolitan Edmonton area, and (g) willing to participate in a minimum of three interviews. The primary informants were interviewed in the last six weeks of pregnancy, within two weeks postpartum, and six weeks postpartum.

Six women participated as secondary informants (Sarah, Linda, Marie, Rita, Carla, and Cindy). They did not meet the strict primary informant criteria; however, they were able to contribute to the data by further expanding the information and the theory being generated. Although each secondary informant had a perinatal loss in the first pregnancy, three of the women successfully delivered live children since those losses. The experiences of these women were included to investigate the influence of having been successful in the mothering role on the process of livebirth following stillbirth. The secondary informants were interviewed one time only.

Another woman who participated in the study (Lucy) had experienced a stillbirth 31 years previously. She was selected to contribute because of her ability to give some perspective on the effect of time on the process of livebirth following stillbirth and to verify the process.

The age range of the primary and secondary informants was 23 to 39 years. Ten of the participants were married, and one was in an ongoing relationship. The education completed by participants ranged from eighth grade to university degrees. Some of the women worked as homemakers, and others were employed outside the home as professionals. The gestational ages at which the stillbirths occurred ranged from 20 weeks of gestation up to and including term labor. The causes of the stillbirths varied.

The study focused on the experiences of women during pregnancy and birth following stillbirth. Despite the women's awareness of the purpose of this study, they all included the experiences of their previous pregnancies and deliveries in the telling of the current experience. The women deemed it necessary to include the stories of their previous losses in order to understand the context of their subsequent pregnancies. It is with the description of the previous loss that the story of subsequent pregnancy begins.

Reliving the Previous Loss:
The Worst Has Happened

As is common with pregnant women, these women knew that there was a possibility that something untoward could happen to their babies during pregnancy and birth. However, when the stillbirths occurred, they were perceived by the women as the worst thing that had ever happened to them: "I know what it is like to give birth and to have a stillborn baby and, I mean, what is worse than that? Nothing" (Grace).

The women indicated a variety of grief reactions that are well documented in the literature: anger, shock, disappointment, emptiness, horror, and denial (Kübler-Ross, 1969; Lindemann, 1944): "I was so mad. Really angry. I didn't care anymore. I just didn't care. . . . I put myself into shock, like, both mentally and physically" (Linda); "It was just that I felt, you know, very disappointed. You know, not disappointed, lost" (Lucy); "The horror of it all just hit me" (Grace).

Disillusionment

For these women the experience of stillbirth shattered their whole lives. They could not believe that such a devastating thing could have happened to them:

> And when it did happen, you can't believe it. Like, you know, now you are a statistic [laughs], you know, you are not just one of the regular people, you are one of the people that it happened to. And it's just incredible that these things happened. (Marie)

For many of the women the loss of the unborn child was the first time they had ever had anyone close to them die. The unknown experience of grief may have compounded their feelings of sadness: "That was the first time in my whole entire life that I had not been able to have something that I wanted to. I had not had losses either. I hadn't had significant people die" (Carla).

The women's confidence both in the process of pregnancy as being a normal event and in the health care system was shattered: "I never assumed that anything would go wrong. I didn't think anything of it. . . . I never knew that babies died actually, to be honest, I just didn't. I just sort of thought that it was taken for granted" (Sarah).

The disillusionment that occurred with the stillbirth made the women feel vulnerable regarding pregnancy:

It will never be the same again, I know that. . . . You become sort of, "Well, it's not really." You just become sort of skeptical. . . . It is like a little knowledge is quite dangerous really. . . . If you don't know things can go wrong, then you don't think about them. But when you hear things that can go wrong then all of a sudden you start thinking, oh god, maybe I can get that! You almost become paranoid. (Sarah)

The experience of stillbirth left the women with a feeling of having failed. They felt that they had failed in one of the basic tasks of being a woman and that their bodies had failed them:

And the other thing I never noticed or I never thought that women would feel that when those babies died you felt less of a woman. Why you looked at women who had babies or children that, I shouldn't say you looked at them with envy or you felt lesser of a person. And it was just I had never thought that one could feel that, you know. (Sally)

The women felt not only the failure of not producing a live child but also the failure of not having a child to mother. There was a loss of the plans and dreams that they had of becoming mothers: "Not being where I wanted to be at that time. And that wasn't what was planned or dreamed about or anything like that" (Grace); "And then I planned so much with Joseph, like I quit my job and I did this and I did that and I had everything planned out perfectly and then it all got screwed up anyway" (Sarah).

Blaming Themselves

All the women sought causes for their losses and often ended up blaming themselves. The causes of self-blame were many and varied. They included such things as marital problems, moving to a new residence, sexual intercourse, and physical activity. One of the most common causes of guilt was working too hard during the pregnancy:

I don't think I would have worked so hard, because I did. I kept working and I worked very hard. I worked day and night and Sundays. I was pretty stubborn and stupid in that way that I didn't realize that you had to slow down a lot. (Linda)

The women often could recognize that their self-blame was irrational, but the guilt feelings persisted: "I did a significant amount of blaming myself. You know, well, we shouldn't have done this and we shouldn't have had sex. I mean people do those things when they are pregnant and they don't have miscarriages" (Carla).

It was not uncommon for the women to review their antenatal care and evaluate it to determine whether any blame could be placed with the medical staff. This evaluation had significance in the subsequent pregnancy in determining whether the woman would seek prenatal care from the same physician. Five of the women sought antenatal care from another doctor in the subsequent pregnancy:

> This was the question that I think it always nagged me in the back of my mind that Dr. Jones sent me home on that Wednesday. . . . And, of course, you know, you are trying to decide shall you go back to the same doctor. Was there anything they could have done? (Sally)

The guilt women felt regarding the stillbirth tended to continue unresolved. Grace said, "It's just like it happened yesterday, that I had done that. That I had killed her." At a later interview, she reiterated, "I don't know if it will ever be resolved."

The women felt additional guilt when they perceived that they had failed others by not producing a live child: "I woke up again and then it hit me that our daughter Vicki . . . was three and one-half and so she was really looking forward to this baby. Here I am without a baby" (Lucy); "You are feeling more sorry for people around you. Like my mom and dad were just having a terrible time and I just sort of felt really bad for them. I felt really bad for my husband" (Sarah).

Fearing Recurrence

With the occurrence of stillbirth, the women had become disillusioned and perceived that perinatal loss could conceivably happen to them again. Fear of recurrence was triggered at the time of the stillbirth, but the confirmation of the next pregnancy provided a tangible thing to be lost. This manifested itself as feelings of anxiety. Guilt over the previous loss was carried into this pregnancy too.

Going through the process of pregnancy provided the scenario for reliving the previous loss and fearing that the outcome would be the same: "Oh my god! Is something happening to this one too?" (Grace).

The vast majority of pregnant women fear the possibility of something untoward happening to their unborn children, but for these women who had experienced stillbirth, their fear was of recurrence rather than occurrence and was based on their own personal experiences:

The first pregnancy too I remember having concerns but they weren't as real as this time. This time it is more real for me to think that I am not going to have a baby to hold. You know, it's more of a reality for me. . . . Those fears that every first-time mom has before she has even given birth or had a stillbirth, those are present but they are not as real as they are to me. Like these things can happen to me. (Tina)

Fearing recurrence caused a decrease in confidence about a positive pregnancy outcome. The women remained unconvinced that they would deliver live babies: "I will believe it when I see it or hold it" (Grace); "According to my [blood sugar] record, I controlled it very nicely too [gestational diabetes], but until the baby was born I wasn't sure" (Helen); "You might not get toxemia, but there are so many other things out there that could happen" (Marie).

Fearing recurrence of loss was not resolved with the birth of a live child, but continued into the postpartum period:

I was still picking out all these negative things that were coming at me. I couldn't understand why they would say, "He's a healthy boy," yet he has jaundice. And it's the same when she was born, Jane: "You had a healthy baby girl." Well, I mean, like nothing was wrong with her [she was healthy but dead]. Well, you guys are giving me mixed messages here. (Grace)

After the baby is born they have some monitors to monitor the baby's heartbeat and everything? Because we heard they have some, like sudden infant death babies. (Helen)

Not only did fearing recurrence continue into the postpartum period, but three of the women also experienced the fear of recurrence in additional pregnancies, despite having borne live children following stillbirth.

Anxiety

The fear of recurrence manifested itself as anxiety. The women perceived that the uncertainty associated with fearing recurrence was even worse than knowing a bad outcome: "We can just get it over with no matter what we are faced with, but get this pregnancy through" (Grace).

Anxiety was evident early in pregnancy and represented a long waiting period to the women before the anxiety would be resolved. As Sarah noted at 23 weeks' gestation: "So like it is going to be an awful long pregnancy. . . . It is just getting by day to day. That's all really. Actually, you wish it were over. . . . I just hope it is all over soon."

It was apparent that anxiety increased as the women approached term. Women who had previously delivered live children following stillbirth remained anxious during pregnancy: "I think that you could have 20 babies and you would still be nervous" (Marie).

Anxiety related to labor and delivery involved both concern for the baby's well-being and concern over being able to cope with the labor. The women could not picture themselves delivering successfully:

> But this time I don't associate labor with giving life. Like it's like it's associated with death. Like it's just, "That's how it ends" sort of thing. . . . Like you still are always thinking, well god, I just can't believe this is actually going to live. And you can't believe the labor part where they actually cry. . . . Like I think about that a lot, like if it's going to cry, I hope it screams. (Sarah)

Fear of the outcome of the labor made three of the women dread the prospect of actually having to push the baby out. As a result, they wished to avoid labor and delivery altogether by having a cesarean section:

> I was thinking that I would go for the cesarean and ask the doctor and tell him for emotional reasons I can't go through. (Sarah)

> Oh yes, you had a baby. You had a stillborn but I almost feel like I would probably be more retaining this time. Harder to let go, whereas before I didn't have a major problem at delivery letting go and having the baby come out or anything like that. (Grace)

In a later interview, Grace commented:

> I was really hesitant and really lots of times wouldn't push as hard as they wanted. I don't know if that happens anyway, but I was just laying there and gave these little wimpy pushes too, you know. Part of that is tiredness and part of that is, you know, I don't know if it was just me holding back or not.

Feeling Guilty

The women carried the guilt they had experienced for the stillbirth into their next pregnancies. They feared that if they repeated whatever they felt guilty about in their last pregnancies, they would jeopardize their current pregnancies. Most of the women attempted in their current pregnancies to remedy, by their actions, the things they thought had caused the stillbirth and thus to decrease the risk of the stillbirth being repeated:

"I try to do anything which I thought last time was not enough. I try to make it up this time" (Helen).

In order to prove to herself that she had not been responsible for the stillbirth of her first child, in her second pregnancy Grace wanted to indulge in doing the things that she had felt guilty about:

> So I think when I got pregnant again, rather than avoiding doing those things that I had done before which a lot of people say, you know, they are so cautious and they are not going to, everything is going to be different this time, I think I indulged more in doing the same things because I wanted to, I still had to prove in a sense to myself, that's really screwy, but was it that thing in fact. (Grace)

In a later interview, Grace commented, "I was almost wishing things would happen just so we could make sure that isn't why."

Significant Dates

Two dates or time periods were significant to the women. The first was the calendar date on which the stillbirth occurred. Three of the women became pregnant again within three months of their previous stillbirth losses (physicians often recommend that a woman wait a minimum of three months following stillbirth before conceiving again). For these women, the anniversary of the stillbirth coincided with the expected date of confinement for the next pregnancy and precipitated residual grief: "I just got sad about her that she died at that time and was just sort of reliving how I was feeling, you know. I think it was really just I was more emotional about her" (Grace).

The second period of time that was significant was the gestational age at which the stillbirth occurred. Although confidence in the subsequent pregnancy increased somewhat once this point was passed, fear of recurrence continued throughout the pregnancy:

> One of the things that happened in the pregnancy with David that was really good for me was I guess, like I said June 19th was the day that our baby died, so on the anniversary of his death was the day that I turned 28 weeks with David. It was just the way it worked out. So it was a really really sad day for us because of the grieving on the anniversary, but it was also a very happy day because we knew we had made it to 28 weeks. (Marie)

For those women who had stillbirths some years previously, the anniversary remained as a time to remember the child who was lost:

I know every year on September 15th I always think and it was in 1980 when I lost the baby so it is like it is very easy to keep track of how old it would have been, like 9 years old and stuff. I think of what it would be like to have a 9-year-old son. . . . I mean the last time I cried about that baby was last September 15th. And maybe the next time I cry about that baby will be September 15th coming up. (Carla)

Attempting to Replace

Following the occurrence of the stillbirth, the reaction of the women was to get pregnant as soon as possible to replace what they had lost:

I just had to [get pregnant], I could not wait. . . . For some reason it was really important for me to get into that. It was just because I felt ripped off of everything and my arms, you know, everything was just so empty that I just couldn't take it. (Grace)

That was to replace [wanting to get pregnant right away]. I tell you, I wanted to get pregnant immediately because you just die inside. (Sarah)

Women who did wait longer than three months spoke of wanting to get pregnant earlier. Sarah, who was pregnant within four months, said, "I waited long enough; I wanted to get pregnant right away as soon as it happened but the old body just said no, it just wouldn't." Marie, who waited six months, commented, "I should have waited longer but if it was up to me I would have gotten pregnant right away. I just wanted to have a baby so badly. Six months was about as long as I could wait." Although these women willingly became pregnant again in order to replace the child who was lost, they resented it when this was suggested by others:

I remember one of the nurses coming in also and sat with me for a while. Her advice was, "Try to have another child as soon as possible to fill that void." At the time, I don't know, you are not thinking that clearly. You are just thinking of your loss and I guess trying to adjust to it. (Lucy)

Although the women desperately wanted to be pregnant again, they felt ambivalence once the pregnancy was confirmed:

When I first found out that I was pregnant there was a lot of ambivalent feelings because you kind of have to, for the first couple of months, accept the fact that you could have to go through this again. (Tina)

I feel really mixed up about this pregnancy. . . . I thought for sure I was pregnant. So I was hysterical. Like all of a sudden I was just hysterical thinking, oh god, I am pregnant again! So then I go to the doctor and have the test and he said, "No, you are not pregnant." Then I am devastated because I'm not pregnant [laughs]. (Sarah)

Even Marie, who had successfully delivered a live child since her still-birth, felt ambivalence at becoming pregnant again: "This is my third pregnancy, so I have already had a live child. But even so I was still quite leery about getting pregnant."

Becoming Pregnant

Once the women had their pregnancies confirmed, they had to face the reality that they were carrying another child. The women also had to work through residual grief as their pregnancies progressed. They had a need to replace the child who was lost, but with the confirmation of the new pregnancy, they were faced with the reality of this child replacing the stillborn child. This led to confusion over wanting to replace what was lost while at the same time not wanting to negate the child who was lost:

Yes, no, but then, on the other hand you sort of do [want this baby to replace the stillborn child] but you know that it can't. They are two distinct people. It gets a little blurred sometimes. . . . I just thought, I just wanted another one. I wanted to hear crying and I wanted to hear all that kind of stuff. So it was like replacing something that you had lost. (Sarah)

The short pregnancy spacing may have contributed to the women's fusing the two pregnancies in their minds:

But I am glad [I didn't get pregnant immediately] because otherwise I would have confused the two pregnancies because even waiting the length of time that I did [four months] sometimes, it seems like a blur. I have just been pregnant for almost two years now. . . . It feels like I have been pregnant all along now. Just continuing on. (Sarah)

I almost started feeling that it was the same baby once I started getting close to that time, about 28 weeks. (Grace)

All the women verbalized concern over wanting a healthy child, regard-less of the sex of the child: "We don't mind if it is a girl or a boy as long as it is healthy. We will love a healthy baby" (Helen).

At the same time, the women thought that if this child was the same sex as the child who was lost, they would be more likely to fuse the two children. It would also be a reminder of their grief: "Maybe it would be even better for me, which is crazy but just to have a boy because I am so conscious of, initially that I'd put anything on, like, I don't want to do all that replacing bit" (Grace). At a later interview, Grace said, "What if it was a little girl? How would I be looking at her? Would I be looking at her as, could this almost be like Jane? Like her?" Marie also commented:

I wanted David to be a girl. In the beginning of that pregnancy I really thought he was a girl. And I guess I wanted him to be a girl so badly because I didn't want to be reminded or I didn't want him to look like our first child or have any resemblance or anything.

Carla used the name for her stillborn child in the name for her next child, and this created fusion of the two children for her: "And then there is another Samuel Brian really but it is two babies. Sounds kind of strange. . . . So he carried a piece of that baby."

Differentiating Between the Pregnancies

As well as experiencing the fusion of the two pregnancies, 10 of the women referred to attempting to differentiate between the unborn children. Whereas fusion appeared to be an unconscious act, differentiation appeared to be a conscious attempt to distinguish between the two pregnancies and the two unborn children.

It appeared that coming to know the lost child and mothering the lost child made differentiation easier in the next pregnancy, as the lost child was more likely to be perceived as a distinct individual by the mother. The mother's experience of her lost child was gained through fetal movement, fantasizing, viewing the lost child on ultrasound, and holding the lost child:

I have sort of fantasized about their personalities, so it has really made them individuals. (Marie)

I think it does [have its own personality], I think they are all different because Joseph, he never kicked like that at all. (Sarah)

So I haven't denied it at all and that's really helped me to work through and to accept this next pregnancy because it isn't the same as the other one. You know, there is a different baby inside. And I know that because I have held that other one. They didn't sweep it away from me and put it away in the morgue or whatever. This baby is going to look different and is going to be different. (Tina)

Sarah acknowledged that coming to know the stillborn child was difficult: "It is just that you don't really have anything to compare it to. Like if, if, if he had lived, even for a couple of days." For Sarah it was important to acknowledge the lost child during the subsequent pregnancy. Perhaps this was to help her differentiate the lost child from the live fetus:

Yes, I am really glad I have them [pictures of Joseph]. Just lately though, you know. It must be the maternal instinct or something that you get because before, I never looked at the pictures for like three months after it happened. I never, I wouldn't even look. I wouldn't do anything and then when I was pregnant, all of a sudden it seemed very important that he couldn't lose his place in the family.

Except for Carla, the women did not wish to use the name of the stillborn child for the next child: "We had a name picked out. . . . No, no, no, as much as we like the name we didn't [use this name for any child born later]. That name was meant for someone else" (Lucy).

Dealing With Residual Grief

The subsequent pregnancies caused fulmination of the women's grief. They were reminded of the loss of the previous child and at times were overcome by sadness:

When I did get pregnant I was still grieving and am still upset about my first one. It's still too sad. I mean I can talk about certain elements but it's still very hard to talk about her and how she looked and everything yet I did it when it first happened but it's awfully hard and will always be. . . . I wanted to talk about that [stillbirth] rather than talk about me being pregnant again. (Grace)

And every once in a while I will have a relapse and think back about the first baby [cries]. (Rita)

Marie acknowledged that although the grief never completely goes away, it is lessened with time: "You know, I don't think there is enough time in the world to get over grieving. I don't think you ever really get over it. I just think you learn to live with it."

By just going through the experience of pregnancy again, the women were forced to relive the loss. Things such as going back to the hospital for nonstress testing or for delivery rekindled the memories and fostered the fear of recurrence:

> I was right next door to the room that I had been in when my first baby died. . . . And when they started [inducing] I asked them to turn the monitor away from me so that I couldn't see the heartbeat because I had watched my first baby die. I had seen his heartbeat go. And I didn't want to see that again. (Marie)

The experience of having lost a child made the women very aware of the value of having a live child:

> I felt so bad for him. That is how I felt the most. I feel that he has been cheated out of life. He never got a chance. Sometimes with David I think, "Oh, you are so lucky to be here, David. You just don't know how lucky you are." . . . Oh god! For sure, I appreciate him so much more. (Marie)

> You certainly realize when you lose a baby that you have lost a very precious thing, you know. (Tina)

Enduring Fear of Recurrence

Throughout their pregnancies, the women were faced with conflicting feelings of fearing recurrence while at the same time feeling confident that things would go well. It was as if fearing recurrence and feeling confident were on a balance scale. Fearing recurrence was always present, but it was less pronounced at times when the women felt confident. Linda, who was carrying twins, had a dream that demonstrates this dichotomy of feelings:

> About three nights ago I had a dream that I couldn't make it to the hospital and that I had to have an emergency C-section. . . . And so they cut me open and they pulled out the first baby and he was a boy and he weighed about 10 pounds and he was really healthy and good but the other one was really deformed and dead.

A number of things appeared to foster confidence in the women. Quickening, or the presence of fetal movement, reassured women of fetal well-being: "I think my baby moved at 19 weeks. Then we felt safer" (Helen); "I am feeling really quite good about it and confident, the baby's moving a lot" (Tina); "I know it feels good because the baby is kicking me and stuff. That is the one thing that I really find, if the baby doesn't kick me, I really start to have a fit" (Rita). Normal results of antenatal screening tests increased the women's confidence: "Actually yesterday was the first time I heard the baby's heartbeat and that made me feel better" (Carla). Of the three women who had successfully delivered live children following stillbirth, two felt their previous success increased their confidence in this pregnancy, whereas one did not:

With this one I was more confident than with David. (Marie)

Yes, it does [increase my confidence to have a live child]. Because it helps you to think more positively because after having lost Melissa, when I miscarried I didn't think anything was possible anymore. It was so negative and stuff. But now I feel a lot more positive. (Rita)

Not really, no [having two children that survived does not increase my confidence]. Not really, no it doesn't. I suppose that it should. (Carla)

The gestational age also seemed to play a role in whether or not the women were confident. Confidence appeared to be low early in the pregnancy and when approaching labor and delivery: "Well, I found that the first three months were quite hard and I am finding right now is quite hard. Somewhere in the middle, in between, you're starting to cope again" (Sally).

Although fearing that perinatal loss could conceivably occur again, two women also expressed joy regarding fetal well-being. This joy was for the fetal well-being of the present pregnancy, regardless of what the outcome might be:

I feel very positive because the baby is alive inside and well inside of me now. To me, that is something very special. It's something that I don't take for granted or think that the only thing that matters is that this baby is born alive, for the baby is alive inside me now. (Tina)

One of the parameters of fearing recurrence was the acknowledgment that the possibility of having another perinatal loss was not under the woman's control. The women sought to maintain control over other aspects of their pregnancies as much as possible, perhaps to compensate. For Tina, maintaining control over her emotions was very important:

A person just has to take every day and prepare yourself and remember that you are going to have to go through all this. It doesn't matter what you do, you have to give birth to this baby [laughs]. And you don't really have much control, you know. You can choose to have control over how you respond but you are not really going to make much difference. You can fight it or you can go with it.

Tina felt satisfaction that she had maintained control during labor:

And really my pain tolerance was pretty high because I had really powerful contractions according to that little monitor there and I dealt with them just fine. And that made me feel good too. I was successful doing that, maintaining your control. (Tina)

Grace, on the other hand, who had labor induced, felt labor was not in her control, and this caused her some distress. She regretted losing control over her own body:

No one was really saying except Bill [husband] finally [said], "It is your body and you can decide what you want to do with it." . . . Like even if I'd had the choice, who knows how that delivery would have gone or that labor. I tend to think I would have been more positive about it. I don't know. (Grace)

Marie felt very positive that she had accepted the responsibility involved in embarking on a high-risk pregnancy and had control over this decision: "I knew what could go wrong but I did it anyway because I wanted him that badly and it makes me feel good that I took control and gave life to this person that I wanted so badly."

Resisting Attachment

One result of fearing recurrence was resistance to attaching to the unborn child. All the women who participated in the study were hesitant to attach to their unborn babies antenatally for fear that the fetus would die and they would once more be hurt: "Don't do it. You're just getting in worse, you know what can happen. . . . Not getting that huge closeness or really emotional about it like you did with your first one at the beginning" (Grace).

When the women found out that they were pregnant again following the stillbirth, they wanted to maintain a low profile and conceal their pregnancies from others for fear that the loss would recur:

And then I was scared to death and I didn't tell anybody, well, I told my husband but that was it. But I didn't tell a soul. Not anybody. It was easier that way for me because I really didn't have to talk about it because I just wasn't ready to talk about it at that particular point. (Sarah)

I didn't tell. Oh, I think probably I was past my three months when I told them. . . . The first time . . . you were just bubbly. You were just totally excited. . . . You want to hide it . . . what we were thinking is, let's go over to Europe and have this baby. And I just don't want anyone around. (Sally)

Concealing their pregnancies permitted the women to resist attaching to their fetuses. The women were ambivalent about being pregnant again and did not want to acknowledge the presence of their unborn babies:

But I think for the longest time, the best way to describe it is, I didn't acknowledge this pregnancy. . . . This is just something which you would like to hide. (Sally)

When we first got pregnant you were just sort of ignoring it in a way, part of you was, "Oh yeah, you're here, yeah." Not getting that huge closeness or really emotional about it like you did with your first one at the beginning. . . . I didn't tell anybody. Like I felt okay about it but . . . I didn't want that attention on me again. . . . People are always talking about the baby and . . . you're not really there at that time. (Grace)

Fearing recurrence not only led the women to fear that they would not deliver live, healthy babies but delayed their acknowledgment of the reality of pregnancy itself. Perhaps because the previous pregnancy did not produce a viable child, the "unreal" feeling of the next pregnancy was increased:

It's hard for me to relate that there's somebody inside there at times too and I'll believe it when I see it or hold it. (Grace)

Like I couldn't believe that in two weeks I would go into labor. . . . It seems very far. Very unreal. (Sally)

With this baby I don't know what it is. . . . It is almost like I am still getting used to the idea of being pregnant, I guess. I don't totally block it out of my mind but it would be almost as if you were talking to someone who a month ago went to the doctor and found out they were pregnant. But it isn't. I found out in November [said at 28 weeks' gestation]. (Carla)

For the women who did not have the experience of mothering a live child, fearing recurrence led to a sense that their pregnancies lacked reality and disbelief that they would deliver live children. This lack of reality in turn led to their inability to picture themselves in a mothering role:

> It is hard for me to picture myself giving birth to a live crying baby. It's hard for me to even look forward to, to picture myself as that. . . . Just the reality I guess of raising a child and being a mother to that child. It has never happened to me before. I am a mother but I haven't experienced what most normal women experience. . . . Because I have never experienced a normal delivery, a normal child, a normal baby, I've never had that, I don't know. There's that hope I guess. I'm not being negative about this delivery, I am just saying that I have a hard time visualizing myself in that role. (Tina)

The women who had experienced mothering a live child were better able to fantasize about mothering their babies from their current pregnancies. Marie fantasized about repeating the positive aspects of her previous mothering experience:

> Yes, yeah, now that I have a live baby and I know what it's like. I know what it's like to get up in the middle of the night and feed them. I know how wonderful it was with David to get up and nurse him. It was so comfortable and relaxing and loving just to lie in the middle of the night in the quiet nursing your baby and getting them back to sleep. Holding them all the time. I just love to hold them and rock them and read them stories and sing to them. . . . I guess because I know how wonderful it is to have a baby. It's not that I'm not enjoying the pregnancy or that there is any problems or anything like that. It's just I look back on when David was born and when I was in the hospital with him and I remember lying in bed and having him lying next to me and just looking at him and thinking, oh god, he's so fantastic. He is so beautiful. And it is such an incredible feeling having this child. That is yours. That you produced. This is healthy and alive. And it is so nice to take care of them and to nurse them. To hold them, you know. For me it is like what I was born to do. Yeah, I don't know. I don't know why. I just really want to have this baby now.

Following stillbirth, the nursery that had been prepared was a concrete reminder of the failure to have a live child to mother. The women remembered how painful this experience was:

If I could go to first-time mothers I would tell them, "Don't do anything until your baby is born," you know. Because there are just too many memories, you know. (Marie)

When I found out I was pregnant . . . we went out and bought everything. Moved. And there was the baby's bedroom which when the baby was dead and I came home, it was still the baby's bedroom. We ended up having to leave and move to another place because it was like, which bookshelf should I put the books on? Well, the one in the baby's bedroom. Well, it wasn't the baby's bedroom. There was no baby to go in that bedroom. But it was still referred to as the baby's bedroom. (Carla)

As a result of this previous pain, and connected with their hesitancy to fantasize about the future mothering role, all the women hesitated to prepare nurseries in anticipation of their coming babies or to make other concrete plans for the future:

I haven't planned anything for it. I haven't done anything. . . . But you don't really. I don't anyway really think about the future. I just try and get through. And usually I always plan, I am the type of person [who likes] to know what is going to happen. . . . And then I planned so much with Joseph, I quit my job. . . . I had everything planned out perfectly and it all got screwed up anyway. So I think, well, you know, this is obviously something you can't plan. (Sarah)

Like I haven't really prepared much. . . . This time, no. And yeah, I've changed the room too. . . . All I was doing was bringing some of the baby things over to the other room but I didn't set it up or anything. (Sally)

Preparing the nursery was also tied in with the residual grief that women felt over the loss of their previous children. Hesitancy over preparing the nursery was not just because of fearing recurrence of the loss in this pregnancy; the women also wanted to avoid reliving the pain of the loss:

Well, the nursery was done for my son, Joseph, and I still haven't gone in there. . . . I have dealt with a lot of it but that is one thing that, I just closed the door and the room is just sort of there. I figure I will have to go in there pretty soon. Going out and buying new stuff for this one, no, I don't want to do anything and I don't want any showers or anything. (Sarah)

I still have diapers and things like that from the first time. That's hard. (Linda)

In resisting attachment, the women were reluctant to personalize their unborn babies in any way. Helen did not want antenatal knowledge of the gender of her unborn baby, as she did not want to get to know it:

> My husband says it is not good to know it [the gender of the baby]. If you know it, it is going to be too close. We have more confidence right now but he is still thinking the baby is not ready to be born yet and he doesn't want to be like, the relationship to be too close and later on he will be more upset in case something happened.

All of the women were reluctant to think about the antenatal development of the unborn child. Although they sought some reassurance from health professionals in the form of information about fetal well-being, they did not seek information about fetal development or prepare for labor and delivery:

> I was really into it [prenatal education] the last time. Every week I knew what was growing and what was happening but I don't this time. . . . But as far as the stages, I wasn't really as interested in saying, "Now the hands are this far now," whereas before I would give Bill a blow by blow about where the baby was at. So yeah, that was kind of it. And I think that's part of it again, not wanting to get that close or being that total part of it too. (Grace)

Two of the women verbalized that they recognized a hesitancy to attach to their unborn babies and felt guilty about this: "You also have the guilt feeling that maybe you are not expecting this baby enough" (Sally).

Protecting the Unborn Child

Fearing recurrence fostered the women's behavior in protecting their unborn babies. All the women made concerted efforts to protect the unborn babies within them. They attempted to do what they could in order to prevent recurrence of the loss: "That was the only thing I was concerned about. I only thought about the baby. I tried to do anything not to hurt the baby. That was the only thing I was concerned about" (Helen).

The women gave of themselves to ensure that their unborn babies would be healthy. Often their behaviors were intended to amend in their current pregnancies what they thought may have caused the stillbirths in their previous pregnancies: "My main project every day was keep watching my diet and nutrition and blood sugar. . . . You know, it is worth it to quit your job and it is worth it to eat well and control your diet well" (Helen); "I think I took extra precautions to make sure I wouldn't miscarry or anything like that. I made sure I rested and so on" (Lucy).

Three of the women expressed concern that the stress they were experiencing in their pregnancies because of fear of recurrence would adversely affect their unborn babies:

> I probably put this child through just as much stress if not more than I did the other one. . . . I believe that the baby's going to be alive but is it going to be brain damaged now because of all the stress I've had or is it going to be this or this? (Grace)

> And I think about what this baby knows is going on. If this baby can hear a lot or if it can know what Mommy's feeling or knows if Mommy's upset or having a bad day. (Marie)

Seeking Reassurance

The women were anxious to be reassured regarding fetal well-being. Helen blamed her lack of information about pregnancy and toxemia for contributing to her stillbirth, and thus being informed in the next pregnancy became extremely important for her: "Last time, like my husband was thinking that we didn't have enough information maybe. . . . This time he's more careful than before. He borrowed all the books from the library and even purchased some books from the bookstore." Monitoring fetal well-being was important to all the women: "You know, I would check and see if there was any spotting" (Grace); "I bought a blood pressure measurement thing and I test my blood pressure myself, every day, twice a day. . . . And I even bought those tests to test the protein in the urine myself" (Helen); "I wish I could wear a monitor around, you know, 24 hours a day to make sure" (Marie).

Although the women were happy to have nonstress testing and ultrasound performed to monitor fetal well-being, they perceived more invasive antenatal screening, such as amniocentesis and oxytocin challenge testing (OCT), as a threat to fetal well-being: "I think that is where some of my apprehension came from last week. Why do you [obstetrician] want to do the test? These two tests? This OCT test twice?" (Grace); "But I talked to my husband and my husband doesn't want to do it [amniocentesis] again if the baby is normal unless we must do it, otherwise we don't want to do it because there is another risk there" (Helen).

Despite the reassurance provided by the antenatal screening tests, the women were not totally relieved of their fear of recurrence:

> I thought, well, now they have done all these ultrasounds they've measured [and] it's growing. Well, they've seen it's a fairly big baby. Every time I go for my nonstress tests and they make all these comments about the baby. Yeah, I believe the baby's going to be alive. . . . It's reassuring to go to the doctor and hear her put the stethoscope on in terms of that I can hear it, that's reassuring. But these other test things are just sort of getting to me. (Grace)

Fetal movement was significant to the women in signifying fetal well-being, particularly for the women whose first indication of stillbirth was loss of fetal movement: "If I don't feel the baby move I will call my husband and he will be concerned about it" (Helen); "I love it when they move. I think it is the most incredible experience in the world when the baby starts moving. When they don't move you are terrified" (Marie). The presence of fetal movement reassured the women that the child might survive: "But every time it kicks I think, oh my god, my god, it's still alive! Every day I will be waiting for that little kick" (Sarah).

Seeking Safe Passage

Preparing to give up their unborn babies proved to be an anxious time for the women. The women had dichotomous thoughts regarding delivery; they wanted to keep their unborn babies inside them for protection and yet at the same time they were anxious to have their babies delivered, particularly if they perceived that their babies were unsafe being inside them. Grace noted, "Sometimes I really just want it to be all over with and just hold this baby and other parts of me [are] just, maybe this is too quick." In a later interview she said again, "Part of me just didn't want to give the baby up in the state it was in because I knew it was safe and secure in there already." Sarah, too, expressed similar concerns: "If the baby could survive right now [23 weeks' gestation] I would just say, let's do something, because I am afraid. . . . It might have a better chance of living out."

The women who made these statements regarding being anxious to have their babies delivered also expressed opposing views of wanting to keep their babies inside of them: "So with this labor, my biggest fear is like, it is alive inside me, so why can't we just keep it inside there?" (Sarah); "I know enough that if these nonstress tests are run and the baby is in a healthy environment, the baby is just as well off if not better off inside me until term" (Tina).

The women's hesitancy about delivering their babies might have been based on their previous experiences of giving birth to "death." They might have associated delivery with their babies' dying and therefore wanted to protect their unborn children by maintaining them in the womb. Sarah verbalized these concerns: "But this time I don't associate labor with giving life. Like it's associated with death. That's how it ends sort of thing."

Following the occurrence of stillbirth, it was important to the women in their next pregnancies that their physicians acknowledge their fear of recurrence:

> And I think the strange part about it was I couldn't find a doctor who could understand how concerned I was that it would happen again. The first family doctor that I came across said, "Well, these things happen and it won't happen again." And I was sort of left thinking, well, I would rather be prepared for it happening again than to go about it as if it is not going to happen, you know. (Carla)

Mothering a Live Child

The birth of a live child was a significant event that marked the end of the pregnancy that followed the stillbirth. The reactions of the women to the births of their live children included relief that the babies were alive and happiness that they, the women, had been successful in producing live children: "Oh, I felt so happy. Very happy. And then they told me that, when I heard the baby's cry, I felt so happy and the baby seemed so normal and looked healthy to me too" (Helen); "Relief, relief! We actually had something!" (Rita).

Accepting the Live Child

In the postnatal period the women had to accept the live babies they had delivered. Grace compared her child with other children in the nursery, fearing that something was wrong with her child:

> I would go by and they would tell you not to look at other kids but you would go by these full-term kids and their eyes were open and his were going [she squints her eyes closed], you know. I was just comparing and

thinking, jeez, you know, maybe he's not as healthy as everyone had said when they felt him and everything. (Grace)

In the process of accepting their babies, the women had to differentiate their live children from the previous stillbirths. Ease of acceptance appeared to depend on the importance of the sex of the child to the mother. For many of the women, the sex of their babies did not matter as long as they were healthy: "This doesn't really matter [the sex of the baby]. . . . We didn't mind, a boy or a girl is all alike" (Helen). For Carla it was important that she replace the male child who was lost with a male child for her husband:

> I didn't really care when I was pregnant the first time whether it was a boy or a girl or not. I felt, in a way, better that my husband ended up with the boy that he lost because he seemed to have been more involved with that baby than I was. Like seeing him and all that stuff. So it is like I sort of replaced the first baby with Randy for my husband.

Grace wanted to mother a girl and lost this opportunity when her female child was stillborn. Although she delivered a healthy male infant, she still longed for the female child who was lost. Grace felt that having a child of the same sex would have made acceptance of the new child easier. At the same time, she realized that she would have been more likely to consider the live child as a replacement for the stillborn child if the two had been the same sex:

> I don't know how I would have related if it was a girl but I think at times it might have been easier in a way to have a girl. I don't really know. . . . I'd probably be putting more on it because she was a girl too. In some sort of a weird way or maybe it's not so weird, I'd always be looking at her like maybe this is Jane back again. You know, maybe it is her coming, you know, whatever your beliefs are in reincarnation or whatever and maybe I would be, I don't know, it's hard to say. (Grace)

Interestingly, Helen expressed this same desire to be the mother of a girl infant, but readily accepted the role of being a mother to a boy once she saw her son: "At the beginning, I thought I would like a baby girl better. . . . Since I saw this little guy I don't mind. Yeah, it is the same to us. It is the same."

Despite the presence of the live babies, the women came to realize that these babies did not replace the ones who had been lost:

I will look at him and just sort of think back on what she looked like. I'll
be sitting around sometimes in the evening and I will just start to cry and
say that I just want her too, you know. I don't know, there is still that
emptiness too. Like even though he is here. (Grace)

Fearing Loss

Although with the birth of the live child the mother's fears of having
another stillbirth were resolved, fearing recurrence of loss was carried
into the postpartum period. Grace's son developed hyperbilirubinemia,
and Carla's son was born prematurely. These threats to their infants'
well-being probably fostered these women's fear of recurrence. In Carla's
case, there was a definite possibility that her son's life was in jeopardy,
whereas in Grace's case the neonatal jaundice was a minor physical
problem. Despite the differences in the possible consequences to the
infants' welfare, both mothers reacted the same. Both were afraid that
perinatal loss would recur and, despite reassurances from the medical
staff, were not convinced that their babies would survive until the physical
problems were resolved: "I wasn't really in that celebration mood once
the baby was born. . . . I was really worried . . . and wondering if this
baby's okay. You know, are they telling me everything? Everything
cleared up so well but I had to see that, again, for myself, for him to
come out of it" (Grace); "I guess there was always this thought or this
fear that I was going to go to the hospital this one day and he wasn't
going to be there anymore. Even though the doctor said he was fine"
(Carla).

Resisting Attachment

Even prior to her son's developing jaundice, Grace wanted only passive
interaction with her baby. She wanted to know that the baby was all right,
but she did not want to be actively involved: "He's been on my tummy
but take him away. Not take him right away but just let somebody else
hold him or do something with him." Grace also commented:

> I had asked Bill to go and get him before I went to bed so I could see him
> before I went to bed. And he wheeled him down and everything. And I just
> said good night. I didn't hold him or anything like that. I was just sort of
> looking at him in bed, I didn't feel like picking him up then.

It took Grace until two weeks postpartum to be confident that her son was going to be all right. She started to feel confident once the jaundice was resolving and she was past her due date:

> I had people phoning me in the hospital, "Oh Grace, I am so happy. Congratulations, da da da da." And I'm going, yeah, but he's got . . . and I was talking about his health [laughs]. I wasn't saying, oh jeez, yeah, thanks, it's so nice and I'm really happy. . . . I wasn't hugely ecstatic. Yesterday [two weeks postpartum] was the first day I picked up the phone long distance. I was really feeling good about him and started to feel really happy because he's healthy, he's gaining weight and doing what he should be doing.

Unlike Grace and Carla, the other nine women expressed more immediate attachment to their liveborn babies. Helen had confidence in her son's well-being as soon as he was born and expressed her love for him:

> Even before I saw him I already loved him. . . . But to me, maybe I already had very good confidence. It seemed that my baby was so strong and healthy. I didn't wait that long. The first minute I saw him I was quite happy already. I was quite confident already, yeah.

Protecting the Child

Protecting the child was important in the intrapartum period, when fear of loss was still extreme. Tina was relieved that the nurse who cared for her during labor had the knowledge and skills to protect her baby:

> I had an excellent nurse and she gave me oxygen. . . . I don't know whether the nurse knew that I had had a stillborn . . . she was an exceptional nurse. I was lucky. I am sure not all nurses are like that. She was extremely expert at it, what she was doing.

Just as fearing recurrence carried on into the postnatal period, so did protecting the child. It took the women a while to adjust to their new babies and to feel confident in the mothering role:

> Maybe I was looking at him as being fragile or maybe I would have been overprotective anyhow. I am not too sure. I think when the jaundice thing came and everything, that's when I sort of panicked and blew it all out of

proportion not knowing once again what this whole thing was about and thinking, oh god! Is something happening to this one too? (Grace)

Acknowledging the Lost Child

The birth of the live child rekindled grief over the lost child:

I think I remember the degree of my loss, like it is such a precious thing. Like that can be easily forgotten or overlooked over a period of time. You do forget a little, you know, about the value and you kind of see this little bundle of joy here and you remember that you had one before too. (Tina)

In Grace's comments it appeared that grieving for the lost child had been delayed by the subsequent pregnancy and then was rekindled with the birth of the live child:

I have been more upset about Jane than I was at the beginning, you know. Because I was so absorbed and worried about this pregnancy when I was pregnant at the end. When I got home I'd sometimes bake and stuff but lately it seems that I've had periods that I have been upset about her.

In congruence with accepting the live child, there was a need among the women to acknowledge their lost babies. They did not want the existence of their live children to negate the loss of their stillborn children:

And I think there is still that thing, "Is this your first child?" . . . We went to a shower up where I worked, Allen and I on Thursday and someone said, "Oh, congratulations on your firstborn son." I really hung on those words, I was really glad she said "your firstborn son," like, it's not your first baby. (Grace)

The women anticipated the task of telling their children about their stillborn siblings: "He [husband] asked me, when he grows up will I say anything to Allen [the baby] about her? And not to go way overboard, he's saying, 'What will you let him know?' And I am saying, yeah, yeah, you know" (Grace); "And then you decide when should you tell this one, this one, that his brother died. And you know, you do think about that" (Sarah). Carla and Lucy continued to acknowledge their stillborn children, although their losses had occurred some years previously: "I think the point is that the baby will always be a part of our family and rather than be a secret, that baby should be a part of our family" (Carla); "Since we have lived in so many communities whenever we go back to that area we always go up and take a look at the grave and tidy it up. . . . I mean that is about all you can do" (Lucy).

In caring for their live children, the mothers were faced with sharing between their stillborn children and their live children. The nursery, articles of clothing, and maternal love were recognized as being things that were shared between the two offspring: "If I ever thought that my sadness over losing the first baby would affect Randy and Randy thinking, 'Well, you don't love me because you love that other baby more' or whatever, I would die" (Carla); "I was wondering if I would have as much love or as much care for this baby or the next baby as I did for her. . . . Wondering if they have enough love to carry over for the next one" (Grace).

It was important to the women that nursing staff acknowledged the previous lost child during the current pregnancy and childbirth. They appreciated it when nursing staff recognized their concerns antepartum and intrapartum and provided additional support:

> And she [social worker] told me that the nurses asked her how I was doing and if I was coping okay and they were quite concerned and stuff. And I remember thinking that that was just wonderful of them. That I had come through this and I had a live healthy baby and they were still concerned about me. So that was really good. That was really nice. (Marie)

Three of the women did not perceive that they received the assistance and support they required in the postpartum period. They felt that the postpartum staff did not acknowledge that a previous child had died and assumed because of their parity that the women were competent and confident in the mothering role:

> They had on my records that this was my second. And I guess maybe for medical reasons they need to know that but, as far as any help or anything I guess they assumed that I knew everything and I knew nothing. . . . I really felt neglected in the hospital. . . . I just didn't feel like I was getting a hell of a lot of support. (Grace)

> Well, as far as nursing care goes, I don't think that when I had Randy that the nurses were even aware that I had had a baby. Well, I would imagine it says under those things, one, zero, one or whatever. . . . That Randy was baby number two and that baby number one wasn't alive anymore just by the numbers that they write down. (Carla)

Perceptions of Others

The women's beliefs about the perceptions of others pervaded their experiences of pregnancy following stillbirth, and so some comment on this is warranted in this discussion. The women were very conscious of how other people might view their situations. They often commented that their experiences were different from what other people might think. There also might have been dissonance between the women's experiences and their own expectations of what those experiences might be like.

The women recognized that other people did not understand the significance of their loss:

Because they figure that because you weren't actually bringing that child up that you can't miss it. Or miss the whatever. They don't understand that [sighs] having it growing and feeling the expectations, you know. Wanting to be that mother and then all of a sudden, nothing. They don't understand the attachment you felt. They say, "Oh well, it just wasn't meant to be." They said that! (Linda)

And his mother's belief for our first baby was that he wasn't a baby because he died in utero and I never got to hold him and I never got to change his diapers and nurse him or whatever. So he wasn't a real baby. And she said to my face, "You are not grieving for a real child. You don't know what it is like to have a real child." (Marie)

The women even thought that their husbands could not understand their loss:

I get the impression that Larry didn't realize exactly, you know, because he is a man and he doesn't know what a woman feels about her baby or whatever. (Tina)

A man could never understand. My husband, he lived through it and my husband can't even understand what I went through. Because . . . to him it was like, you know, it wasn't something alive yet. Like when it laughs and crawls on the floor and stuff like that, I think that is when men get more . . . (Sarah)

Grace was resisting attaching during labor and delivery and postnatally in this pregnancy. Others did not realize this and mistakenly assumed that she would be ecstatic about becoming the mother of a live child:

I can't really say I was excited during the whole thing, I mean, you know, because I had a few nurses I knew up there [caseroom] already and people saying, "Well, now, it's going to happen. You are going to have a baby tonight" and all this. I wasn't getting really ecstatic or thrilled. It seemed the people around me were more excited about it than I was. . . . And I almost started feeling guilty about that, you know, you hear everyone else being . . . I sound like a morbid person but everyone is so excited when the baby is born.

Others mistakenly thought that the grief over the stillbirth would be immediately resolved with the birth of the live child. They assumed Grace would no longer have a need to be involved with the parent support group in which she had actively been participating: "One of the girls said, 'Well, do you still want your name on the brochure, your number given out?' And I thought, 'Yeah, yeah.' Like it was just after he was born. I don't know if they thought . . . " They failed to realize that once stillbirth occurs, it changes a woman's life forever.

The Process of Livebirth Following Stillbirth

The critical juncture in the process of livebirth following stillbirth is the occurrence of the previous stillbirth (see Figure 5.1). In order to understand this process fully, it is necessary to go back in time to consider the antecedents to the stillbirth. The women were transforming to motherhood. The occurrence of stillbirth interrupted this process. The worst had happened; their fears were realized when stillbirth happened to them. They experienced not only the loss of their children but also the loss of the mothering role, a loss of control, and a loss of confidence in their own ability to produce live children.

For women who were pregnant for the first time since having a stillborn baby, the themes of the replacement of the mothering role and, to a lesser extent, the replacement of the lost child were dominant. In the early stages of pregnancy the lost child and the current unborn child became fused. Some differentiation occurred following fetal movement and ultrasound, but separation of the two was not complete until after the birth.

The third theme was fear of loss of this child. The fear of loss was not just a fear of the recurrence of stillbirth but also was a fear that anything untoward would happen to this child. This fear of recurrence of loss also occurred with women who had had live births subsequent to stillbirth. This fear appeared to influence attaching behaviors. Early in pregnancy

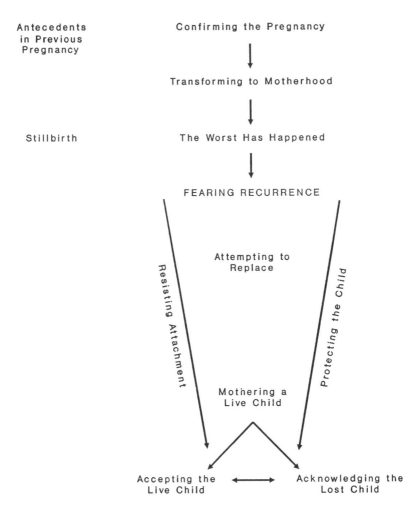

Figure 5.1. The Maternal Processes of Livebirth Following Stillbirth

the mothers delayed telling others about their pregnancies. Mothers with
no previous live children did not fantasize about their unborn children.
They avoided personalizing the children: They did not want to know the
children's sex and they did not want to choose names for the children.
Later in pregnancy the mothers did not select baby clothes or prepare

nurseries. The mothers recognized their hesitancy to attach to their babies and felt guilty about this. Hesitancy to attach to the unborn child seemed to decrease once quickening occurred, once the fetus was viable, once the gestational age at which the previous loss had occurred was past, and generally with time.

Protective behavior was evident in the mothers' adapting their lifestyles, for example, eating differently or giving up work early if they believed it to be beneficial for their unborn babies. The mothers did not want information on growth and development of the unborn babies, but they did want information about fetal well-being. As labor approached they expressed concern that their unborn babies were safer inside than being born. They had many concerns about induction of labor and found this threatening. The women felt relief when their babies were born. With the birth of the live child each woman, with the exceptions of Grace and Carla, felt success at having fulfilled the mothering role.

Following birth the mothers appeared to complete two tasks: acknowledging the stillborn child and becoming acquainted with the new baby. Through this process, differentiation of the newborn from the stillborn baby took place. The fear of recurrence of loss did not appear to dissipate with the live birth, as indicated by the mothers expressing high levels of anxiety over minor health deviations such as an elevated bilirubin level. Two mothers who had babies with problems (neonatal jaundice and prematurity) continued to resist attaching. The other mothers seemed more confident in accepting their babies. Birth rekindled grief as the mothers recognized that their live children would not replace the children they had lost. Putting their live babies in the nurseries and dressing them in clothing meant for the children who had died precipitated their grieving. In addition, the presence of the live child made each mother more aware of the value of the child who was lost.

In summary, although the women who experienced stillbirth were deprived of knowing these children, they were in the process of transforming to motherhood and attaching to their newborns, and consequently the loss was devastating to them. The stillbirth loss affected the subsequent pregnancy, with the women fearing recurrence of loss. Fearing recurrence resulted in anxiety and resistance to attachment, both during the pregnancy and in the early postpartum period. As the women established positive relationships with their live newborns, they had a simultaneous need to acknowledge the babies they had previously lost through stillbirth.

References

Bergum, V. (1989). *Woman to mother: A transformation.* South Hadley, MA: Bergin & Garvey.

Bourne, S. (1983). Psychological impact of stillbirth. *Practitioner, 227,* 53-60.

Clark, M., & Williams, A. J. (1979). Depression in women after perinatal death. *Lancet, 1,* 916-917.

Dunlop, J. L. (1979). Bereavement following stillbirth. *Practitioner, 222,* 115-118.

Furlong, R. M., & Hobbins, J. C. (1983). Grief in the perinatal period. *Obstetrics and Gynecology, 61,* 497-500.

Kirk, E. P. (1984). Psychological effects and management of perinatal loss. *American Journal of Obstetrics and Gynecology, 149,* 46-51.

Kowalski, K., & Bowes, W. A. (1976). Parents' response to a stillborn baby. *Contemporary Obstetrics and Gynecology, 23,* 1113-1123.

Kübler-Ross, E. (1969). *On death and dying.* New York: Macmillan.

Lindemann, E. (1944). Symptomatology and management of acute grief. *American Journal of Psychiatry, 101,* 141-148.

Stringham, J. G., Riley, J. H., & Ross, A. (1982). Silent birth: Mourning a stillborn baby. *Social Work, 27,* 322-327.

Wolff, J. R., Nielson, P. E., & Schiller, P. (1970). The emotional reaction to stillbirth. *American Journal of Obstetrics and Gynecology, 108,* 73-76.

6

Becoming the Mother of a Preterm Baby

Barbara Brady-Fryer

Research conducted with mothers and full-term infants has provided a conceptualization of attachment or relationship formation. Attachment has been depicted as a process that begins during pregnancy and continues in the postpartum period. Evidence exists that supports a concept of the mother's attachment to her infant evolving through her increasing awareness, during pregnancy and after birth, of the child's unique characteristics and capabilities (Cranley, 1981; Gottlieb, 1978; Leifer, 1980; Rubin, 1975, 1977; Stainton, 1985a, 1985b). "Mothering," through contact with and caring for the infant, facilitates attachment, as does the infant's increasing responsiveness to caretaking (Gottlieb, 1978; Stainton, 1985b).

When an infant is born preterm and hospitalized in a neonatal intensive care unit (NICU), the customary mothering role is difficult to realize because the care of the newborn is, at least temporarily, the responsibility of professional caretakers. Maternal activities that focus on the tasks of identifying and claiming the baby are inhibited. The infant's condition may prohibit the mother's holding, touching, and caring for him or her, and the infant may have limited ability to respond to her caring efforts.

AUTHOR'S NOTE: This research was supported in part by the Alberta Association of Registered Nurses and the Alberta Foundation for Nursing Research.

Little is understood about the mother's subjective experience of relationship to a hospitalized preterm infant. How is the untimely end of the pregnancy incorporated into the developing mother-infant relationship? In what way is the evolution of that relationship continued after birth when "normal" maternal activities are not possible? What is it like for a mother to give the care of her newborn over to strangers? How does a woman "mother" a child under such circumstances?

The purpose of this study was to examine mothers' descriptions of attachment to their hospitalized preterm infants and to identify factors that influence their developing relationships. For the study, mothers were encouraged to talk about what was important to them, focusing on their experiences during and shortly after their infants' hospitalization in the NICU. The six women who participated in this research were "successful" multiparas, each having previously achieved a full-term pregnancy and the birth of a healthy child. It was assumed that each informant had developed through this previous experience an outlook, a mind-set, or an image of herself as a mother. Prior to the birth of this infant, she had no knowledge of a personal, maternal role in relation to a hospitalized preterm infant.

Each study informant met the following criteria: gave birth to an infant born between 25 and 34 weeks' gestation no more than 2 weeks prior to study admission that was expected to remain in hospital for at least 2 weeks, had delivered and kept at least one full-term infant previous to the preterm delivery, was married or involved in an ongoing relationship, was able to speak and read English, and was willing to participate in at least three interviews. The informants were interviewed several times over the course of their infants' hospitalization and at least once after their infants were discharged.

All informants were living with the fathers of their preterm infants at the time the study took place; five were married and one mother was involved in an ongoing relationship. Their ages ranged from 26 to 36 years, and their education ranged from 10th grade to an undergraduate degree. The gestational age at which the preterm births occurred ranged from 26 to 34 weeks, and the length of hospitalization from 23 to 109 days. The infants experienced complications associated with preterm birth to varying degrees, including respiratory distress, apnea, bronchopulmonary dysplasia, and problems with feeding. All infants were discharged from the NICU to home; however, one infant later died of respiratory and cardiac complications.

Prebirth Experiences

Most women experience some degree of relationship with their unborn babies during pregnancy. Study mothers gave evidence of that prebirth relationship through their postbirth reflections on their communication with their unborn babies and their commitment to their pregnancies:

> Well, like all the time I was in there [the antepartum unit in the hospital], I knew she was going to be little and premature . . . [because of placenta previa] and it seemed to make her that much closer, I don't know why, maybe 'cause just her and I were there, going through all that together. You know, before she was born the nurses asked me, "Well, how do you keep going, how do you, you know, not get really upset and everything?" and I just used to tell them, well, every week I'm here is a week better for her, so it was the only way I could look at it, otherwise I think I would have gone crackers sitting in here. (Anne)

For all of the study mothers except Anne, the labor and preterm birth of the infant were surrounded by surprise and confusion:

> I didn't believe it. Initially at home I thought, this is false labor, and kind of joked, well, this can't be happening, but I always knew things were different, so at first I ignored it and then I came to realize this is serious and this is very scary because it's not supposed to happen now. (Pam)

Initial Reactions

The appearance of the infant after birth proved disturbing. The mothers' reactions were, in part, influenced by their previous mothering experiences and their recollections of their previous children:

> I felt a little disheartened to see how small a baby of that size really is. . . . You forget how small babies are anyway and then to see one like that, it's really little. . . . Nothing prepares you for seeing a baby that tiny. . . . I mean my oldest boy was a small baby but not 1 pound, 11 [ounces], I mean that's small. (Sue)

The mothers were shocked by the appearance of the life supports connected to their infants:

When we first went to see her and she had an IV [intravenous] in her head, she had something in her arm and her arm was all done up and in her belly button and in her foot, she had tubes down her throat and I thought like, this is prematurity, this is too much on the brain. (Emily)

A preparatory tour of the NICU before her infant's birth did not protect Anne from a negative reaction to the technology: "I knew she'd have it [scalp intravenous], but it looked different on other babies than it did on my baby."

Accepting

Study mothers had not expected to "fail" in pregnancy, and with the exception of Anne (placenta previa), they searched for a cause for their preterm births:

I didn't really think that I was doing anything to hurt the baby but I wondered after if I should have rested more. The doctor said that rest wouldn't have [made a difference]. . . . I don't know. It's not something that I really dwell on a lot I don't think but I wouldn't say I'm comfortable with it yet. . . . In my reading I search for little clues but I don't think it's so much to, what's the word I'm looking for, to blame myself but if I ever got pregnant again I'd want to know what to avoid, I just don't want to do that again, you know. When I was in the hospital, I can remember thinking that I was afraid to call him [husband]. . . . I was afraid that he was gonna . . . blame me. . . . I wouldn't have been surprised if he'd try to find something wrong that I'd done to cause this. But he's been completely, completely the opposite. That would have been hard to fight 'cause I [had] enough trouble with my own guilt and searching for what I did wrong without somebody else doing [it] to me too. (Mary)

Accepting meant facing reality and continuing on, despite negative feelings:

Well, I guess I just have to [accept it]. I do, I feel really bad about what's happened to him [hydrocephalus, intraventricular hemorrhage—IVH] because he would have been a normal baby; there was nothing wrong with him when he was born and now he's got who knows what. . . . It's really disappointing and saddening in that way. I'm never going to feel probably completely okay about it even if I knew exactly what it was. (Mary)

Study mothers were also keenly aware of what they were "missing" compared with their previous birth and postpartum experiences. Intimacy with their newborns in the NICU setting was not possible and was sadly missed by study mothers:

I mean you can't touch them but then at least you can sit and you can open . . . up [the isolette] or you can talk to them 'cause you feel kind of . . . like you want to say things to them, like I wanted to talk to them but you didn't really say what you wanted to say 'cause there was always somebody around and they're buzzing around your face, especially at [the NICU] 'cause they couldn't leave the baby because they have to be there to make sure everything is cool. You couldn't say what you wanted to say. Like they don't mind and you know they don't care but it's none of their business. You want to say it to your child and you want it to be on a one-to-one [basis], not one and a neighbor. (Emily)

Discharge from the hospital without their babies was difficult for study mothers:

A lot is just the idea. You have a baby, you're supposed to take it home with you, just not leave it laying there. . . . That's my baby and I shouldn't have to leave her there. . . . It's not so hard as when I was in the hospital and first left her but still, you hate to go and leave her. (Anne)

Eventually, study mothers appeared to reach a point where their own guilt and disappointment receded from primary focus but a sense of loss and sadness remained a part of their day-to-day reality:

Sometimes it feels like I'm missing and something's slipping away, but it isn't really I guess. . . . It's more like I'm missing that part, that it's something that I kind of . . . want or long for, I don't know. I'm trying not to use stupid words but it is almost kind of like an ache or something. I don't know. And you know, I still enjoy the things that I do with the other kids, not all the time, that's true but . . . when I do manage to relax a little. I mean it's not just saying that my whole life is without meaning now, that's what I'm trying to say because it isn't that bad . . . it's just that a part of it that doesn't feel whole. Right. (Mary)

Jacky found solace in her children at home, despite the less-than-perfect situation with her preterm infant:

I wouldn't say it's a gap 'cause like it can't be any other way, like I can go home and hug my other two kids and we can think about him, that kind of makes up for it, I don't know. It's not that I feel empty or anything. . . . No, [it's] definitely not [the ideal situation]. . . . It is for him in that he needs the care but it isn't for us.

Finding Strength

Informants turned to previously established sources of support during the time of crisis:

Mostly, I'm drawing a lot on my faith, my religion and things at this point. . . . Yesterday was really hard for both of us, neither one of us were doing very well and so we arranged to have another blessing for our baby and that helped me. (Mary)

The mothers also drew strength from their marital relationships:

My husband has been able to come through in that area [child care] for some reason 'cause normally he's quite an out-of-patience sort of person and he's really seen the need with the other children and he's been able to fill that better than I have. He's spending extra time with them. . . . One thing that really helped [with breast milk pumping] was my husband's support, it was really important to him that I breast-feed so that helped a lot. If he was against it too, I would have been hard-pressed to carry it through 'cause I can't have him upset all the time too. (Mary)

Happy homes provided welcome respite for informants. They saw evidence of their ability to mother their previous children appropriately and believed they were creating good lives for them within their own homes:

If I didn't have them I think I'd be totally zonked out. . . . I would feel like a complete failure. . . . In this situation the best thing I have is my other children to . . . For one thing I know they're normal and we did things right with them, so to speak. So I have the confidence that we have two other children and I can go home to them and create a good life for them. (Jacky)

Finding time for the newborn often meant taking time from siblings and other family members, leaving little personal time. Strength came from decision making and commitment to decisions, no matter how taxing the routine:

And I had this tremendous sense of the umbilical cord still connecting us. I didn't want to be away from him. . . . I have felt right about what I am doing. I mean I've heard a lot of mothers say to me, "Gee, you must really miss your kids and you must feel guilty about being away" and yes I do, I really miss my kids and I feel guilty about being here but it seems to have been the right thing to do. . . . We worked out what my husband was going to do, how the children were going to be cared for, and everything else. It's just a matter of setting priorities and then working everything out. It's when you don't set priorities and you don't know where you're going and you don't know what your goal is, that all of your energy is pulled here and there. . . . It was a matter of just sort of channeling my energy to the one thing that I felt I could cope with and that was being here. (Sue)

Jacky opted for a different plan that better suited her personality and her family's needs:

And I'm not so sure it's good for me to be there all the time. I find that the other girls that come in here all the time, they're in the hospital, they live, die, and breathe their baby. Whereas I get out into the traffic and my kids and my husband and get my mind on other things. . . . I've got to believe that's best . . . for me because I am a worrier.

Becoming Hopeful

Hope for the future depended on the mother's awareness of signs of her infant's progress, whereas despair was aroused and deepened when the infant suffered setbacks and deterioration:

Both my husband and my . . . feelings have pretty well fluctuated with the baby's daily condition. . . . It's funny but like even the tiniest little setback will just practically throw us into despair. You know, they're just up and down, up and down. . . . Actually we're not really taking it that well now. (Mary)

Repeated setbacks in her son's progress made Mary want to escape the NICU: "I just got down so bad, really, when he started to get sick again I didn't even want to be there. And usually I'm quite the opposite, like I've always wanted to be with him as much as I could." As the despair deepened, relatively innocuous signs of possible problems were blown out of proportion, moving Mary further away from hope:

And like I'm getting less and less stable now, like I was telling you, his temperature went down a bit the other day and I was just totally hysterical and today, I just went in that milk room and I mean I just sobbed my heart out.

Signs of progress, on the other hand, moved mothers toward hope for the future. Physical movement of the child's isolette through the NICU from the intensive to the convalescent teaching unit (CTU) was an important, tangible sign of progress for informants:

> Once they're in the CTU it's more like a nursery and it's everyone's happy 'cause now they're okay, there's nothing wrong. . . . That was so good because everyone can laugh, like the nurses are laughing there, not in the second row where it's so serious. (Pam)

Infant weight gain and the removal of technology were interpreted by study subjects as signs of progress, which they welcomed with guarded optimism:

> I'm not confident in that I'm a pretty guarded person but everyone else seems to be so very confident and they told me yesterday that he'd be home in six or seven weeks and that he was going to be fine, so I really have no reason to be apprehensive but it's still at the back of my mind but I feel pretty good about it. I'm still just as concerned because he is in the intensive care unit and things could turn, you know. He could have a setback and things will be back to square one tomorrow. (Jacky)

Establishing Mothering in the NICU

As their hospitalized preterm infants' conditions stabilized, study subjects began to search for ways to mother them. The urge to touch and hold their newborns was very strong, but fears held the mothers back:

> When my baby was a pound and a half I could reach in and touch him but I was afraid to. There were times when I stood by that isolette and all the machinery was going and he was in, sort of, one of his down days and I could remember standing there and thinking, I should touch him, I want to touch him, but I'm afraid to. What if I make something happen? What if his saturations go? What if he has a bradycardia because of this? All these kinds of things, hesitating to touch him and yet wanting to so badly and then thinking, Don't be stupid, get your hand in there and touch him. I mean literally having this conversation in my own mind, opening . . . up [the

isolette] and touching him and then standing there bawling like a baby. A sense of relief. He's all right, I touched him, I'm all right. (Sue)

At times, holding and touching the baby did not seem worth the risk. The mothers often did without the gratification of touching in order to avoid harming their babies:

> But we kind of worry about putting added stress on the baby. . . . Then last night we didn't want to bother him. They asked us if we wanted to [hold him] but we said, no, just put him back [in the isolette]. . . . If it's gonna upset him or anything I don't want to do anything to aggravate the bleeding [IVH]. . . . I don't want to do anything at all that would hurt him, and I can still hold him and touch him in the isolette. (Mary)

In the early neonatal period, the infants were perceived by study mothers to be inactive and unresponsive. This perception appeared to dampen the women's desire to interact with their babies. Study informants also expressed strong feelings of inadequacy regarding infant care; initially, at least, mothering of the infant had no operational definition: "There's very little that a mother in here can do for her baby. . . . It's such a feeling of helplessness and frustration, of futility, of uselessness, standing there and being of no earthly use to your own baby" (Sue). As time passed, however, they did learn ways to become more involved in the day-to-day physical caretaking of their infants:

> I try to make him more comfortable and like I can move him around a little bit and put his hand on . . . I took some little socks down for him to wear. I do as much as I can, you know, I just can't really do that much but the few little things that I can do. . . . I took some little toy down there and like we talk to him about it and I sing to him and actually all my family visits him a lot. Besides myself and my husband, there's always at least three or four people that visit him just about every day. (Mary)

As the infants grew stronger and were physically able to be more active, their responsiveness to care increased. Jacky's comments underscore the importance of this responsiveness:

> Like yesterday was the first time I really looked into his eyes and he made me figure, well, I have a baby here. No, it's the truth, like I looked at him and he looked back at me and that's the first time I've experienced that with him, whereas the others, it was very early. But I find, too, that I feel differently about the baby that . . . at first he wasn't a baby, I don't know

what he was. I didn't feel for him, you know. But now when I go in, like I hold him in my hand and he looks at me and opens his eyes, so like he's starting to be my son now. I look at him and I wonder what kind of baby he's going to be. I search for his character but I don't know yet. But I think it's just the beginning of a relationship when that happens, when you start to look at each other and hold him.

Early on, study informants could only look forward to participating in feeding, and the anticipation of breast-feeding was an important expression of commitment. Five of the six study mothers used breast pumps to maintain their milk supply for future breast-feeding as well as to provide expressed breast milk for gavage-feedings, "with the thought of starting to breast-feed at some point soon, then that will mean a lot more too 'cause then I get to hold him more . . . especially when he's out of his isolette, that will be very, very nice" (Pam). Breast-feeding helped to minimize the mother's frustration with the situation in general: "Well, I've found that nursing helps because I get to have him out a lot more so I hold him, talk to him and stuff. The rest of the time I just want to get out [of the NICU]" (Mary). Breast-feeding provided a key to a future of more "normal" mothering:

That's going to be the pivot point where, as soon as he learns to nurse, he can come home. But he's more or less my baby now, like I can come in and demand nurse him you know, whenever he needs it. Or that's the point that we're leading to, like I guess it only starts once a day or whatever. (Jacky)

The mothers spoke of their abilithy to observe, interpret, and store information about their infants' cues and responses to various interventions. Their comments convey an understanding of the uniqueness of this aspect of mothering, realizing the value of this information and attempting to share it with the professional staff:

For me there is no question, this is my baby. I've watched this baby every day except those 12 days. I know him better than anybody, I know his patterns, I know his behaviors, I know what makes him happy, what makes him uncomfortable. . . . I try not to be pushy, I try to say things in such a way that it's conversational . . . introducing information into the conversation without being overly forceful about it. And sometimes I feel phony doing that. . . . Like it's not something I should have to beat around the bush about. I should be able to say, "These are the things that my child likes and dislikes and I have noticed these patterns in his behavior" because I have a tremendous amount of information about this baby that you'd have to go back and read a file this thick to begin to know him like I do. . . . I'm not saying that every mother has the capability to stand and make observations, but if you have a mother who can observe these things, she should be part of the care, I mean, a primary part of the care of that baby, not just peripheral, not just an interested spectator, a bystander. (Sue)

The terms *bonding* and *attachment* have been used in the professional and lay literature since the 1960s. Study mothers were familiar with the lay interpretation of the concept and compared their developing relationships with their preterm infants to those established with their previous children. Several mothers feared their developing bonds with their infants because of the possibility of death: "It's almost like you're scared to get close to him because you might lose him. . . . [At first] I was just following his medical progress" (Jacky). Others remembered immediately feeling close to their babies:

> I bonded very easily with my kids, like when you hear about the people that have problems with postpartum blues, that breast-feeding doesn't always start off right and you don't always bond right away, like they try to warn you about stuff like that. But I always felt close to the baby right away . . . all my babies and this baby too. (Mary)

Informants' perceptions of their bond to their infants were influenced by their faith in its reciprocal nature. Not all the mothers believed that their infants recognized and were bonded to them:

> Like how can [the baby], when he sits with me and I talk to him or cuddle him in there every day for a half an hour or whatever, can he distinguish between me and a nurse that does the same thing three or four other times during the day? He can't. It would be nice if he could but, you know, like there's warm and loving nurses in there that coo to him and everything else and they're very gentle with him too. . . . Unless they [infants] have a keen sense of . . . a smell or a feeling that they can distinguish a mother from a nurse, I don't know. But at this point I don't think he can, I honestly don't believe it. (Jacky)

Mothers who were convinced that their infants knew them relied on the infants' behavioral cues for that belief, interpreting smiling and settling as positive responses:

> His response to my voice . . . and my touch. Quite often when he's fussing and really aggravated by some procedure, maybe gavage-feeding or something of that nature, I will put my hands in [the isolette] and he settles down within seconds . . . so he knows, he definitely knows me. (Sue)

The lack of opportunities for normal parenting had a negative effect on the mothers' perceptions of the bond:

> We haven't been parents to him yet . . . like our other children. We haven't guided him through his first two months, the hospital has. We've barely got to touch him the first two months. . . . I think it's a different sort of love. . . . In retrospect, I think we'll . . . love him more or he'll always be more special or special in his way because of what he's gone through. . . . Maybe we'll overprotect him or whatever, I think we'll more than make up for, we'll try to make up for the first three months of his life when he gets home. (Jacky)

In retrospect, Jacky became convinced that an unconscious bond to her son had always existed:

> We take pictures of him every two weeks . . . and when he was born and even at two weeks, we thought he looked like a perfectly normal hap[py] . . . healthy baby and now when I look back at those pictures, I can understand how my brother couldn't look at him. . . . Then I thought, jeez, he looks in great shape. Like that's gotta be that parental thing that you won't realize that, that's a strange feeling. 'Cause I remember my husband commented to me when we saw him first, "Well, jeez, he doesn't look bad considering what he's been through, he looks good." We even said to ourselves, he looks just like [sibling]. . . . He's in better shape than [sibling], 'cause [sibling] was all bumped and bruised and he had bruises all over his face. . . . We said that he looked better than him but now when we look back at those pictures we're just overwhelmed. . . . Like his skin's just hanging there and he's lying there like that.

With this realization, Jacky expressed her concern that such "blind parental love" might hinder her objectivity toward her son:

> That's strange isn't it? That's why I would think that we could . . . easily go through fine for the next five, six, seven years and not realize that he has a problem, just because of our love for him and our . . . need to want him to be normal.

Establishing Relationships in the NICU

Nurses spend more time than any of the NICU staff in contact with parents, and their influence affected the ways in which these women could mother their babies. Study mothers were able to identify characteristics of a "good" nurse. The nurse's ability to maintain what was perceived as an open, warm attitude toward each mother was important: "At first it's a shock to go in there. . . . If you get a really nice nurse . . . they'll explain to you the whole situation and you'll go home feeling so good" (Jacky). Nurses who recognized mothers and conveyed a sense of welcome were appreciated, as were nurses who made an effort to involve mothers with their infants:

V encouraged us to talk and encouraged us to stroke him right away and at first to talk was very hard because, gee, talking through an isolette. . . . She [nurse] was very, very good. And I was saying, "I'm scared, I don't want to touch him," and she was saying, "Don't say that," just very nicely, not forcing or . . . very calm, quiet. She was a good first nurse to have on I think. Very good. (Pam)

Nurses who were "motherlike" in their care of the babies were appreciated:

I think I told you already what the nurses did. . . . You can tell the difference that [they] tried to make, that [they] weren't [just] caring for the baby, that they tried to make him really comfortable and stuff too and a lot of them will talk to him and he needs some of that stimulation so that he's not just there being worked on all the time. When they are a little bit attached I really like that, I think that he's going to get better care then. (Mary)

Some nurses were perceived as caregiving experts who worked at not getting involved with mother or baby:

Sometimes I'm disappointed when I go in. . . . There have been a few nurses that are very detached and some that don't even really want to talk to you about much and that kind of disturbs me. Like I like the nurses that feel like they can talk to me and that I feel are being really open and honest and that notice little subtleties and share them with me and actually it's very important to me. And some of them don't share a lot. I'd say that most of them do but I've noticed that the more that the nurses have J the more open they become. I think that they get to know the baby, I guess that makes it a little easier for them to share things and maybe they just don't have a lot to share at first. . . . All the nurses are so different too, actually a lot of them do try and make him quite comfortable but it's more a kind of a lot of times it can be a kind of clinical touching and . . . that's not true for all of them, a lot do spend the time just touching him and stuff too, but I would think that they work at not getting too involved. (Mary)

The mothers regarded NICU nurses as individuals with needs and personalities of their own, but stated that not every nurse working in NICU "has what it takes":

> I think that the ones that are successful at it, from the minute you get in there they're talking to you, they explain what they're doing and [ask], would I like to try it? Or "Here, I'll show you how," and some of them don't even come over and say hi or anything. Then when they come over to change a diaper they just whip in there and whip out of there again, they don't wanna hang around. . . . They could take time out to explain to you or whatever and some of them just don't have the personality for it. . . . Some of them don't realize what you're going through. I don't know whether they do or not but what they say gives you an indication that they have no idea that you're going through. But they're there to care for the child, they're not there to analyze us, like how can they deal with the stress of working in there and then have to deal with us too? That's a full-tilt job. That takes a special personality to work in there and obviously some of them don't have it. (Jacky)

Study mothers felt intimidated by a dogmatic nursing approach:

> They'd come across as a complete authority instead of a person that wanted to. . . . You know how you're intimidated by that. . . . It's like talking to a doctor, right, like you don't always feel comfortable with a doctor when you go in and see him so you're scared to bring some things out, right? It's the same with some nurses, like you're intimidated so you don't open up to them; you have to have a special skill not to be intimidating so a parent will open up to you. . . . Like if I won't open up to them or a parent is scared to open up to them and express their concerns then it doesn't do any good if they're talking to us anyway. (Jacky)

Coping with rules and regulations was difficult for the mothers, especially as it appeared that rules varied depending on the nurse. Rules enforced without input from the mother lessened her feeling of ownership for the baby and caused friction in the nurse-mother relationship:

> When you're in the hospital I feel like you should do it their way so they're happy. It's their nursery, it's their place, their responsibility. I guess they should do what they want but it's not their baby. 'Cause you think, god, maybe I'm doing something wrong! Maybe I'm not diapering her right. Maybe she's not comfortable laying like that. 'Cause every time [the nurse is] there I feel like I have to ask, "Do you guys want her laying on her back?

Want her laying on her stomach?" You know, "How do you want me to lay her?" And I thought, I'll lay her any way I want to lay her. (Emily)

Occasionally, mothers were able to achieve a measure of control over enforced routines, ironically, with the help of nurses:

'Cause when they changed his bath time again, we just got so that we would both be here at 7:00 and bathe him and be done by 7:30 or so, so they can feed him at 8:00, and well now they say, "Well, now we don't want you to do it until 8:00." But I had a good nurse on and she says to me, "Well, forget that, you do what you can do and the nurses can work around you." Which is right 'cause we just got used to this. . . . She [nurse] made a point of educating me, just how to put our foot down and say, "This is what's for us." (Pam)

While their infants required care in the NICU, the mothers felt it was their duty to cope with rules and regulations, personality conflicts, and the negative interactions that were sometimes part of their relationships with the NICU nursing staff:

And he's mine now but he's not mine because if he was mine I would be holding him all the time, I would be hugging him and loving him and you know I can't take him out so . . . I can stroke him, but I don't have a say, really, medically in what's going on with him. I can't change this, it's not like I'm in my own world and I can tell you to leave my house whoever you are, I can't do that. . . . I can't allow myself to resent it because that's the way it has to be . . . because when he gets home he'll be home and that's when I'll have my baby. Like right now, you guys need to do what you have to, I'm not going to fight that but I know the difference. (Pam)

Informants described making concerted efforts to "keep the peace." For study mothers, things were "hard enough" and they felt more comfortable when cordial alliances were maintained:

I am the type of person that would tell somebody what for without any hesitation, but in there I never did. To the surprise of my husband, I'd go out and walk around. Go phone my Mom or something. (Jacky)

Well, it is, it's exhausting. . . . It just is you know, when you have to be . . . the nurses can be quite emotional too, they have their own personalities and they don't want to be . . . I mean they're just questioned and hounded all day too by everybody and I realize that but they kind of have to put up with me and I kind of have to put up with them. . . . I'm really worrying about their feelings, worrying about the nurses all the time and I'm tired of that too. Like trying to get along with everybody when I'm feeling so frustrated and stuff all the time. I just want to get back to the worrying about the usual things like what we're gonna have for supper and not anybody's feelings and stuff. (Mary)

In the mothers' minds, there was another, more ominous reason for keeping the peace and avoiding conflict:

On one occasion when it [conflict] happened, I was absolutely devastated by it but rather than show the nurse how she had affected me on the off chance that it would jeopardize the care given to my baby I removed myself from the situation and went elsewhere and sat down and had a damn good cry, because, you know, all the tension that builds up from that kind of interaction has to come out somewhere. (Sue)

The mothers admitted that they did not have the knowledge or expertise to provide much input into the care given to their infants. Despite their ignorance, however, the mothers needed a great deal of faith to entrust virtual strangers with the total care of their infants:

I mean you can talk to the nurses, you can talk to the doctors, but in terms of the actual medical care that is being given, it's out of your hands and it's a very frightening thing. I mean you have to have a great faith in what's going on, a faith in the people who are handling your baby, and there are times when the person who is handling your baby is not the one that you would have chosen to be taking care of him. Sometimes it's an outright dislike, I mean just like anywhere else in the world, in life, you don't get along with 100% of the people and there are times when you're faced with the situation of watching someone you don't particularly like handle your baby in a way that you don't particularly like. (Sue)

In establishing trust, a perception of recognition, openness, honesty, and true caring on the part of professionals was important to the study mothers:

That's the way I feel about the doctor too. He's really shown quite a lot of interest in . . . he remembers things, he's got such a good memory. . . . He knows when [husband] goes to work, he knows when he's going to be home and he remembers things about my children, and he's said that he's really become quite fond of the baby and I just trust him completely and it does make us feel 100% better. I really appreciate the feeling that the doctor shows toward us . . . and the same with the nurses. Actually, I guess it makes us trust them more. . . . I have more trust in the ones that I think really have a true concern, not just a medical concern. (Mary)

Trust in the professionals caring for the baby grew as the baby progressed: "I don't know, it just, maybe it happens over time. He's getting better so they obviously cared for him the right way" (Jacky). The mothers described a desire and a need to know about their babies, and the perception of openness and honesty in information sharing was crucial:

Don't be cautious about what they tell the parents because the nurses that would talk to me, I really liked them the best; the ones that would tell me as much as they could, those were the ones I liked. I have had a couple that almost acted like it was a secret or something and I didn't like them that much. (Mary)

When time was taken by professionals for communications that involved explanations of complicated conditions or treatments, informants felt empowered in their role as mothers:

Actually, you know, I appreciate somebody thinking that there's a chance that I might grasp it because some of the doctors won't even say boo to you. Or tell you anything, so whether or not I understand it all was beside the point; the fact that he tried, that he assumed that I might understand really was good. And I did basically understand it but not to repeat it that well. But it gave me an understanding at the moment [of] what was happening. (Mary)

Defensive reactions in response to mothers' questions created confusion and resentment:

It's like hitting a person when they're down, if someone is in my situation, seeing something done to the baby, some procedure, and simply asking questions about it and I am met with a very defensive attitude, it only confuses. . . . Basically all parents are looking for is not explanations of the nurse's behavior but explanations of the procedures and sometimes they don't take it that way, sometimes they respond in an agitated way, maybe they're having a bad day, everybody does but in this situation, it kind of blows things all out of proportion. (Sue)

The mothers saw themselves as major stakeholders in their infants' outcomes and spoke of their right to be informed about the babies' conditions:

> I heard some parents who make suggestions or ask questions were told more or less to mind their own business. I prepared myself; I thought, if that particular individual ever responds to me that way, I'm going to ask them, "Whose business is it then, since the child cannot speak for himself?" This is my baby, I have the greatest stake in this baby's life. . . . You'll have him here for a week or a month or three months, I've got him for the rest of my life and whatever is going on here is my business and if I want it explained someone should be prepared to explain it, not tell me that it's not my business. (Sue)

Opinions varied in the study group as to the benefit of other relationships that were established over the course of the infant's NICU stay:

> There's a camaraderie amongst the other mothers, we all know each other by first name, I don't know half the last names here but I know everybody by first name and we keep up to date on how we're doing and take each other out to lunch or go shopping together, just to get out of here sometimes, just to have a shoulder to cry on, just to get through a critical time when one's own family can't be there. I find that talking with the other mothers is a tremendous help, we're quite close-knit, we spend a tremendous amount of time talking, trying to cheer each other up, doing things for each other. (Sue)

In contrast, Jacky avoided mother-to-mother discussions:

> Well, the worst thing that you could ever do is to go into the [breast] pump room and listen to everybody's problems. That's why I pump at home, 'cause you go in there and somebody'll be saying, "Well, you know . . . ," and then you wonder, whew, at least my baby didn't get that [or] all in all, is this what's to come? or something. Like I find that they depress each other more than . . . I say, "How are you? How's the baby doing?" and stuff like that, I mean that's all there is in our lives right now. . . . It helps to talk about it but still you wonder, oh no, is this what I'm in store for? Maybe I'm wrong in that, but I feel like we should be cheering each other up instead of telling each other what could go wrong next. And that's the way it got, like I don't know whether they're sadists but it's like they thrived on it. If something went wrong, you got more pity type of thing. . . . Why would you want to drag yourself down like that? You just went further down the gutter.

Coping With Relationships at Home

The disruption in "normal" family life precipitated by the preterm birth and the events that followed had negative effects on siblings. The study mothers expressed guilt over their lack of attention to siblings at home during their preterm infants' hospitalization:

> We have two other kids at home too, 4 and 6 years, and it wasn't fair to them. We couldn't go on like that. . . . We were trying to do things with the kids and spend time with the baby and take care of the kids at home too, like not to disrupt their schedule too much. . . . The kids haven't been on time for school once since the baby was born I'm sure. (Mary)

The mothers were not surprised when siblings expressed their frustrations by acting out:

> We're just treating him [sibling] the way we always do basically, I mean trying to be as consistent as we can and setting the limits and not trying to change too much stuff, but you can't do anything with him, he isn't responding to spanking or he doesn't care what the punishment is, he doesn't care what it is. (Mary)

They described some difficulty in their attempts to involve siblings with the hospitalized newborn:

> I understand how much she's [sibling] hurting, it's very hard; last night she refused, she doesn't want to be around D at all and that's understandable, but we are only with him for two hours in the evening, we're here with the pump, we don't have to be here for so long 'cause it takes half an hour to pump, her good time would be half an hour and she gets restless. This past week it's, "I don't want D, I don't want to see D." (Pam)

Ultimately, family needs as a whole took priority, with study mothers devising solutions that were best for all concerned:

> I've got more of a routine now, I have a morning shift and a night shift and the afternoon is for myself, well myself and mostly [sibling A]. . . . [Sibling B] doesn't get home from school till 4:00, so then we can have dinner together and then I go again [to the hospital]. I tried nursing him [preterm infant] five times on Saturday and I think they could just wash the floor with me at the end of the day, like I was like a dishrag. That was too much,

I think it won't work out, it won't work out with the kids either. But if I can keep it to these kind of two shifts, I think it'll be all right. (Mary)

The involvement of extended family members with the hospitalized infant was controlled by informants:

We just didn't tell them that they were so ill because it would just kill them. . . . They are the first twins in 33 years, so it's a big thing at home right now and to tell my grandmother something like that, like she'd panic . . . so we just didn't tell her. We figured that once they're out of the danger zone then we'll explain all the tubes and all that. All the other things that have been going on that we haven't been telling everybody because we didn't want to worry them. (Emily)

Pam shared details of her infant's condition, but on her terms:

Just my family . . . I've told "No comment back unless it's positive." . . . I mean I know better now that because initially I didn't know he was going to live, I don't need you going, "Ohhhh, that's terrible, why is this happening? Why is he having bradycardias?" Because that's normal and I've explained and explained. Don't go like that anymore because it scares me. 'Cause then I get scared, I mean I don't trust my instincts or . . . I have to go with what they [NICU staff] and . . . I've told my mother, "Whatever I say, do not comment," because her comment sets me off to a panic.

Making the Break From the NICU

When the movement of their infants toward wellness seemed guaranteed, the mothers began to consider making a break from the NICU. At this point, they began to visualize themselves in the role of primary caretaker, and with technology removed, the possibility seemed more realistic:

'Cause at first I realized that I couldn't do anything anyway, with all these . . . like it hurts to just go. . . . All you could do is just stand there and look at her more or less and, you know, put your hand in and touch her hands or something but it seemed like if she got a little better then I figured, well, I should be able to do that for her, especially after she got off her IVs and that. (Anne)

Pam expressed the urgency she had begun to feel:

I'm sure they were doing what they had to and everything, they weren't holding him back but to me, I felt they were and that he was ready. . . . He was off his monitors, he was in a cot, and I thought he was going to get more infection being in the cot in their environment than in mine, my environment at home 'cause there's all kinds of people coming. . . . And I was going to get a lawyer, I was, that was it, that's all I felt was that it was time and that's it. They didn't know I was going to get a lawyer but that's how urgent or how strong my feelings were.

Informants expected their fears to persist in the home environment:

Is he going to have bradycardias at home, is he going to have apnea? We worried about apnea with my daughter . . . SIDS [sudden infant death syndrome]. I did, my friends don't. I'm the type that checked on her [sibling] all the time. (Pam)

The mothers began to talk about preparations and plans for homecoming:

In terms of his health, yes, we will make allowances, we will not take him to large crowds you know . . . and have people coming with colds or anybody who smokes or [has] pets or paint things or anything like that. . . . I know what I'm going to face at home. I know we're going to be hermits for a year or so. (Sue)

Jacky intended to incorporate her preterm infant quickly into the existing family lifestyle: "[We're going on a] family holiday. . . . [We'll] take him to the mountains his first weekend home." The mothers were confident that their newborns would be well accepted by siblings but predicted a period of adjustment:

I mean it never is [easy] when you bring a new member into the family . . . but I'm sure they'll [siblings] adjust well. They're very . . . very stable, they haven't been whining and crying and, you know, having nightmares and wetting their bed because I'm not there. . . . They have that, the years of growing up in a caring family. (Sue)

The mothers felt that they were likely to be overprotective toward their preterm infants and planned to make conscious efforts to avoid this, in the best interests of their infants:

If we're not going to let him learn how to walk because we're so afraid he might fall and hit his shunt or something, then he won't learn to walk. I mean we could slow him down by getting too worried about things like that. I'm assuming, nobody's told me that, but that would be, that's the kind of attitude that I have. I can see where if you just kind of acted on natural impulse you might tend to do that but, I mean, I want to make a conscious effort to encourage him as much as I can to be independent and to grow and stuff. (Mary)

Mothering at Home:
Role Transition

The preterm infant's discharge from NICU precipitated a change in the developing mother-infant relationship. A period of transition began at discharge, as the mothers, for the first time, assumed total responsibility for their infants:

> I think I could see that he was ready [to go home] too. He was just kind of waiting . . . and it seemed like that to me too. But even though . . . I say that I didn't really like it there [NICU] that much, you still get kind of attached to the place, you know. [It was] a kind of strange feeling, I wasn't excited about it at all until half an hour before and I had to, quick, get ready and get him dressed and then I was practically hysterical. I wanted to cry and I was just scared somebody would look at me and that would be the end of it. I was really excited right before I came home but not at all until then. I don't know how to explain it, kind of, not annoyed, but like, I don't know, hard to explain. Not at all what you'd think. Like now they're kicking me out, kind of thing. (Mary)

Fears and mixed feelings notwithstanding, the positives in having the infant at home far outweighed the negatives:

> We're the ones that decide what happens to him and what . . . he's out of that atmosphere where he gets his diaper changed 12 different times during the day and he gets six different techniques; it's different, that's the way it has to be in there, like without them he wouldn't be right, so you're so grateful to them, but on the other hand it's nice to get home and get back to our own routine too. When you're going into the hospital four times a day you can't, you don't have any. As soon as we got away from that hospital, like we were great. Well, then you have normality again. (Jacky)

Not surprisingly, there were some residual effects of the care:

I still kind of catch myself, even here [at home]. You know what I did, I take his temperature and wonder what his head circumference is and stuff like that, and noticing if he's going to the bathroom, if they're wet or not and like things that I've, like perhaps getting to the point of counting voids and stuff, where I never did that with the other two. Like I feel like I'm kind of doing something I shouldn't be doing if I'm administering his vitamins, I need to ask if I can change his diaper and does anyone want to see if he peed or not. (Mary)

In the home, the mothers seemed to need to get to know their infants all over again, interpreting infant cues and behavior:

He's just really good. Very quiet but confusing because I don't know what he wants. . . . He grunts and groans and whether that means gas or that he wants to nurse, and so he's fooling me a lot during the night 'cause I'm thinking he needs to nurse. And sometimes he just needs to be held for some reason and that's enough, that'll get him over it or we walk around with him to get the gas out . . . he's very gassy. But that's part of his grunting and groaning and I guess that's what preemies do. Like all those faces and I was really concerned. (Pam)

Informants described some difficulties in dealing with health care providers practicing in the community. Uncertainty or negativity on the part of these professionals hit study mothers hard during this period of role transition:

We were doing very well because he was home, that's all I think us moms are waiting for, you get to the point where well, he's healthy now or he's off the monitors or whatever, it's time to bring him home. And then we took him to the pediatrician and then he said he was quite concerned about D being so premature, coming home so early; he was quite confused because the doctor at the hospital let him out. And then he said, also, he [the baby] can catch infections quite easily right now. . . . So we have to keep him bundled up like in the hospital with his hat on and everything. So we went back to being afraid again. First we were happy . . . and I don't like that. But he [the doctor] sort of looked at me and said, "Well, he's home too soon, he's not even five pounds yet." And I should have said, "Yes but were you a mother, six weeks of going through times of being, coming home empty-handed?" You know, like "You don't know . . . buddy." (Pam)

That negative reaction led to renewed fear for Pam and shook the foundations of the confidence that she had so painstakingly built:

Right now I'm just trying to deal with it, trying to say, okay, well, prepare yourself if something happens, but I don't want to. . . . I don't want to, then so I'm sort of pulling back from [the baby] saying, well, you know, I'm scared I'm going to lose him again. So I'm pulling back and trying not to get too attached, which isn't right.

According to study informants, siblings, for the most part, reacted positively to the preterm infants' homecoming:

It didn't seem to bother them [siblings], though. Like even when we went and picked her up [at the hospital] they were all excited and taking a peek in her bed all the time. If she's sitting in the chair here, they both have to climb up and kiss her . . . she's had so many kisses. [They] give her dolls to try and hold. They loved her. They didn't like it this morning when all those people [visitors] here holding her. (Anne)

Extended family members presented problems for the study mothers once their preterm infants were at home. Informants tried to control the situation, focusing on a return to "normal" family life:

Like I said before, I thought I would be possessive and that too many people handling her bothers me a little bit. This morning my husband's sister came from Saskatchewan and a couple of her friends and her kids and they all passed her [preterm infant] around, and I said, "Enough, she has to go back to bed now." She's kind of a novelty, everybody's coming to see her, all the relatives. (Anne)

The mothers continued to be concerned about the intellectual and physical normality and the potential disability of their infants following discharge:

We can't really do anything until we see, like we're scared to do anything 'cause we don't know what he's going to be like. It's like the thought entered my mind to ask the doctor whether he knows if he's [preterm infant] going to be slow or anything like that but it's almost like I'm scared to . . . but it's such a stupid question I guess no one really knows. Nobody knows the answer, right? What can you do or say that . . . that leaves a lot of uncertainties about his development and stuff. Things that are inside his head instead of outside. Like, outwardly, he's actually doing very well but it's the things that aren't tangible, you can't see and you can't really understand and that's kind of what's hard for us. (Jacky)

Informants also monitored their infants for signs of normality:

> He lifts his head, he can turn his head from side to side. . . . His eyes appear
> to both work simultaneously, which is encouraging. . . . His sucking response
> started weeks back, and I thought that was a very encouraging sign. (Sue)

Reflections

At the final study interviews, which occurred after their infants were
discharged from the hospital, the mothers spent some time reflecting on
how things had changed for them as a result of their experiences. Sue
described the vivid impressions of the NICU that she still recalls:

> I found it [NICU] quite alarming initially, I know why they call the
> monitors' signaling systems alarms, it's because it's very alarming, you
> know, you see lights flashing and buzzers sounding and when it involves
> your own baby, it just is a wrenching experience. I mean like on many
> occasions I thought I was going to need the CPR [cardiopulmonary resus-
> citation]. It's a terrible thing to go through.

In contrast, Mary described positive feelings about the way she had
managed her infant's hospitalization:

> I think he really needed me for that two months and I feel that it helped
> him to have me there. Who knows what would have happened if, you think
> about other babies whose parents can't be there or aren't there for whatever
> reason and they just lay there day in and day out and a lot of them, it seems
> like they do just kind of deteriorate. They don't move on and I don't know.

Feelings of regrets about the preterm birth persisted:

> [My husband has] more guilt than I do. . . . He'll say, "Gee, you know, you
> told me that you felt the baby dropped and why didn't I take you more
> seriously?" and "Why didn't I tell you to lay down and when they told me
> you were in the hospital why didn't I just come down and supervise it
> myself?" Like all these things that he could have done differently. . . . I
> don't know, he said about a week ago, he said, "I think that this has just
> ruined my whole life." Like it's really affected him. . . . He [husband] is
> just quite single-minded anyways because for me I still have, like to me,
> he [preterm infant] is here, I still have him and I have [husband] and we

have a good marriage still and we still have the other two kids, like I
certainly don't see it as the end of my life. I'm not saying that it hasn't
changed but it hasn't made it necessarily more gloomy, I wouldn't say. But
his [husband] life is gloomy now, for a while anyway. He said, "No matter
what I'm doing, if I'm sitting at dinner or I'm at work or anytime that I'm
just sitting any place I just can't stop thinking about him [preterm infant]
and why did it have to happen to him?" It's just really getting to him. (Mary)

Jacky wondered whether she would have done things differently if she
had it to do all over again:

If I had been a stronger person I would have aborted the pregnancy. I just
kept thinking, well, I have two little blond heads, there's another one in
there, I can't do this. No, if I could do it over again, I wouldn't have went
through the pregnancy. Not that I'm not grateful for [preterm infant] but I
think it could have turned out bad too. . . . It could have been a very
traumatic thing for the family.

For others, lingering feelings of regret as well as a desire to complete
childbearing on a positive note led to thoughts of another pregnancy:

You have such a tremendous sense of failure in delivering a baby prematurely, it's like you've only done half a job. Something has remained
undone and I think that's one of the reasons that I have been so busy trying
to do things, I want to get something done to completion because I didn't
do a good job with the baby. I even had the feeling a few weeks back, maybe
I should have another one just to see that I can do it right. I mean what an
irrational thought, but that's the way I was thinking. (Sue)

Looking back on their experiences, the mothers were sensitive to their
increased sense of personal vulnerability:

I can't hardly think of anything that could be worse [than the preterm birth]
except maybe having a live child die or . . . an older child, a child that
you've gotten used to . . . being murdered by a rapist isn't very good either,
but I think it does fit in those categories. And I've kind of changed in that
regard that something did happen to me and now I'm not, this is going to
sound really stupid, I shouldn't tell you this but you know that silly killer
that's been out, that's killed those two women and you think, well, it was
two of them and you never think it'll happen to you. And I don't have that
feeling anymore. Like that feeling is gone. Like I think anything can
happen to me [now]. (Mary)

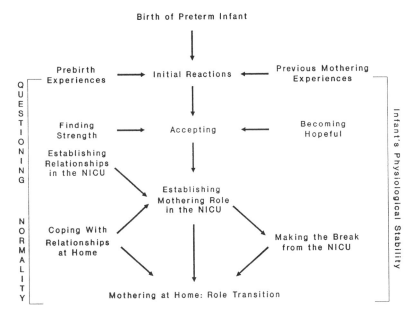

Figure 6.1. Forging the Role: The Process of Becoming the Mother of a Preterm Baby

Summary

Women who deliver prematurely experience an abrupt termination of their physical attachment to their unborn babies, but the evolution of the mother-infant attachment relationship continues. The findings of this research identify a process that may be called *forging a role*, which gave mothers access to that attachment relationship in the postpartum period; these mothers forged a role in relation to their preterm infants and thus were able to express their attachment to them. This process is outlined in Figure 6.1.

Forging a role is best characterized as a series of successive steps that are influenced or dependent on certain conditions. The mothers' progression through these steps ultimately resulted in the formation of a new role as mother of a preterm infant. The postpartum evolution of the attachment relationship between mother and infant continues unabated in the event of preterm birth and hospitalization of the newborn. Those women who deliver prematurely experience persistent feelings of guilt, sadness, and regret about the birth.

The concerns of the women in this study have implications for health care professionals. A mother's confidence and ease in being with, touching, and caring for her preterm infant comes gradually as time passes and with improvement in the infant's condition. Women need support and encouragement to become involved in their infants' care, and such involvement empowers women in their roles as mothers and provides an outlet for expression of commitment to their infants.

Family problems, time limitations, conflicts with professional staff, and the infant's condition place constraints on the mother's inclination and/or ability to participate in the care of her hospitalized preterm infant. Caregivers should attempt to assume nonjudgmental attitudes and avoid labeling mothers or parents as difficult or hysterical. Commitment to a plan for involvement in infant care can help mothers of preterm infants to attain a sense of control and to prioritize other responsibilities.

The relationship between the mother of a hospitalized preterm infant and the NICU nurse is potentially very powerful. Nurses working with these mothers must walk a fine line between displaying an attitude of knowledge based on confidence and clinical expertise and displaying an attitude that reinforces the mothers' feelings of uselessness and helplessness in caring for their infants. Nurses need to be sensitive to the mothers' feelings of ownership for their infants and strive to establish partnerships with mothers.

Mothers' potential contributions in terms of awareness of their infants' patterns and responses to care should not be underestimated. Because mothers are the only persons who spend time with their infants on a consistent daily basis, they can often provide vital information, helping caregivers to bridge the gaps created by days off, shift changes, and varying patient assignments.

References

Cranley, M. S. (1981). Roots of attachment: The relationship of parents to the unborn. *Birth Defects: Original Article Series, 17*(6), 59-83.

Gottlieb, L. (1978). Maternal attachment in primiparas. *Journal of Obstetric, Gynecologic, and Neonatal Nursing, 7*(1), 39-44.

Leifer, M. (1980). *Psychological effects of motherhood: A study of first pregnancy.* New York: Praeger.

Rubin, R. (1975). Maternal tasks in pregnancy. *Maternal-Child Nursing Journal, 4*(3), 143-153.

Rubin, R. (1977). Binding-in in the postpartum period. *Maternal-Child Nursing Journal, 6*(2), 67-75.

Stainton, C. M. (1985a). The fetus: A growing member of the family. *Family Relations, 34*, 321-326.

Stainton, C. M. (1985b). *Origins of attachment: Culture and cue sensitivity.* Unpublished doctoral dissertation, University of California, San Francisco.

7

When a Child Has a Birth Defect

M. Gail Diachuk

Although pregnant women often fear they may give birth to abnormal children, they still imagine babies who are normal and healthy at birth. Down syndrome is a relatively common genetic anomaly, but to date no work has been done that identifies the impact of a baby born with such a birth defect on the mother herself. The joy of anticipated motherhood requires that the baby be perfect. What uncertainty does the birth of a handicapped child create regarding the child's future?

The purpose of this research was to document the experiences of women who had given birth to children with Down syndrome, to listen to their stories as "lived-through" or "recalled" experience, and to identify a shared experience by analyzing their stories. Three of the babies in this study were physically healthy; the other two had cardiac anomalies that led to respiratory problems, leading to several hospitalizations over the course of the study. All the mothers were perceived by community health nurses to be adjusting to their babies' condition. Indeed, the nurses acted as gatekeepers, preventing access to mothers they believed were having trouble adjusting to their babies. Thus this shared experience comes from mothers the nurses believed were "doing well" and who would thus have the energy to take part in the research.

AUTHOR'S NOTE: This research was supported in part by the Dr. Jean C. Nelson Award, the Alberta Foundation for Nursing Research, and the Alberta Association of Registered Nurses.

The women willingly shared their stories with me. They expressed gratitude that someone wanted to listen to their stories rather than give them information or suggest what they should do. The sample consisted of four mothers whose babies were affected by Down syndrome. Transcripts from another study were used, with permission, to obtain data on a fifth mother (Terry). The mothers ranged in age from 31 to 38 years; all were married, and the husbands' ages ranged from 31 to 40 years. All the women had previous pregnancies that had resulted in normal children. All the births occurred between 37 and 40 weeks of pregnancy. There were three females and one male infant. Two were small for gestational age (4 pounds, 9 ounces; 4 pounds, 14 ounces) and two had a septal defect. In three instances the genetic aberration was a trisomy 21; in the other babies a chromosome 21 translocation was identified. At the time of the first interviews the infants' ages ranged from 8 to 28 weeks. A total of three interviews were conducted with each mother, each lasting from 60 to 90 minutes, with a mean of 75 minutes. At the final interviews the infants' ages ranged from 19 to 44 weeks. The two infants with heart defects were hospitalized for upper respiratory infections and croup between 5 and 7 months of age. At the time of the interviews, all of the four children had the marked facial symptoms that clearly identified them as having Down syndrome. Because it was believed that the grief reaction of the mother to having a handicapped child might interfere with her ability to focus on attaching behavior, it was decided that the first interview would not take place until the infant was 6 weeks of age.

None of the women interviewed had a family history that would indicate the possibility of having a child with Down syndrome. Each of the women described her pregnancy as normal, and none experienced anything that would suggest to her or her doctors that a genetic abnormality was present prior to birth. It was assumed that the process of maternal-infant attachment began during the normal pregnancies experienced by these women. The desire to continue the attachment relationship with the expected child was a driving force in the process of maternal role formation in the postpartum period. The major differences between the expected child and the actual child contributed to the difficulties in maternal role formation. An assumption is made that the formation of the maternal role is ongoing and continues to develop as the mother grows in confidence and competence while meeting the needs of the child throughout the child's life.

Although the experiences of each of these mothers were unique, commonalities were found that led to the discovery of the process of maternal role formation following the birth of an infant with Down syndrome. The direction of the steps taken in the formation of the maternal role was fairly consistent in the experiences of the four primary informants. The variation in the amount of time spent in each of the steps of the process was a result of differences between the mothers' experiences. The process of maternal role formation begins with the pregnancy, continues to develop with the birth experience, and is ongoing as the child matures.

Overview of Maternal Role Formation

Each of the four primary informants experienced a normal pregnancy that suggested to her that she would give birth to a normal healthy infant. These women's expectations for the maternal role were based on their prior experiences as mothers of at least one other child. In addition, the mothers' ages influenced their expectations for healthy children. The two mothers of advanced maternal age were aware of their increased chance of a genetic abnormality in the infant, but, like the other mothers, did not think that it would actually happen to them. All of the mothers had heard about Down syndrome, but Sandy was the only mother with personal experience involving children with Down syndrome.

The birth of the infant initiated feelings in the mother of uncertainty about her ability to nurture her child. The mother's expectations of her role in the birth and the newborn's status were affected by her previous childbirth experiences and her ability to recognize abnormalities at the time of the birth. Both the gender and the health status influenced the mother's relationship with the newborn. Both Sandy and Norma were separated from their newborns following birth. These two mothers found this separation to be a hindrance in beginning the attachment process with their babies.

The next major step in the process of maternal role formation related to the mother's reaction to the diagnosis. The time at which the mother was informed of the diagnosis of Down syndrome and the way in which she was told had an effect on the mother's reaction and her ability to relate to the infant. The mother's perception of the care received from health professionals was associated with her finding the strength to accept the diagnosis and become involved in mothering the child. Simultaneously, the mother's involvement in taking care of the child was associated with her level of acceptance.

The responses of family, friends, and others in the form of support or nonsupport became important factors influencing the mother's willingness to establish a relationship with the infant. Acceptance of the diagnosis and positive feelings toward the infant were important factors in determining the mother's readiness to inform others about the diagnosis of Down syndrome.

All of the mothers found that the return home marked a major change in their ability to mother their Down syndrome children. The mothers now had control over the care of their babies and were able to establish some sense of normality in the home environment. Being at home helped the mothers to focus on the normality of the infants rather than on the abnormalities. Indeed, throughout the process of maternal role formation the mothers frequently questioned the presence of abnormality in their children. The mothers often compared the babies with other children to promote their own perceptions of normal progress and development.

The integration of the child into the family was associated with the mothers' feeling more confident and competent in the maternal role. At this step in the process of maternal role formation, all of the mothers found it important to focus on the present rather than worry about the future.

Expectations for the Maternal Role

All of the mothers experienced what they thought were normal pregnancies, which indicated to them that the outcome would be healthy babies. Although the mothers had heard of Down syndrome, none of them thought that it would happen to them with this pregnancy. The amount of prior knowledge and personal experience with Down syndrome varied for each woman. However, the amount and type of knowledge did not influence the mothers' expectations for normal babies.

Antenatal Expectations

It is commonly accepted that most pregnant women begin to develop relationships with their unborn babies. The mothers in this study tried to develop a sense of knowing something about their unborn babies by evaluating their own health during the pregnancy. Sally described her pregnancy as normal and her expectation for a normal baby:

> I was expecting a normal baby. 'Cause my pregnancy was really good. . . .
> I didn't even gain that much weight, I only gained 17 pounds, which was
> nice. But I was never sick with morning sickness, I felt really good when
> I was pregnant.

After the birth, Sally recalled that her husband was upset that an amniocentesis was not done, but her response was, "Like the doctor said, there was no history of it in the family, there was nothing wrong with the pregnancy."

Norma's healthy lifestyle during the pregnancy suggested to her that she would have a healthy baby: "I had a really good pregnancy and I didn't do anything, you know, I drank very little and I didn't smoke, you know, I exercised and that kind of thing." Sandy's healthy pregnancy gave her no indication that anything was wrong with the baby:

> Nothing, I had an absolutely wonderful pregnancy. I was healthy. We did everything, swimming. And my size was about the same and my weight. I don't think either of the doctors ever suspected anything. . . . I never thought about it once because I had such a healthy pregnancy.

Mary was living in an ongoing relationship with the father of her child when she found out she was pregnant. She related her initial response:

> To tell you the truth, I had considered terminating when I found out I was pregnant. Just for the sake that I've already had three kids and I really didn't know whether I wanted another one or not. And it had nothing to do with the fear of anything that would be found.

Mary's healthy pregnancy gave her no indication of any problem: "Nothing was wrong with my pregnancy, everything was perfectly normal. Nothing gave me any reason that anything was wrong, nothing at all." Mary's feelings about the pregnancy changed as her boyfriend became excited about becoming a father for the first time:

> After we had decided to go ahead with it, yeah, then we were excited. And it was fun for me because he was just like a little kid with this whole thing. His first and only. And he was just fascinated. It's kind of what made it for me because everything was so exciting and new for him.

Prior Knowledge of Down Syndrome

All of the mothers had heard of Down syndrome prior to the birth of their babies, but none of the mothers thought that she would have an affected child. Sally had the least knowledge about the disorder and seemed to be the least prepared for the possibility of it happening to her. When asked if she had heard about the condition prior to the birth, Sally responded:

Just very casual. I just never paid any attention. In fact there was a show on TV a couple of weeks before she was born on Down syndrome. My mom phoned and told me about the show and I wouldn't watch it. I said to her that I wasn't going to watch it and she said, "Why?" and I said " 'Cause I don't want to know about it."

Later Sally was annoyed that she had not watched the show, but at the time she thought it would never happen to her: "No, you always think there's nothing going to be wrong with your baby, it'll be born normal. You don't want to think the opposite. Now, I could kick myself now for not watching it."

Norma was aware that Down syndrome was associated with advanced maternal age and she felt that if she had been older, she might have been more prepared for the handicap: "I think if you were older, then you would expect it more." Both Sandy and Mary were over 35 years of age during their pregnancies and were aware of the increased risk of having a handicapped child with advanced maternal age. Mary thought about the possibility during the pregnancy: "I think I was a little bit leery or apprehensive all through my pregnancy. Simply because nothing was ever wrong, I never felt any different but just because of my age, I think." Sandy felt prepared for the possibility of having a handicapped child with her first child, who was born two years earlier, when she was 35 years old. However, she was not prepared this time:

And with her I never thought about it once because I had such a healthy pregnancy and when she was Down syndrome, that was the shock because I thought we talked about this so much and I was so prepared last time, not this time.

Although Mary and Sandy knew that prenatal diagnosis was available to them, neither of them had an amniocentesis. Mary chose not to have the test for financial reasons, but Sandy's reason for not having prenatal diagnosis was different:

We wanted a family. And we just discussed that we were going to have the children we get. We think we can take care of them. . . . We discussed that and we thought, well, if we get a special child, we think we have got enough love to give to a special child too.

Norma was the most educated of the mothers and had the most prior knowledge about Down syndrome:

At least we had enough knowledge, we knew what Down syndrome was. And when they said that she had trisomy 21 . . . we understand that. I have graduate work in special ed[ucation], so it wasn't like it was a total shock. Like we both know about chromosomes.

Both Sandy and Mary had had some personal experience with handicapped children when they were younger. Sandy had had some personal experience with children with Down syndrome when she was a child growing up near an educational institution that housed mentally retarded children:

We always knew kids who had Down syndrome and we knew they were different but they still played baseball, so who cares. And I always wondered about their capabilities. I always felt they were untapped. And, of course, we are talking about 25 years ago now.

Mary had heard about Down syndrome but had little specific knowledge about the condition. She too had some childhood experiences with handicapped children that she felt helped her deal with having a handicapped child:

The cerebral palsy telethon. My father used to run this thing when he was alive. And I used to go with him, along with him to several classes, just to go with him. . . . I felt that I've kind of been around the handicapped kids, even though that's going a way, way back in my lifetime.

Initiation of Maternal Role Formation

The process of maternal role formation was initiated by the birth of the infants. The newborn characteristics, including gender and health status, had effects on the immediate maternal-infant attachment process. At the time of the births, the mothers' previous maternal experiences tended to help them feel ready to cope with their new maternal role. Although their past experiences did not prepare them for the birth of an infant with Down syndrome, all of the study mothers felt more able to cope with the handicap because of their prior maternal experience.

Comparison of Present to Past Birth Experiences

All of the mothers had experienced vaginal deliveries with their other children and did so again. The maternal role was initiated by the onset of labor, when the mothers began to experience the pain of childbirth and remember their past childbirth experiences. Mary's labor was induced, and she recalled her thoughts at the time that labor began:

> And it did start to get me into labor at about 3 o'clock in the morning but it lasted for about an hour, just enough so that it was a reminder of what that horrible pain is like. And then I went back to sleep.

It was common for the mothers to compare the current birth with their past childbirth experiences. Two of the mothers had uneventful labor and deliveries that they described as easier than their first:

> It was a very easy delivery, no stitches. I was about four hours from start to finish, we didn't think we would make it to the hospital. It was very, very fast. The total opposite of my first, and I was fine afterward. (Norma)

> For her, it was actually better. . . . Once I went into hard labor, it was maybe an hour and two pushes and she was out. I was really amazed. 'Cause I was expecting a long time, like how I had with my son. (Sally)

Sandy's pregnancy ended three weeks early and resulted in a small baby weighing 4 pounds, 14 ounces. This was very different from her older child, who was born at term weighing 8 pounds, 14 ounces:

> And of course I didn't know what a premature baby was like, like a little baby. And so I was kind of getting that mixed up with the Down syndrome too . . . 'cause I was thinking of a 9-pound baby versus a 5-pound.

Mary's current delivery was different from her other deliveries because of her decision to be induced and have a saddle block to relieve the severe back pain she was experiencing during the pregnancy. However, she felt that her previous experience helped her to cope with the delivery: "Well, if I didn't know what I was doing it would have made it a whole lot worse. You know, so I look at it that way too."

Infant's Gender

It was common for the expectant mothers to desire an infant with a particular gender. Each of the mothers in this study gave birth to an infant having the desired gender. As noted by Rubin (1977), disappointments related to a desired gender take time to overcome and may "delay or limit" the attachment process. Having infants with the desired genders may have helped the mothers to attach to the infants. Mary, the only mother to give birth to a boy, summarized her feelings upon learning she had a boy:

> And so I guess when John was born, number one we wanted a boy very bad because Ted is the only boy; he comes from a family of five sisters and he's the only son. And I was the only one that could have given him a boy to carry on the name. Okay. So then we were thrilled about the fact that he was a boy and that was number one.

Three of the mothers said that they did not think that it mattered whether it was a boy or girl as long as it was healthy. Sandy seemed surprised at how pleased she was to learn her baby was a girl:

> When she was born I gave it all away. I always said that I didn't care if it was a boy or a girl and I still don't. But when she was born I said to my husband, I mean I always said I don't care if it is a boy or a girl, "I got my girl, hon." I was excited that she was a girl but I was devastated that she should have Down syndrome.

Sally admitted that she was hoping for a girl during the pregnancy even though she would tell people that the baby's gender didn't matter: "So I was really looking forward to having a girl so that I could dress her up and all the things that you want for your daughter." After the birth of their daughter, Sally's reaction surprised her husband: "In fact, right after she was born, I held her. And my husband was amazed 'cause she was still covered with blood and I just grabbed her 'cause I was so happy it was a little girl." When Sally was asked if the ordeal of giving birth to an infant with Down syndrome was made easier by the fact that the baby was her desired girl, she responded:

> No, I think if she would have been a boy it would have been the same. To me that really didn't matter if it was a girl or a boy 'cause I would have still loved it just the same. I just kept saying if only when it was born it was born healthy. No. No, just I'm glad she's a girl so I can dress her up in pink.

Newborn Health Status

The infant's health following the birth was another factor that seemed to influence the mother's ease in attaching to the baby. Mary's baby had no health problems and the Down syndrome was not evident immediately following birth. However, because of her age, she was concerned and asked that the baby be checked for any abnormalities: "Of course right away they checked for the normal things that Down's babies would have, the heart murmur and all this and that and he doesn't have any of that. He doesn't have any health problems." Mary said that having a baby with Down syndrome did not "faze her," partly because as an infant he was no different to raise from her other babies: "I would have had more concern, of course, if there had been physical problems, especially with the heart." Two of the study mothers had babies who were diagnosed with heart defects. Sally was scared about having a baby with a heart problem:

> The doctors came from cardiology. I was amazed at what they said 'cause when they came in they said she had a hole in her heart. They said, "Don't worry, she's not going to die on the spot." I looked at them and that really scared me. And I thought, okay, that was the furthest thing from my mind, but I guess for them they have to say it that way, to make you feel better. But that was the only thing that scared me was when they came and said that she wouldn't die on the spot and for a couple of days after it bothered me, 'cause I thought, could she? You know, is there really a problem in that? But then after they told me that it was not really that major and I wouldn't have to really worry about it.

Sally was told that heart surgery would not be required until the baby was about 2 years old, and that no other problems were present. She began to feel good about the infant's immediate good health:

> Yeah, it probably is a lot harder for somebody who has had a lot of problems right from the day when they came out of the hospital. . . . So you feel lucky after you hear other people's problems and you think, well, I have really no problems.

Norma's infant presented at birth with multiple problems related to the heart defects and had to be transferred from the community-based hospital where the baby was born to a hospital with a neonatal intensive care unit (NICU). A few days later the baby again experienced difficulties and was transferred to another NICU that had the capability of working with babies with cardiac conditions:

> Probably because of the heart condition was one of the reasons she was so small. They wanted to keep her for growth. Then at four days old she went

into congestive heart failure twice and at that point they transferred her [to the university-based NICU].

Norma found that the infant's health problems added to the difficulty in adjusting to the situation: "I think we had accepted the Down syndrome long before that but it was a different kind of adjustment, of course, just having a new baby with health problems." The need to adjust to the diagnosis of Down syndrome became secondary to the other, more urgent, health problems: "One extra problem that I have to deal with. I would have to say that probably we are more concerned about the heart at this time because it is more of an immediate problem." Sandy's premature baby added to her problems in coping with the Down syndrome: "So I was getting confused with what was Down syndrome and what was premature. . . . She could suck, that wasn't the problem. 'Cause she was tiny and she was falling asleep."

Recognition of Abnormality

Three of the study mothers became aware of the possibility of an abnormality at the time of the birth, but none of them thought it would be Down syndrome. Sandy's premature labor indicated to her that a problem might exist for the infant. However, Sandy thought that the nurse's request to have the baby removed from the caseroom was because of the baby's size: "And I guess partly too she was 4 pounds, 14 ounces. She was little. Yeah, but she was healthy and strong and a good color and everything, so there was no problem there." Norma also thought that her infant's abnormal appearance was related to her small size:

> He [the doctor] suspected that something was wrong right at the point of delivery and the only thing I noticed abnormal at that point is that, I had her but I didn't have her for very long, but I did notice, they told me that she was very small, you know they're all wrapped up so much, it's hard to tell much anyhow. I guess she was so small, like my son was big, he was [8 pounds, 7 ounces] and he was round and everything. She looked kind of peculiar but I hadn't really noticed much and I guess when the doctor had suspected something he called his pediatrician to have a look and see what he thought.

Sally recalled hearing the doctor voice some concern about the infant, but she did not think that it was important at the time:

> When she was born I can remember the doctor saying something to the nurse about her tongue sticking out, but at that time, I didn't pay much

attention. I just thought, you know, how babies have so much stuff in their throat.

Although Mary could see no problems with her infant at the time of the birth she was concerned about the baby because of her age:

> When he was born and they give him to you right away and I just [subconsciously] checked, physically-wise I could see nothing and it was basically because of my age that I was a little bit leery. . . . The two doctors that I had deliver John didn't seem to feel that there was any cause for worry . . . no, they didn't. I guess once they started getting my feelings and stuff, they went ahead and had the genetics people test him.

Being an Experienced Mother

All the mothers found that their prior experience with motherhood helped them to cope with having infants with Down syndrome:

> And I don't know, I feel a little bit fortunate because I've got three other children. And I've had the experience of that. Now if this would have been my first baby even though he doesn't have the physical problems that make it any different to raise this baby from any other baby, I think it still would have bothered me because it would have been new for me. But being an experienced mother, if you want to put it that way it doesn't phase me in the least. It really, really doesn't. (Mary)

> I'm glad she wasn't my first. You have some sort of an idea of how to take care of a baby. You know, no matter how much you know, you know yourself, when a new baby comes home it's still a stressful time. So I am kind of glad that she wasn't my first, to have all the problems that she does. I think I probably might have had a harder time coping. (Norma)

Although Sandy found her prior experience as a mother to be helpful, she also found it to be a hindrance. She had difficulty getting her infant to breast-feed, which was very different from her first child:

> I wasn't a first-time mom so I think they [the nurses] sort of figured I knew what I was doing, but I had never dealt with a preemie baby. I mean [my older child was] 8 pounds, 14 ounces, I mean I nursed him on the table and away we went, that was it.

Maternal Reaction to Diagnosis

Each of the mothers in the study needed time to recover physically from the labor and delivery in order to be able to cope with the information about Down syndrome. The ways in which the mothers were informed of their infants' condition and the support they received at the time of telling affected their initial reactions to the diagnosis.

Recovery From Labor and Delivery

Each of the mothers had the opportunity to hold her infant after the delivery. All of the infants were in stable condition immediately following the birth, including the two infants with low birth weights. Therefore, each of the mothers left the caseroom relieved that the labor and delivery were over and pleased that her infant was born safely: "The minute John was born I was crying because it was such a relief. And because it was a boy I was just so thrilled, that's just the way I respond sometimes, I cry" (Mary).

After her baby was born, Sandy was separated from her, and Sandy was concerned about this:

> She was born and we saw her and I held her, like she was on my tummy. . . . I held the baby and then she just said, "Have them take the baby out. I need somebody to take care of the baby." She didn't overreact or anything, she knew already that the baby had Down syndrome. And then, I had an intern too so the doctor and the intern were stitching me up. And after that we kept asking, where was Miranda? And the doctor said, "I'm just going to see your baby and then I will come back."

The doctor returned after seeing the baby and told them about the Down syndrome. Sandy was still in the recovery room with her spouse when they were informed of the diagnosis. This mother was glad to be told right away: "Well, the way we were told was the best, for us, being told right away."

All of the study mothers, except for Sandy, went to their postpartum rooms and spent time alone with their spouses. In each case the father left the hospital for a few hours, at which time the mother was able to get some rest. All of the mothers, except for Norma, stayed in the hospital for five to seven days. Because her infant was transferred to another hospital, Norma requested to be discharged home within 24 hours:

Overnight. She was born Thursday and I came home Friday morning. I would have come home Thursday night if they had let me. . . . You don't want to sit on a maternity ward when your baby's not there and you're feeling blue anyway.

Although it was an easy delivery, Norma still needed time to recover from the multiple changes that occur in the mother after birth. She found herself unable to visit her baby in the first 24-hour period:

They told me they would give me a day pass the day she was born, the Thursday right after they transferred her, but I just couldn't at that point. I was too tired and too weak and too everything else to go at that point. I needed to get myself together before I did that.

Even after discharge Norma had little time for recovery, as she went home to care for her 2-year-old, manage her home, and find the time and energy to visit the new infant, who was in the NICU of a hospital 30 minutes from her home. Norma's difficult time with recovery may have added to her negative reactions to becoming the mother of a sick infant with Down syndrome.

Being Informed of the Diagnosis

Norma was the only mother who did not feel ready to be told about the diagnosis. She described her experience:

A doctor. A stranger actually. She was born about quarter after 4:00, and about 7:00 the next morning, a gentleman, I was half asleep, said, "Hello, I'm doctor so and so, I've been called in to look at your daughter because of these things," and then walked out. . . . This was a two-minute deal and then left.

Norma thought she should have been allowed to complete her sleep before being informed of the diagnosis: "I mean it's not easy ever to find out things like that but I think there's better ways than others to tell someone. I don't know. Not to wake me up with the news, that's for sure." Two of the mothers, Mary and Norma, were alone after their husbands had left the hospital when they were informed of the diagnosis. Mary did not mind that her spouse was not present, as she thought that it was important to know the diagnosis as soon as possible:

I wanted to know the sooner the better, it really didn't even occur to me to have Ted there. It wouldn't have made that much difference. I just wanted to know. 'Cause something like that, well the first thing that any mother says is, "Is he all right?" And you know if you have any kind of doubt in your mind whatsoever, the sooner the better. So that's really the case. Whether Ted was there or not it didn't make any difference to me.

Norma would have liked her husband present for support:

Yes, just for support and I think it would have been easier on him too. Rather than having to come home and start his [phone calls to tell people about the birth] . . . and then having to turn around and come back [to the hospital] and that type of thing.

Both of these mothers had never met the physicians who came in to talk to them about their babies' condition: "I really couldn't tell you what his name was . . . and it was about an hour before Ted and his family came in to see me that night, that first night and just the way that he [the doctor] was so unfeeling that didn't help at all" (Mary). Both Mary and Norma would have preferred to have been informed by a familiar physician: "Yeah, it wasn't my family doctor. I think that I would have preferred that he was at least there" (Norma). In addition, Norma thought that the doctor should be willing to spend some time with the parents when informing them about Down syndrome: "I think from the doctor, I mean, was fine but I think that they should be willing to spend time with the mother. . . . I think they need to spend more time in bedside manner than just the clinical facts." Norma also believed that her experience of being told about her infant's handicap was negative and hindered her ability to adjust to the situation:

I think it makes a big difference in adjusting at the beginning, how you're told. I've talked to other people who have said the same thing. You know, I think a lot of the support groups have gone out to start to talk to medical students and I think that's really important. I mean it's not easy ever to find out things like that but I think there's better ways than others to tell someone.

The other two mothers were told of the diagnosis with their spouses present. Sally's physician waited to inform her about the diagnosis until her husband had returned to the hospital. Sally was pleased that her spouse was present, and she was satisfied with the way they were told: "I was glad the way I was told. They weren't mean or nasty, they were very polite and explanatory. It was nice." Sandy had recently moved to the city, so she was told by a general practitioner who had seen her only a few times prior to the delivery. She was given the diagnosis while in the recovery room with her husband:

> But anyway, he went and he came back after he had seen the baby. He said, "She's okay but there is a problem," and he said, "She has Down syndrome." Just like that, like he didn't hold back from us at all . . . this doctor and he stayed and talked to us, like he wasn't going to just take that as carte blanche.

Sandy felt that the way she and her husband had been told as a couple was best for them:

> No, I was very happy we were both together. We talked so much together that we really did accept it. Like we knew it was a possibility so we just said, you know. But if I had been alone—I had to have somebody to talk to.

She and her husband had positive feelings toward the baby following the diagnosis: "We just both looked at her and, gee, she looks pretty good to us. And she's just so cute, so she has Down syndrome, we're not turning her in. No, no we're not sending back this version."

All of the mothers, except for Mary, preferred to have their spouses present when told of their babies' condition. Mary's situation was different, as she had a concern about the baby's health status and requested an examination by a pediatrician. Therefore, she felt it was appropriate for her to be informed of the diagnosis as soon as possible whether or not her spouse was present. The experiences of these mothers suggest that the manner in which a mother is informed about her infant's handicap and the time at which she is informed can influence her initial feelings of attachment to the infant.

Initial Reaction

The most common reactions experienced by the mothers were shock, denial, and grief. Other initial reactions that were identified were fear, disappointment, and shame. All of the mothers except for Mary experienced shock as their initial reaction to the diagnosis: "I think it's a shock. Like I definitely went through shock, I know that" (Sandy); "I think if you were older, then you would expect it more. The shock. Total unacceptance in the beginning" (Norma). Sally was the only mother who said she was scared when she was told that the baby had Down syndrome.

Mary said that she did not experience shock because the diagnosis was a confirmation of what she had thought possible because of her age: "Like I said, that had always been in the back of my mind that that would be a possibility." Both Norma and Sandy discussed the denial that they experienced after hearing the diagnosis:

> You go through a whole cycle of things. Denial: It's not there. Why me? (Norma)
>
> And I know I went through denial 'cause she seems so normal. . . . I can't believe this. I mean you tell me so intellectually I believe it but emotionally, I know I denied it until he finally phoned with the results and told us. (Sandy)

All of the mothers experienced an initial sense of guilt for different reasons. Mary thought it was her fault because of her age: "I was upset for 24 hours 'cause I went through a thing of baby blues, plus I went through a thing of thinking that it was my fault 'cause of my age, you know, I went through that thought." Sally worried about postponing pregnancy: "What [had I] done wrong? Yeah, and why did I wait so long? Maybe if I wouldn't have waited so long to have her, maybe this wouldn't have happened. All those type of things run through my head."

All of the mothers said that they cried a lot for at least the first 24 hours. The study mothers described this emotional state as being upset or bothered by the diagnosis: "I was upset with myself in the beginning, at the very beginning, like in the hospital. . . . I was upset for 24 hours . . . so I was crying or getting over crying. I was sort of in spurts off and on" (Mary); "At first I was upset and tired. . . . I cried much more than he [her husband] did, which is natural" (Norma). Sally said that she was bothered by the diagnosis for about 2 weeks. After that time, she experienced disappointment: "Disappointed. I waited so long for her 'cause my older boy will be 10 in the spring." Norma was the only mother to discuss the negative thoughts that she had during the first week after the birth:

> So you would go through a period of feeling, well, maybe she would be better off, it would spare everybody in the long term, kind of thing. And then you would feel guilty because you felt that way at the beginning and then you would think, oh my god, this is my baby and I wish it was dead! kind of thing and she's not. So you go through a real realm of real nasty, real ugly thoughts for a while. That lasts for the first week, you know, you're just on a real roller coaster. . . . That's the time that's the hardest.

When your mind is stuck with all these negative things, I mean no mother wants to have these thoughts about her own kid.

A preoccupation with the diagnosis made it difficult for each mother initially to get to know her baby. When reflecting back on this period, Norma recalled how her thoughts were always on Down syndrome:

> I think that when the news is new, it's 24 hours a day, 60 minutes an hour, that you think about it. It's just your entire life revolves around Down's basically, especially when she was still in the hospital, the first two or three weeks anyhow. That's all you think about. You wake up in the middle of the night and that's all you think about.

Mary said that she was initially self-conscious about having a baby with Down syndrome. She dealt with it by taking the baby with her everywhere in the hospital:

> As time went on I was there and John was with me and I would take him in to where we had meals and all this and that. Nobody, nobody noticed it. . . . I felt a little bit [self-conscious] for a while. I really did quickly get over that.

Of all the study mothers, Sandy's initial feelings of attachment to her infant seemed the least affected by the diagnosis. However, she too recalled how she spent the first night crying as she worried about both how she would care for the baby and the baby's future:

> So they gave me something and I probably slept for two or three hours and then I woke up and I reconciled the first of my tears and then slept. But, of course, I was bawling and everything 'cause I was kind of upset and you have to determine if she is going to be married, and going to have kids, and how she is going to take care of herself when she is 80. And I had to get this all figured out in my mind and I was crying and that, and the nurse came in and she said, "You've got red cheeks," and I said, "Well, I've been bawling."

The initial reactions experienced by these mothers dampened their desire to take on the maternal role and influenced their attachment to their infants. Both Mary and Sandy seemed able to get over their initial grief sooner than Sally or Norma. Mary said that she was upset in the beginning for about 24 hours, whereas Sandy was eager to be with the infant and begin breast-feeding immediately. Both Sally and Norma said that it took at least one or two weeks before they were not "bothered" by the diagnosis. However, all of the mothers continued to experience a sense of loss related to having a child with Down syndrome rather than a normal child. Mary and Sandy were the two mothers of advanced maternal age and were more prepared for the possibility of their children having handicaps. In addition, these two mothers had personal experiences with handicapped children when they were younger, which they both described as positively affecting their attitudes toward the handicapped.

Maternal Acceptance of the Diagnosis

In addition to the physical recovery from the labor and delivery, the mothers required a certain amount of emotional energy to be able to accept the diagnosis and continue in the process of maternal role formation. While the babies were in the hospital, supportive health professionals helped the mothers to find the necessary inner strength for acceptance. In addition, the mothers gained strength from their spouses and their spiritual beliefs. As the mothers became more involved in caring for their babies, they simultaneously became more accepting. Their feelings of attachment for their babies became stronger with the developing maternal role.

Finding Strength

The feeling that they were responsible for their babies' condition made it difficult for the mothers to feel good about being mothers of children with Down syndrome. All the mothers said that the guilt was relieved by their gaining more knowledge about the condition. For example:

What the doctor told me and that it made me feel a lot better knowing that it was not anything that I did. But up until when he [the medical geneticist] explained everything, then you get kind of weird feelings that maybe if I had done this or done that but he said there is no way no matter what you do or did, it didn't cause her [to be] like that. (Sally)

Well, I just wondered if it was something that had caused my eggs to be damaged or something along the way. But yeah, that was the only thing I went through but it was just made so clear to us so many times. (Sandy)

Gaining knowledge from health professionals helped the mothers get to know about Down syndrome and feel more comfortable in being with their babies:

I asked a lot of questions. I think I bothered everybody, I asked so many questions. I spent most of the time in the nursery. . . . They did the best that they could. The only thing is that it was too much too fast to absorb and that's why this lady from genetics, she was a big help to me. She talked slow, she'd repeat things, she came back maybe the next day and repeat what she told me the day before . . . then I spent a lot of time with him [the baby]. (Mary)

Because for them it's their medical terminology and they just rattle on and expect you to understand what they are saying but I have to say that the doctors at the hospital were very good and the nurses, they really helped me a lot. (Sally)

The mothers felt stronger about being able to cope with handicapped infants when they perceived that health professionals were supportive. Initially, Mary felt bad about not having had amniocentesis to determine if her baby was normal. However, her doctor talked to her after the birth, and his support relieved her guilt and made her think about the positive side of having gone through with the pregnancy:

He came into the room and he told me, "Don't even think about it twice because . . . are you going to make the decision that you are going to terminate it?" And he said, "Especially as much as you wanted a boy." And so he says, "In a way, this way you weren't [confronted] with a decision to make." Which is true, I mean he was trying to give me other alternatives, you know make me think differently . . . and so my doctor was very, very helpful to me and it really made all the difference in the world. He really did.

Mary also received support from a few other professionals in the hospital: "And the lady that I became friends with that did my ultrasounds all the time, she was a big help to me also . . . reassuring and so were a couple of the nurses that were in the nursery."

Terry said that the support from the hospital staff helped her to realize that her experience of having a baby with Down syndrome was not a bad thing:

Well, I have to say the whole staff there at the hospital was so supportive it was just like I had gone to heaven for a while 'cause everybody was just so [good]. When I read stories of other people's experiences that were so bad, you know, when they discovered their baby had this problem, like I couldn't think it was a bad thing that happened to you because so many people were so great.

Norma and Sally had the opportunity to speak with a nurse at the hospital who had a child with Down syndrome. Both of these mothers gained a more realistic image of Down syndrome that helped to reassure them about being parents to their children:

> What really helped us is there is a nurse at the hospital that has a daughter that is 9 . . . with Down syndrome and the second day she was working and my mom and I were there and she came over and stopped and said . . . she "would like to talk to you about my daughter." And brought us a picture and we sat and I bet she sat and talked to us for at least two hours, more than that. And I think that that was kind of the turning point for me, she had been in, she was about three days old. (Norma)

Sandy awoke from her first night's sleep and began to worry about how she should care for the baby. A nurse reassured her that she should care for the baby the same as any other baby: "Anyway she said, why was I crying? I said, 'Well, how do I treat my baby?' She said, 'What do you mean?' and I said, 'Well, do I treat her like a normal baby?' She said, 'Yes.' " Sandy was also concerned that her baby might not have the will to live. The nurses reassured her and helped her to feel more secure about the infant's health:

> I thought, I wondered if she had a will to live. So I said that to the nurse. "Of course she's got a will to live. She's just small," . . . one of the nurses told me. The ones I was telling you that need the commendation. I was worried she wasn't strong enough to suck; she said, "She's strong enough" and, of course, she was.

Both Norma and Sandy talked about their spouses as being a source of support. Norma found that she needed some time alone with her spouse in order to find the strength required to cope with the situation: "My mom and dad had come up that night, we were still trying to work through things ourselves and we weren't really ready to work through things with other people." Two of the mothers felt that their spiritual beliefs helped them to be more accepting of the situation. Mary's spouse had been thought to be sterile because of an injury, yet Mary had learned she was pregnant. She found the strength to accept the birth of a handicapped child by believing in the powers of fate: "He really couldn't be accepted anymore than what he is right now because I feel that he was born to me for a particular reason somehow." Sandy believed that she owed the birth of her special child to the powers of God. Her spiritual beliefs helped her to accept the responsibility of being the parent of a handicapped child:

> And when she was Down syndrome, that was the shock because I thought we talked about this so much and I was so prepared last time, not this time. And I thought there's God, He gets you, He plays tricks on you. . . . Well no, we discussed that and we thought, well, if we get a special child, we think we have got enough love to give to a special child too.

Becoming Involved: Mothering the Infant

As the mothers gained the emotional energy to face the diagnosis of Down syndrome they were able to come to terms with their negative feelings through acceptance. As a part of the process of maternal role formation, the process of accepting was multifaceted. Each mother had to come to accept the diagnosis, the maternal role in caring for the baby, and the infant as her own child. Becoming involved with their infants helped the mothers to gain acceptance.

Accepting the Diagnosis

Immediately after hearing the diagnosis, all of the mothers, except for Sandy, withdrew from their babies. These mothers needed time to think about the diagnosis and gain the emotional strength that was required to accept the infants' condition: "I think I maybe would have not believed them if she had been laying there beside me. This way it gave you time to think about it" (Sally). Norma did not accept a day pass to see her baby at the hospital to which she had been transferred a few hours after birth: "I needed to get myself together before I did that" (Norma). Sandy's reaction was different from that of the other mothers; she wanted to see the baby immediately after being informed of the diagnosis. She was upset at being separated from her infant:

> We both said, "Can we have her?" and he kept talking. And we said, "Can we have our baby?" And finally he brought her to us and that to me was the worst trauma I had to go through was not to be able to have my baby. . . . He came right back and let us be with her and we took some pictures and everything.

Sandy's reaction may have been different because she did not believe that the baby had Down syndrome, as the baby seemed so normal. She said she did not fully accept the diagnosis until the chromosome results came back positive for trisomy 21:

> Well, sure and I knew, like I knew she was Down syndrome. I knew 'cause I knew to look at her. But by the same token, when I was just watching her I thought, well, maybe she's pretty normal, so when he did actually say it I thought, well, that's good, now we are past that. Get on with it, you know, don't waste any more energy.

Initial Mothering

After initially being apart from their infants, the mothers wanted to spend time with the babies so that they could get to know them. Mary said, "You've got to get to know the baby. And you know, of course, when they are an infant there is every day something different." She got to know her baby by keeping him with her all day while she was in the hospital:

> I didn't breast-feed, so . . . what I did was he stayed with me all day long up until about 10 o'clock and then I put him back in the nursery so that the nurses could watch him. . . . As time went on I was there and John was with me and I would take him in to where we had meals and all this and that.

Norma said that she had to work on bonding with her baby by going up to the hospital every day to see the baby in the NICU: "We took turns going up, we were there every day pretty well, at least once, usually two or three times." When Norma was asked what helped her to get to know her baby she said, "Nothing in particular, I don't think. Like I can't think of a certain event or, you know, I suppose it is just a natural mother-infant bonding."

Some health professionals helped the mothers to be with their infants. One of the nurses helped Sandy to be comfortable in being with the baby and caring for her: "I said, 'Well, can I hold her?' She said, 'You can hold your baby.' She took me to the nursery. After that as soon as I knew where the nursery was, that was where I lived."

Two of the mothers wanted to breast-feed their babies but were confused by the mixed messages they received from alternating nursing shifts:

> It was really weird because one shift they were encouraging you to nurse her and the next shift they were encouraging you to bottle-feed her and they just wanted to get you out of the hospital, anything to get her gaining weight, right. (Sandy)

Terry did not begin to breast-feed until the fourth or fifth day because the nurses were bottle-feeding or gavage-feeding the infant. Terry was pleased with the support she received from some of the nurses and recalled the nurse who encouraged her to breast-feed:

> When Mrs. Smith comes on you get her to help you with the breast-feeding. And she is just great. Tips, and I think her motivation is and just her personal attention and she came all the way down to get me when it was convenient for her all the way down from another floor and she would sit me down and just say, "Well, you've got lots of milk there and here we will get the baby on," then take in the baby's mouth and how to get it open and get the nipple in it and just saying, we have another kind of pump here that you can use and it was so much better than those horrible bulb ones. . . . She's really a high point.

Sandy remembered a nurse who made her feel uncomfortable about her decision to breast-feed her infant:

> I know from one nurse I got the feeling that it was like, and this might have been my perception and it could be wrong, like I might have been oversensitive but I got the feeling that she thought, just feed him, give her a bottle, she's got Down syndrome, what are you worrying about? Who cares? As for me, my feeling was, all the more reason to do as much as you can for her.

Being able to breast-feed was important to these two mothers because it helped with the maternal-infant attachment process. Sandy described how important it was for her to breast-feed and her disappointment with the baby's initially needing a nipple shield:

> Oh well, I would like to have her nursing, nursing. But I'm certainly satisfied with second best. I just miss the bonding with the one on one. Like I like the feel of nursing. So if I can get her to latch on a couple of times a week, it satisfies my brain a bit.

Terry felt that it was important for her infant's emotional needs to breast-feed but realized that the baby tired more readily when nursing: "I think in her little heart she prefers to nurse but she doesn't get enough out of it." Norma tried to breast-feed her infant, but the baby became tired too easily from the exertion, so instead she pumped milk and gave the baby the breast milk with a bottle. When asked if it bothered her that she was unable to breast-feed the infant, Norma replied, "It didn't bother me. My son nursed for about three months and that was just fine. She [her daughter] had milk for about two and a half months, so they both had about the same."

The hospital environment inhibited the mothers from being involved with their infants. Mary spent most of the time in the nursery for the first few days before the baby was allowed to be with her during the day. When asked if she was encouraged to spend time in the nursery, Mary responded, "No, I mean no they [staff] didn't. This was before he was able to come and stay with me most of the time during the day because he was there for a week, I was also, six days anyway."

Sandy was not allowed to have her baby in her room. She found the separation from her infant to be a hindrance that she had to overcome in order to get to know the baby:

> Well, the first night, it drove me crazy. They wouldn't let me hold her and like it drove me nuts and then finally at 5 o'clock the next morning they showed me where she was and they couldn't get rid of me, they could try and I still looked at her at night and everything. They'd phone me and I'd come running down and feed her. She was never allowed to stay in my room until I got discharged.

As they spent more time with their babies, all of the mothers, except for Norma, began to realize that the maternal role in caring for a child with Down syndrome was similar to their past experiences with normal children. Mary said it took her 24 hours to become accustomed to having a baby with Down syndrome. When asked if she was comfortable in caring for the baby at the beginning, Mary said, "Um, comfortable? The only way that I can answer that is that the Down's part didn't have anything to do with anything. It was just learning how to handle a baby all over again." It took Norma longer to accept that she would have to be the mother of an infant with Down syndrome. The NICU environment inhibited her from becoming involved in caring for her baby:

> Well, she was in the hospital six weeks, so . . . I'd have to say probably a good two or three months. Once we got over the major health difficulties, as long as they're in the hospital it's hard to treat them like a normal baby, which is what you're obviously going to strive to do. But when they're all hooked up to this that and everything else . . .

Accepting the Infants as Their Own

The realization that a baby with Down syndrome is similar to a normal baby helped the mothers to accept these infants as their own. Sandy said, "Like that's why I say I accepted her totally right from the beginning, but I was probably denying too, just because she seems so normal." Sally did not spend a lot of time caring for her baby until she went home. She said that it took her about two weeks to accept her handicapped infant. As she spent more time with the baby her feelings toward having a baby with Down syndrome changed: "And then when I came home and I saw her and held her, to me she was no different and it didn't bother me anymore." Initially, Norma found it difficult to accept her baby because of the baby's poor health status: "Total unacceptance in the beginning. Or at least that's what I found. I went through a period when she was very ill thinking maybe things would be better off if she had just died at that point." As Norma was able to become involved with her baby, she began to dwell less on the problems and more on caring for the baby: "And then as time goes on you begin to not totally dwell on, on all the problems and you become more involved in just taking care of the new baby. And it settles down."

All of the mothers expressed acceptance of their infants: "We wouldn't trade her now, I mean we wish that she wasn't what she was but I mean I wouldn't want a different baby" (Norma); "I love it. She's mine. I know I gave birth to her and no matter what you say nobody could take her away from me" (Sally); "I just feel that if John had to be born the way that he was, that he's lucky that he was born to me. I'm lucky to have him. . . . I just feel that it's not going to be a problem between him and I" (Mary).

Informing Others of the Diagnosis

Initially, the mothers relied upon their spouses and other family members to inform close friends and family, as they found it difficult to tell people about the diagnosis. The reactions of the people who were told affected the mother's attitude toward being the mother of an infant with Down syndrome, which in turn influenced the mother's willingness to inform other people. As the mothers became more accepting, they found it easier to tell others about the Down syndrome. Simultaneously, informing others helped the mothers to overcome denial and become more accepting.

Receiving Support

In two of the cases, the husbands were not present when the doctors informed the mothers of the babies' abnormalities. Both of these mothers found that telling their spouses was a difficult task that they did not feel prepared to handle. Mary obtained the support of the nurses by making an arrangement with them to inform her spouse of the diagnosis:

> It's just at the time I didn't want to have to tell him 'cause I didn't think that I would be able to get it out. I was pretty upset at the time. So this is why I made the arrangement with the nurses.

Norma telephoned her husband immediately after being told about the diagnosis. When asked if she told him on the phone, she said, "I don't remember. I think I did but he didn't really [understand], he knew something was seriously wrong because I was bawling on the telephone."

Norma and Sandy relied on their spouses as their major source of support. They found that their husbands accepted the infants immediately:

> He's been very supportive, he accepted it right from the beginning. There was never a problem. The only thing that happened to Daddy was he started to smoke again. He had quit but he started the day she was born. (Norma)

> Yeah and he is totally accepting. I don't know if he is going to have a total breakdown sometime or not but he has been so totally accepting of her. She's his little girl. He hasn't cried, and he's quite an emotional person. (Sandy)

Mary and Sally described their spouses as being upset after hearing the diagnosis. However, Mary felt that her husband was supportive as he tried to comfort her:

> So then they all left and came back to the room and he was crying. But he was crying because he knew that I would have blamed myself for this. . . . Yeah and he was trying to comfort me and saying, "Hey, it's not your fault, it's just one of those things."

Sally's husband provided little immediate emotional support, but he too came to accept the baby after she came home:

> He was upset. In fact, he left right after the doctor told us. He left the hospital. And it took him a while to come back. For him, all his dreams

were shattered. . . . But he's accepted her now and he understands more about it.

All of the study mothers relied upon their husbands to inform immediate family about the Down syndrome. Norma's husband had to contact family members twice; he had told them of the birth before being informed of the diagnosis, and he had to call them back again after hearing the diagnosis:

> He had come home, actually what had happened is he had come home and made half of his phone calls and then I called him back to tell him the news. He came back right away and then he called everyone back and [retold] them the news.

One of Sandy's immediate concerns was how her parents would react to the news and how she would handle the situation:

> Actually, the first night, that was one of the most traumatic things for me. And I guess because I didn't know how they were going to react to us. Especially my mom and dad . . . how they were going to react to her and how I was going to react to this whole mess in my lap.

Sandy asked her husband to call her mother the night of the birth:

> I said, "You've got to phone Mom and tell her because Mom is going to go nuts." Like well, you know what moms are like and I suppose we would too, I don't know. . . . So he phoned and he said, "Sandy had the baby. We have a little girl and she is healthy but she's got Down syndrome." And my mom said, "Okay, goodbye." And he said, "You're not getting rid of me that easily." And he made her talk and then he went and spent the night with them and he told them, "Listen, this is our baby. We discussed it before she was ever born and we are keeping her and that's it."

Each of the mothers said that family members who were told of her baby's condition were supportive and accepting of the baby. Sandy thought that her parents' acceptance was related to the way her spouse had informed them about the baby: "And my mom and dad came up the next day . . . and because he had just laid it down on the line and said, 'This is the way it is,' they just came in and they were totally accepting of her." The parents of two of the mothers came to stay with their daughters after discharge from the hospital. Norma's mother helped out around the house so that Norma could spend more time at the hospital with the baby:

> My mom and dad came the Friday, the day after she was born and they both stayed for three or four days. My mother stayed for two weeks. She took over the house and basically my son and that kind of thing so we were free to go back [to the hospital].

Terry was grateful for the help she received from her parents: "Yeah, they were both here and that helped, with the 4-year-old, 'cause she kept Grandpa busy. Oh, it was wonderful! I probably will never realize how much benefit that really was."

Mary had recently moved to the city and had no friends or family living nearby. Mary's father was deceased and her mother was very ill at the time of the birth. Mary chose not to inform her mother, and a few months later her mother died, having never seen her grandson and not knowing that he had Down syndrome. However, after her spouse informed his family about the diagnosis, Mary received support from her mother-in-law: "So she was very reassuring and she kept on saying to me, 'They are some of the happiest children and they are the most loving children.' She did everything that she could to try to reassure me."

After receiving initial support from family members who were informed by their spouses, the mothers began to tell other people. Both Sally and Norma told their other children that the new baby had a problem: "We told him right when she was born that she had a problem, he said that it didn't matter, that he still loved her" (Sally); "We've told him right from the beginning basically. I don't think he totally understands. He has a book [about Down syndrome], friends gave it to him" (Norma). Norma wanted her son to understand about Down syndrome, as she was concerned about the reactions he might have to face in the future from other children: "He knows the term *retarded*, I'd rather he learned it here 'cause I mean obviously as he grows older and goes out more on his own, he will get his."

Sally found that while she was in the hospital she could not tell anyone, other than her son, about the baby's condition and did not want visitors other than the immediate family. Her mother helped her to tell her friends from work:

> I couldn't even get the courage to phone anybody. In fact, I was really stupid, I could kick myself now for that but the girls from work were going to come up and I told my mom to phone them and tell them I didn't want

to see them. And my mom said to me, "Well, why?" and I said, " 'Cause I just couldn't face telling them that she was born Down syndrome."

A support visit from a mother and her 5-year-old child with Down syndrome reassured Sally about being the mother of an infant with Down syndrome. After the visit she was able to begin to face her friends from work:

> I phoned her at nighttime and I said to her that I was going home tomorrow, why didn't she pop over to the house, and she said, "Oh, you want to see us now?" I said, "Well, I just couldn't talk to anybody, I just didn't know what to say." . . . 'cause then the day, well, actually the night, that I phoned her was the day that the lady came from the Gateway which made me feel and realize that, you know, don't be so stupid.

After their initial delay, Norma and Sandy started telling everyone about the Down syndrome. Norma said that telling others helped her to face the situation:

> And as I said, I forced myself right from the very beginning to be honest or not to hide it. I decided then that, you know, this is my daughter and I might as well get used to it right from the start.

Sandy felt that telling people about the Down syndrome helped her to deal with her denial:

> I just started telling people. 'Cause I thought you just have to do it. I didn't want to and I was hurt to say that my baby isn't perfect. You know, we all have that expectation, I think. . . . So I tell people that I know in the hospital, every person I talked with, I thought I've got to deal with this. So every single person I saw I told that she has Down syndrome.

However, after becoming more comfortable with informing people about the baby, Sandy said that she had to use some judgment in deciding who to tell:

> I was from one extreme to another. First of all I just felt I had to tell everybody, so, "Excuse me, could I just share this with you?" And I thought listen, whoa back a little, you don't have to tell everybody. So I get talking to someone and if it's one of those baby conversations, where you're just talking and they say, "Oh gee, your baby's cute," I say, "Yeah."

Mary said that most of the time she would tell people about the Down syndrome. However, she tended to inform people after they had gotten to know the baby:

> I did tell one friend that had known John ever since he was about two months of age and she was totally shocked. . . . Then my next-door neighbor, she works with these types of kids. So she says, "Oh, does he have Down's?" and I said, "Yeah." But that was after the fourth time that she saw him. . . . It's easier for me [to tell] so I don't have to go around wondering if they're wondering. So I just get it over and done with in most cases.

Sally also preferred to tell people about the baby's condition after they had spent some time with the baby:

> But I had an experience, I took her to one of the hockey practices there and none of the moms had known that she was Down syndrome and they said how good she was and that she was holding up her head well. Until afterward, just before I left I told them and they couldn't believe it. So that made me feel good.

All of the mothers said that everyone who was told of the Down syndrome was supportive and accepting of them. However, after telling some people about the Down syndrome, Sally was uncomfortable with the compliments that people gave her about the baby:

> Sure 'cause once you tell them it's Down syndrome, first thing they look at you and they don't know what to say till they think about it for a while. . . . In the back of your mind, you wonder are they just saying it to be nice to you. I don't know, like a lot of times I think well, they say it real serious but inside are they saying it because they don't want to hurt your feelings?

Norma said that it was not difficult to tell family and friends because of all the support that she received from these people: "Actually, family members and friends have just been fine. We have had no difficulty whatsoever with people accepting it."

Coping With Limited Support

It was common for the mothers to say that others' reactions to their babies were related to the time spent with the babies. Norma was concerned that her husband's parents had not accepted her baby's condition. She felt it was because they lived out of town and were unable to see the baby: "I'm not sure my husband's mom and dad have completely accepted it. I think at times that my husband's dad has a feeling that after surgery everything is going to be just fine, but they haven't seen her either." Sally thought that it took her husband longer to accept the baby because he was away from home a great deal:

> I think it took him a little while longer, especially because he was working out of town. So for him, he wasn't home seeing her all the time. And then when he did come home he realized that she was no different than seeing our son when he was little.

Mary thought that her children from a previous marriage would not accept her new son unless they were able to spend time with him: "If they could be around John, you know, but it's not that way so . . . and they can't see him for himself, for [themselves]." Mary's older children live with their father in another country, and she thought that her ex-husband would be nonsupportive and would influence her children's attitude toward the new baby:

> If he [ex-husband] found out he would say something on the order that, "Well, I knew his father couldn't father a normal child" or something, he would say something very cruel like that. He would and then he would repeat it, almost to the word, back to my other three kids. He would not give, he would not explain to them.

Because Mary thought that she would not receive support from these family members, she chose not to tell them about the diagnosis of Down syndrome: "When I tell you that I haven't told the other kids, it's not that I'm afraid to; there are particular reasons because I don't hesitate to tell other people. With this particular situation it is different." In addition, Mary's in-laws initially decided not tell the baby's grandfather about the Down syndrome because they thought that he would not be supportive:

> Yeah, I was told right away when I got back home from the hospital that Ted's dad didn't know. . . . His mom didn't want to tell him. . . . She feels that if he knew it would be any kind of a handicap, not just this, that he would not understand and that he does not accept any kind of person, child or adult, with a handicap.

Mary was upset by the decision not to tell the grandfather and was unwilling to keep the Down syndrome a secret:

> I'm not going to go hiding it 'cause if it is going to be there, it is going to be there. I'm not going to prevent John from thinking or of having the fear that his grandfather doesn't know this. I'll be darned if I'm going to keep John away, you know. And if John has difficulty in whatever in the future and it is noticed by the grandfather, I want him to know now instead of wondering why later.

Mary was relieved and pleased when her husband finally told his father about the Down syndrome:

> And his [the grandfather's] response was, "Well, I guess you're just going to have to love him all the more." That's exactly what his response was and I was very pleased with that because he was not given the chance to even give his opinion and that's why I told you it was upsetting me.

Norma was initially uncomfortable taking the baby out where strangers might see her. She described her own reactions to one negative experience she had while taking her child out to a shopping mall:

> The first time you go to a mall or that kind of thing. I've never had anyone come up to me and ask me if she has Down syndrome. We did have some comments, she has eye trouble . . . but when she was a newborn, they would maybe half close and we have had the comment, or I have, at a shop when she was asleep, this old biddy, "Look at that baby, she doesn't close her eyes right, isn't that weird?" I thought, "That's not all that's wrong with her lady, butt out."

Norma decided that support from others depended on the experience that the people had with Down syndrome:

> Depends on who you talk to. People in the medical profession are usually fairly optimistic, and the people who work with the Down's kids and especially the people who are involved in the area with programs and those kinds of things, are definitely optimistic. The old-school people, no, they're not optimistic. They're like my grandmother and those kinds of people. She went to see a lady who had a Down's baby who is my age now and they don't realize that things aren't the same now.

Maternal Role Transition: Taking Control

A major transition in the maternal role occurred when the mother was allowed to take her infant home. The mothers found that they were constantly reminded of their children's abnormality while in the hospital, whereas the home environment helped them to focus on the infants' normality. Taking control of the decisions regarding infant care was evidence of the mother's desire to do the best possible for the child.

Returning Home

Norma had to wait the longest before she was able to bring her infant home from the hospital. Although she was discharged in 24 hours, her baby stayed in the hospital for six weeks. Norma found it difficult to meet the needs of both her son at home and the baby in the hospital. She described how she tried to juggle these responsibilities:

> That's a hard thing, it was hard when she was in the hospital so much because you are trying to keep some sort of a normal situation here for our son's sake and for your own. To keep your household going and those kinds of things and yet you should be at the hospital. And that was difficult, juggling kind of two different things. As soon as she came home it was much better.

Mary best described the feelings of the mothers as they were in the hospital being reminded every day about their infants' condition:

> Then every single day they were telling me all this information that was so hard to absorb. And telling me all these doctors' names, telling me that there is this sort of thing that is offered for you and that sort of thing that is offered. And I couldn't take it all in. It just made things a little bit harder to not accept but to deal with. Well, everything at that point makes your head swim. Actually I was wanting to get out of there and just go home.

Mary wanted to go home, where her life could be normal again and she would stop being reminded of the abnormality:

> Yeah, exactly, because it really was as long as I stayed there it stayed in my mind more so than when I got home. Not that you want to block it out, but everything at that point had been proven negative other than the fact that he did have it.

Sandy was afraid of going home and having to take on too much responsibility. She and her family had recently moved to the city and had not yet unpacked the boxes in their new home. She described her experience of going home:

> It was good [going home] but it was totally [disorganized] because we were just in boxes. We moved in on the first [of the month], she was born on the third, and I was afraid to come home because I just thought, how am I going to cope? But it was okay. . . . we were a mess but anyway, so it was good to get out but it was a little fearful. I thought, oh my god, how are we going to get a meal in this house and stuff? But we managed.

Focusing on Normality

After the baby came home, each mother was able to focus on the child's normality. Some common words and phrases were used by the mothers to describe the normality of their babies.

No Different

Both Mary and Sally described their babies as being no different from normal babies. Mary said, "Sometimes you gotta just weigh it out and he knows, he's not any different than any other kid that way." Sally believed that her relationship with her baby was no different from what it would have been had the baby been normal. She also described the baby's appearance and motor development as being "no different than if she was normal. . . . No, like I said, I really haven't had to experience any different changes in her except that as she is growing she is doing things that she should be doing."

Just Like Any Other Child

It was common for the mothers to describe their babies as being just like any other baby: "She smiles and coos and that, just like a regular baby. . . . To me she's just like anybody else's baby. She's my baby" (Sally); "She doesn't cry a lot. I was quite concerned for a while. But she has a temper too, you know, like any other baby" (Norma). Although Norma's baby had remained in hospital for six weeks with a number of additional problems, after discharge home, Norma made the decision to treat the baby like a normal infant. Norma decided to take her baby on a trip four days after the baby was discharged from the hospital:

We were determined that we weren't going to hold back. I said to the pediatrician, "Can I take her away?" and she said, "Would you take a normal baby away?" and I said, "Yes." "Then take her, she's the same as any other kid." And I have to admit we have really done that.

Normal

The mothers often used the word *normal* to describe their babies. Mary found her baby to be like any normal baby: "He really is [normal]. I ran into a little bit of colic with him, but that's normal too." Sandy also saw a similarity between her infant and a normal baby: "She just strikes me like I said she's so much like a normal baby that you have to remind yourself because you don't want to set yourself up for a big disappointment."

The mothers would often rationalize that any differences they saw when comparing their own infants' development with other children's development were within a normal developmental range. Mary's child was almost the same age as her friend's baby, who was developmentally ahead of Mary's son, John. Mary would not admit that her infant was slower than the other baby; rather, she rationalized about the advanced development of the other child:

Well, like I told you before [my friend's baby] she's three weeks younger than John and she already pulls herself up to the table, the couch. Oh no, I know she's very early. . . . She's very advanced in her maturing.

Norma recognized a difference in the developmental skills of her two children when comparing them at similar ages. However, she tended to describe the older child as a fast developer and saw her infant as within the normal range:

And the delays are just not there yet. You know, I'm not saying that, she's behind where he was but then he was fast, so . . . He's the opposite, he's extremely bright. . . . It's hard not to compare the two because he was running at a year and walked just before he was 10 months old. You know he was a real goer. He was very independent and that kind of thing. Whereas she's going to be at the other end of the spectrum. She'll be much slower than the normal, not ahead of them. But what's normal?

Caring for the Child

Having the infant at home allowed the mother to make decisions regarding infant care. All of the mothers made statements that demon-

strated their desire to do the best possible for their own babies. In the hospital, Sandy was confused by the mixed messages she got about feeding her baby. However, once she had her baby at home she made a decision regarding breast-feeding and the child began to gain weight:

> It was very difficult 'cause every shift, three shifts [a day] you were getting conflicting messages about feeding her; we gavaged her, we fed her by bottle, we fed her with the little nipple, I pumped milk. . . . When we got out we knew what we were doing so that was good too 'cause we sort of could get away from the conflict. Once we've made this decision we're going with it and we'll see if it works and, of course, she just started gaining like crazy.

Sandy was angry with herself for relinquishing some of her control over her baby's care when she took the baby back to have some blood drawn at a laboratory:

> She [the technician] laid her down on the table and I took her clothes off and she started jabbing and I wasn't holding her and she [the baby] held her breath and she went nuts and I've never seen her go like that . . . and I guess I grabbed her and then she did it and it was okay. I felt really guilty about that because I should have taken control of that situation and I didn't.

The desire to do the best possible for the baby could be heard in Sandy's following comment:

> I know I'm her caregiver and I'm sure there is a bond there. I'm sure she knows who I am and at least I could see that she was so much more settled when I was holding her. I mean it was terrible but she wasn't like she had been abandoned. And that is how she was when she was on that table and that was terrible.

Two of the mothers had to experience the rehospitalization of sick infants. Both of these mothers did not like having their children in the hospital but felt that it was the best place for them under the circumstances. Norma was upset the first time she had to take her child back to the hospital with croup. However, with each additional rehospitalization Norma experienced relief that she would receive the help that she needed:

> It's the best place for her. Her saturation level was, she wouldn't eat. She hadn't ate decently for a week. Like she wouldn't drink, like she'd take an

ounce and she wouldn't eat her solids. And I mean this kid can't afford not
to do that. . . . Yeah, well she needs it, it used to bother me but not anymore.
I mean [the hospital's] the best place for her if she is sick, sick, sick.

After accepting that her infant had Down syndrome, Sally said she wanted
to help her in any way possible: "I look at it this way, there's nothing that
I can do about it, she's going to stay with it, so I have to accept it. And do
whatever I can to help her out."

Often the mothers were unsure about what they should be doing to help
their own babies. All of the mothers, except for Mary, contacted an early
intervention program to learn about early stimulation. Sally explained her
reason for becoming involved in the program: "Yeah, you don't know 'cause
they say they need so much extra work and then you don't know what to do
with them. So this way now I'll start something and I'll know what I am
supposed to be doing." Each of the mothers thought that it was important
to be involved in stimulating the baby to allow the child to develop to full
potential. Norma found that taking care of her baby was a big responsibility: "Yeah, well not work but you always feel that there is something
more that you should do, more exercises or more stimulation or more this
or more that."

After bringing the baby home, each mother said that she did not want
to return to work because she wanted to be involved in the early stimulation program. However, three of the five mothers decided for financial
reasons that they had no choice but to return to work. Sally had concerns
about being at work when the early intervention worker was working with
the baby:

> I might just skip out of work the day that they are going to be there for an
> hour or two, make arrangements and be there. I just don't want to feel left
> out, I guess. It's the beginning part for her and I don't want to miss that
> part.

The mothers who returned to work said that it was important to make
adequate plans for child care so that the baby would not miss out on the
necessary stimulation. Sally's mother was going to baby-sit for Sally and
have the early intervention worker come to her home while she baby-sat.
Terry worked evenings so that her husband could be with their children.
Norma found a baby-sitter:

> And I think the question is whether your child will get the same stimulation
> and the same exercises if you are with them all the time. I've found a

baby-sitter, at least for Lynn. . . . She's [the baby-sitter] excellent. So I don't have as many misgivings as I did.

The two mothers who decided to stay home to care for their infants felt that they could provide the best possible care. Sandy explained why she wanted to stay home with her baby:

Because I want to spend my time with her, I mean you just, why not? I mean you can give her the best I think. Listen to me. Dumb mom can give the best education. You know, you do tons of stuff with them and so why deprive them of it. . . . Well there is just no way I would leave her with somebody else; well, I mean I felt that way with him too. But with her, it's just, like, not even negotiable.

Integration of the Infant Into the Family

Once the infant was at home, family involvement with the baby helped to reestablish roles and relationships among family members. Sandy tried to explain how the addition of a new family member altered her family's life:

It's quite different with the second one where you really have to adjust, well, particularly when you're at home during the day, the threesome and the interaction. Like when your husband's there, that's different because there are two people to draw from, but when it's just you, you have to work out a whole new set of rules and demands, you get smarter on that one too.

Sandy also described how she made preparations to accommodate her son before trying to breast-feed the new infant:

You get creative before you nurse. You get the piece of apple cut up and go with him or you get *Sesame Street* on or you just think of different things or you try to get him to read a book with you or whatever.

It was common for the mothers to find similarities between the new infants and other family members in both appearance and personality. This comparison of family members represented an acknowledgment of the integration of the baby into the family circle. Both Norma and Sally found similarities between their infants' eyes and those of other family members: "She had large eyes like her brother, her dad's color" (Norma); "Yeah, she's got his eye features, his long eyelashes, his same eyelashes as him and a little mouth like him" (Sally). Mary described one of her children from her previous marriage as a lovable child, and she predicted that the new infant would have a similar personality: "Just for no reason at all give you a great big hug, that's the way Reg is and I think John is going to be like that."

All of the mothers said that they took their babies everywhere that they would have taken any new baby. Norma said that her baby was part of the family:

> She's part of the family and she just struts along with everybody else. . . . I don't know how much we changed because she is her. Or whether because we have a new baby. I think probably somewhat of both. We take her and she goes the same place we would take any new baby.

It was important to each mother to feel that the extended family had accepted the new baby into the family. Sandy was pleased when her niece included the baby in plans to go to the park:

> My sister talked to her kids and she said, "Do you want to go to the park with Auntie Sandy and Fred?" Her oldest daughter, who is 3, said, "What about baby Miranda?" And I said, "Well, you can tell Carol she warms my heart." Like we're not leaving Miranda behind.

After her baby's grandfather was told of the Down syndrome, Mary watched for his reactions to the baby:

> Yes, he was fine. After that time I particularly took notice you know, actually he was more attentive afterward. You know there was everybody, I mean there was so many darn grandchildren there, time had to be shared anyway but he would talk to John and he'd take more notice of John, so I felt good.

Sally perceived that her family's acceptance of the infant would influence how her child would feel about herself in the future: "But they came and held her and played with her and talked to her. They weren't afraid to hold her, so that was a good sign. So I think she'll do good."

Integration of the Infant Into the Community

After learning more about Down syndrome, Norma felt that society was better prepared than she had thought to accept people with Down syndrome as members of the community: "Then you learn that things really aren't as bad as you had originally thought they were. I mean the diagnosis is the same but the Down's kids certainly have a place now. Much more so than they did." It was important to the mothers that their children would be accepted by the community. Sandy was pleased to see an adult with Down syndrome attending her church; she saw this as a sign of acceptance by the community: "I thought there you go, no big deal, he's going to church and no fuss one way or the other. He's just accepted as a member of the community so I think that's what I want for her, certainly."

Norma saw her infant as becoming accepted in the community: "Everybody knows her. . . . I go to the grocery store and 'How's your daughter?' Or we go to the drug store and 'Here's Lynn's mom. Now how's Lynn doing?' " Sally also felt that her baby was being accepted in the community: "Oh yeah, the girls in here, the neighbors come for coffee and they want to play with her and they phone and say, 'Well, come for coffee but make sure you bring the baby with you.' "

Taking One Day at a Time

The mothers found that establishing a daily routine helped them to focus on the present. Although they still had concerns about the future, all the mothers found that it was important to cope with one day at a time. Norma was aware that she would have to contend with a number of potential problems in the future:

> You don't know how, you just take one day at a time. You learn, we are learning I suppose all the time. But in particular, you learn that you don't learn what hasn't come yet. I can't be concerned at this point what the speech is going to be or what her reading level is going to be or what this is going to be. It's only one thing at a time.

Both Sally and Mary said that they did not "dwell on the future." Sally said she coped by taking it "day by day." Mary said that if she were to worry about the future she would "go crazy" because her baby was so young and she would know more about his potential by 3 years of age:

> I don't even think about it at all because there's no point really. All I need to do now is know what's available to me and then when the time comes . . . I guess we just take a day at a time if you want to put it that way 'cause there's not really too, too much to talk about until I can find out some answers from these other people and their thoughts as far as whenever the time comes around that they think that John would be able to go to regular

school or whether he has to have extra help or this and that, because until
that time there's really not that much to talk about.

Norma's advice for other new mothers who have infants with Down
syndrome was "probably just to take one day at a time. You can't worry
about what hasn't happened." Sandy agreed that it was important for
parents of infants with Down syndrome not to worry about the future:

> Well that's true too, you do figure that out pretty quick 'cause here you are
> with this little baby that is so apparently normal and you're thinking, why
> am I bothering my brain about when she is 30? Let's enjoy her babyhood.
> You do that and you come to that reckoning pretty quick.

Maternal Perceptions of Competence

All of the mothers perceived themselves to be competent in mothering
their own children with Down syndrome. Mary considered herself to be
a "really excellent mother" and had confidence in her ability to care for
the infant. She did not like to leave her child to be cared for by anyone
else, as she thought that she would be able to provide the best care. Norma
also said that she had no problems caring for her child: "I don't think I have
any problems. No, I think we are coping just fine. Actually, I'm sometimes
surprised that we cope as well as we do." Norma felt confident that she could
cope with any other problems she might have to face with her daughter: "I
mean I'm beginning to wait for the ax to fall or something. I'm not looking
forward to the surgery. That's okay, though, we'll manage to get through
that the same as we managed to get through the other things."

Both Norma and Sandy referred to the mother-infant "bonding" that
occurred in the development of their relationships with their children.
Norma said that this was similar to her relationship with her other child:
"I don't see my relationship with her any different than it was with my
son really. . . . I care for her the same as I cared for her brother." Sandy
said that her relationship with this baby was "special" because of the
child's affectionate responses, especially during breast-feeding:

> The body contact, and she's so funny when she nurses because she holds
> you, they're really touchy little babies, and when I hold her she pats me,
> she pats me and I pat her. She's so affectionate I couldn't believe it. Like
> you know people say kids with Down syndrome are affectionate but already

she is. I love it. She smiles a little bit . . . and she's cuddly and huggy. Good eye, nice eye contact, that type of thing.

Sally was confident that her relationship with her infant was good: "I think we've been good together, she knows who I am and know who she is." When asked how she knew that she was a good mother to the baby, Sally replied:

She doesn't cry and I know she's being fed, she's always changed. She doesn't have a rash on her behind. She's well dressed. I think those are good signs and every time, somebody, these are friends of ours, they say how cute she is, you know her outfit is nice on her. That makes me think that I am a good mother.

Sandy also saw herself as a "good mom" but thought she might benefit from becoming involved in an early intervention program:

I think I'm doing a good job but you think, yeah, I probably do need more, I do need help and that. And I'm looking forward to when we get her into an early intervention program. Well, I'm looking forward to that just because I think you probably get ideas what you may think of but you might not too. Mothers naturally think of things, surprisingly, by accident.

Sandy also thought that her previous experience with motherhood helped her to be more confident in making decisions regarding infant care:

More confidence and it just comes naturally like you really, it's not even a conflict in your brain or up for discussion, you just know. And you know from the past experience of the way things have evolved you have the confidence of having seen it happen. And you just think, we'll know when it's right, no big deal.

The Process of Maternal Role Formation

The process of maternal role formation described in this chapter is summarized in Figure 7.1. In the antenatal period, mothers developed expectations of the maternal role. As with other mothers, the birth of the infant stimulated maternal role formation. All the mothers in this study had had experience with at least one previous child and therefore had

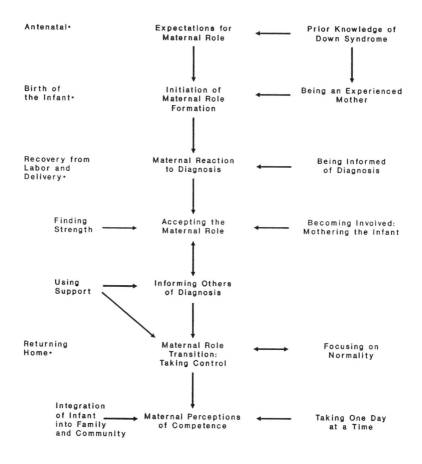

Figure 7.1. The Process of Maternal Role Formation

*Events that determine a time frame for the process

experience with caretaking activities, such as feeding and bathing. When they were informed of the diagnosis of Down syndrome there was initial denial, followed by maternal acceptance. At first the mothers were uncertain of their own ability to care for their newborns, but they soon began to focus on the normality of the babies rather than on the diagnosis. They had a need to be able to take control in order to assume the role of mother. This increased their perceptions of maternal competence. Another critical factor was the acceptance of the children as members of both the immediate and extended family and of the wider community. The mothers coped with the uncertain futures of their children by taking one day at a time and by not looking ahead to potential problems or areas of concern.

Reference

Rubin, R. (1977). Binding-in in the postpartum period. *Maternal-Child Nursing Journal,* 6(2), 67-75.

8

A Search for Understanding

Patricia Beryl Marck
Peggy Anne Field
Vangie Bergum

Words . . . should be discarded as soon as they begin to conceal what they ought to illuminate. Our terminology should be flexible in order to bring more and more of human experience into the range of our theory. (Goldenberg, 1990, p. 215)

In the preceding chapters, the contributors to this volume have explored a wide range of women's experience during the childbearing years. Taken individually, each of these presentations of independently conducted research offers theoretical insights into events that have transformed many women's lives. The women who participated in the studies presented here have spoken about living with infertility (Harris, Chapter 2), encountering unexpected pregnancy (Marck, Chapter 3), carrying high-risk pregnancy (McGeary, Chapter 4), awaiting the birth of a new child as a lost one is still grieved (Lever Hense, Chapter 5), mothering a child who is born too soon (Brady-Fryer, Chapter 6), and mothering a handicapped infant (Diachuk, Chapter 7). The words of some of these women suggest that mothering may also be experienced for a child never born, a child stillborn, and even a child never conceived.

The women in these studies initially regarded childbearing as a healthy process leading to the natural outcome of motherhood. However, as motherhood became a tangible possibility for each woman, unexpected deviations from the natural assurance of becoming a mother also occurred. The "natural order" of healthy pregnancy and childbirth did not necessarily translate into each woman's experience, and the uncertainty of her own outcome became central to her perceptions of herself as mother. Within this pivotal notion of uncertainty, the common feature that emerges for all of the women is that motherhood was not a given. Whether motherhood was sought at all costs or feared, a new role or a familiar one, the uncertainty each woman encountered in this experience of imagining or finding herself a mother defined the nature of her passage through it. To understand these women's stories as a whole, we must move toward a theory of uncertain motherhood.

A search for theory rests on the notion that there are abstract principles to be uncovered that might usefully guide our actions in real, concrete, human situations. Theorizing in this context stems from the stories of women, each a narrative of deeply personal hopes, fears, and pains in uncertain motherhood. Both the commonalities and the differences in the stories speak to the experience of uncertain motherhood. Our goal in this chapter is to develop an understanding of the women's experiences in order to assist caregivers in providing informed care to women during their childbearing years.

The Themes of Uncertain Motherhood

Within these studies, the notion of living with uncertainty during the childbearing years has been derived from several themes that surface and resurface throughout the women's stories. These themes include the *vulnerability* each woman discovers as she realizes that all is not well for her and that her world as she has known it is lost, the *inner dialogue with uncertainty* that is taken up by each woman as she imagines and takes on the role of mother, the *search for care* that each woman undergoes as she becomes aware of her vulnerability with others, and the changed woman who emerges from *living through* possible motherhood, whether or not a child is born.

Everything Has Changed: A Journey Into Vulnerability

Coming to a point in life where "everything has changed" is a perplexing experience, one that unseats a person and transforms every aspect of his or her understanding of the world. As the result of an event or a discovery, even things that are apparently the same as ever are no longer perceived as the same. Mary described this disorientation as the familiar receded after her baby was born with Down's syndrome: "I couldn't take it all in. . . . Everything at that point makes your head swim" (Diachuk, Chapter 7). For one of McGeary's participants, this voyage into the unknown is described with a deceptively simple statement: "Even in my normal everyday life, whatever that is, I'm not sure what it is anymore" (Chapter 4). Having entered a pregnancy that carries some risk, this woman realizes that her world as she has known it is lost.

This loss of the taken-for-granted aspects of life surfaced in all of the studies through the women's words. Whether the discovery was one of difficulty in achieving pregnancy, of an unexpected pregnancy, of a pregnancy at risk, or of mothering a high-risk or different child, a fundamental fact held true for each woman: Her life as lived until now was gone, and what lay ahead was not yet knowable. As each woman moved through this experience, she encountered a different experience of herself, her relationships, and the day-to-day rhythms of life. The world became indeterminate and her journey into the vulnerability of uncertain motherhood began.

Some synonyms for *vulnerable* include *defenseless, untenable, unprotected, exposed,* and *susceptible* (Hayakawa, 1968). The word's etymology also elicits painful imagery; it comes from roots meaning to be wounded, pulled, torn (Barnhart, 1988). What is it like to be laid open to an experience one has not prepared for or chosen, an experience that seems to cut to the core of what one thinks one knows about oneself and one's life? A participant in Harris's study conveyed the fundamental nature of this questioning when she said, "I felt like I was a woman, but when it came to getting pregnant, I felt, I'm not like other women. I can't do it" (Harris, Chapter 2). Sandy described her shock over the birth of her second-born as handicapped after "such a healthy pregnancy. . . . I was so prepared last time, not this time" (Diachuk, Chapter 7).

Vanessa's description of her realization of unexpected pregnancy also speaks of an elemental displacement from her known world: "My heart just dropped out of me. All of a sudden reality hit me. I thought, I'm pregnant, I know I'm pregnant" (Marck, Chapter 3). Yet perhaps one of the most telling impressions of vulnerability is given by Mary when she says of mothering her preterm infant: "You never think it'll happen to you. . . . I don't have that feeling anymore. Like that feeling is gone. Like I think anything can happen to me [now]" (Brady-Fryer, Chapter 6).

Anything Can Happen

The devastating recognition that anything can happen seems almost incompatible with our commonsense understanding of life. How do we act, what are our hopes and fears, when what happens teaches us that we are no longer safe from the unthinkable, the unimagined, the deepest losses of our lives? Sarah conveyed the lasting effects of her experience with stillbirth very clearly in a few words: "It will never be the same again, I know that" (Lever Hense, Chapter 5). Nothing is the same and nothing ever can be again.

For Maggie, the terror and loss she felt in pregnancy as her boyfriend abandoned her transformed to a deeper grief after her abortion. With unexpected pregnancy, she lost her footing in the world of marriage and family that she had planned with a loved one. When her fetus's sex was mistakenly disclosed over the telephone by an anonymous laboratory technician, her loss multiplied. A fetus she felt unable to carry became a baby girl whom she had to name and enter in a priest's log; she had to "do for her what I could" (Marck, Chapter 3). When the unimaginable occurs, we may act in ways we have not envisioned, on knowledge we did not anticipate, and with capacities we did not know we had. We are caught unaware and anything can happen.

These unforeseen moments when "anything can happen" seem endowed with a different meaning in our memories than the taken-for-granted events of former "everyday" lives. Women relived their previous stillbirths throughout second experiences of pregnancy and birth, with recollections so vivid that some spoke of not wanting to give up their unborn babies to birth. Grace talked of her desire to withhold her baby's entry into the world during her labor: "[It was] harder to let go, whereas before I didn't have a major problem at delivery letting go and having the baby come out" (Lever Hense, Chapter 5). Sarah echoed these bodily misgivings about the risks of birth: "My biggest fear is like, it is alive inside me, so why can't we just keep it inside there?"

What each woman remembered about her experience was unique; still, each memory seemed an indelible part of that experience. For Gillian and Ginny, the recollection of general anesthetic loomed larger with each successive test they contemplated to investigate their infertility (Harris, Chapter 2). For Katherine, the internal scars she feared from repeated abortions took up residence alongside the memories of a lifetime of physical and emotional abuse from her father and her boyfriend (Marck, Chapter 3). Other women also conveyed the apprehension embodied within uncertain motherhood as they recalled how technology constantly signaled the fragility of their infants. Repeated equipment alarms in the neonatal intensive care unit (NICU) left them alternating between a dread of touching their children and experiences such as Sue's, in which reaching out left her "bawling like a baby. A sense of relief. He's all right, I touched him, I'm all right" (Brady-Fryer, Chapter 6). As each woman entered into uncertain motherhood, it seemed that everything could be at risk, at any time, in any way. I may never hold my baby; I may never have one. I may touch him; I may watch him die, right within reach of my own hand.

Marie paints this possibility of ultimate loss with terrifying conviction, when she simultaneously describes her first and second experiences of childbirth:

> I was right next door to the room that I had been in when my first baby died. . . . And when they started [inducing] I asked them to turn the monitor away from me so that I couldn't see the heartbeat because I had watched my first baby die. I had seen his heartbeat go. And I didn't want to see that again. (Lever Hense, Chapter 5)

She questions, as she hopes for the best, whether she can make it through anything. An inner dialogue with an uncertain outcome is entered into as each woman struggles, in her vulnerability, to discover her capacity to trust and connect with her possible or real fetus or child. Both because of and despite her vulnerability, each woman searches for a way to mother.

An Inner Dialogue With Uncertainty

In listening to the women's descriptions of their experiences, some of the meanings of vulnerability noted above warrant revisiting: wounded, pulled, and torn. These women experienced pain. It is clear that they have felt many wounds. These women have been pulled, hurt, and afraid; for some of the women the experience of uncertain motherhood tore their lives apart. How can we listen to their pain in a way that helps us to understand their experiences? What do their vulnerabilities reveal to us about their needs?

To address these questions, it is helpful to explore the concept of dialectical thinking. *Dialectic,* in Hegelian terms, is described in *Merriam Webster's Collegiate Dictionary* (tenth edition) as a "process of change in which a concept or its realization passes over into and is preserved and fulfilled by its opposite." Like vulnerability, dialectic embodies the tension and threat that lie between different possibilities, disparate outcomes, or apparent discrepancies that do not add up when we are trying to make sense of a situation. The dialectical principle invites us to use critical reflection and dialogue to resolve such apparent contradictions (Gadow,

1980, 1990, 1992). It provides a way to enter the women's experience of uncertain motherhood.

When we use this dialectical approach to consider the women's stories on more than one level, overt differences between their experiences can be reconstituted into one meaningful whole. On one level, it seems evident that each woman experiences vulnerability in different ways, for different reasons. It could be suggested that the vulnerability of a woman awaiting abortion may have little to do with the vulnerability of a woman trying to conceive or trying to bring a healthy baby to term. Yet, at a different level, each woman's story can be considered not only as one of being or not being a mother, having or not having a child. Rather, the inner dialogue revealed by each woman's words transforms each woman's experience from arbitrary definitions of infertility, pregnancy, and birth to something else: what it has come to mean to her, regardless of her particular outcome, to imagine the possibility of being a mother.

The vulnerability that sprang from imagining motherhood led each woman to search for relationships she could trust, where the possibility could be safely explored. For some of the women, the only connection of safety was internal dialogue with themselves; for others, caregivers, family, and/or friends provided understanding. Ultimately, however, the possibility of motherhood brought with it the vulnerability of possible relationship with a fetus or child, and for each woman it was this relationship that seemed to demand the deepest and most difficult trust of all (Baier, 1986; Bergum, 1989).

Possible Mother: Trust and Vulnerability

In each woman's experience of uncertain motherhood, living with her vulnerability and unknown outcome seemed to become a new "everyday" experience of life. Over time and place, and accompanied by others she may or may not have chosen, each woman seemed to undertake, in her own unique manner, an inner dialogue. Such dialogue sometimes led her to a developing understanding of herself as mother, but this was not always the case. The ambivalence of potential motherhood is captured in Tina's comments as she awaited childbirth while remembering her stillborn baby:

> It's hard for me to even look forward to, to picture myself as that. . . . I am a mother but I haven't experienced what most normal women experience. . . . Because I have never experienced a normal delivery, a normal child, a normal baby, I've never had that. (Lever Hense, Chapter 5)

Prior reproductive losses also left the women in McGeary's study "unable to trust their bodies to carry their babies to term." Mary, in Marck's research, echoed similar qualms. For women in Harris's research, this mistrust extended even further, as most of the women questioned whether their bodies could even achieve pregnancy.

From different foundations this bodily mistrust was reflected in many of the women's experiences. For Maggie, trust of her pregnancy was shed first with her weight and eventually with her abortion. Even Vanessa, clearly pregnant to others, suspended her own belief about the inevitable birth of a child she would need to mother; she could not see herself as a mother. Through her body, each woman understood something about her own way of becoming a mother and found herself more or less able to envision that she could in fact be a mother.

In one manner or another and at one point or another, the task of trusting herself as mother was therefore at issue for every woman. There was no one common juncture where this task became paramount; it seemed instead to be embedded in each woman's unique struggle to balance the scales (Harris, Chapter 2). This balance lay between hope and loss, between a former state of self already altered by the possibility of motherhood and a potential state of self-other, woman-fetus, or mother-child.

In striving for balance, each woman sought to imagine the kind of relationship she could have with her fragile "other": a baby envisioned, remembered, or developing within or a child already born and needing her care. Yet for many of the women such a relationship was unimaginable, especially at times when the pain, responsibility, and vulnerability of loving a child that might not come seemed too much to bear. With no assurance of how her experience would culminate, each woman sought inside of her the knowledge she needed to find safe passage through uncertain motherhood.

Over time, recognizing the uncertainty of her journey led each woman to an even more fundamental truth, the realization that no matter how her experience completed itself, her essential task was to take on and trust a new understanding of herself. That understanding needed to be one that allowed each woman, regardless of her outcome as mother, to find safe passage through the experience of uncertain motherhood to a forever-changed self, one who had survived the inevitable pain that the possibility of becoming a mother would bring.

Negotiating the Risk

Although the need to preserve the self informed each woman's experience of uncertain motherhood, the path toward a new understanding of herself lay through an array of opposing tensions and possibilities. Safe passage did not seem assured by either the alignment with hope or the abandonment of it, by trust in others first and foremost or by trust in oneself alone. At the same time each woman recognized her inherent need to be in a relationship with others, she saw the inevitable need to listen to herself.

Vulnerable to others in her need, each woman entered a state of protective governance (Corbin, 1986; Harris, 1992) to manage and endure her experience of uncertain motherhood. Protective governance was a way to secure a place of internal refuge, a place where the competing voices could be taken into account in an effort to preserve oneself. Experts and others gave the women their opinions as they sought or experienced pregnancy and/or birth, yet each woman also turned to her own inner knowledge of her experience. Although these interpretations might differ, both versions of reality were needed for the women to explore the possibilities motherhood might hold.

Uncertain Motherhood as Hidden Conversation

Many aspects of the women's stories provide articulate descriptions of an inner passage to the possibility of being a mother. To mother, to hope to or to even consider it, was to risk pain unlike any other. The pain risked was found in the difference between *wanting* a child and *committing oneself to respond* to a child: To forfeit the former opportunity could bring disappointment; to lose the latter could mean devastation.

This painful risk was bodily present in ways distinctive to each woman's particular experience and, as it inserted itself into her passage through uncertain motherhood, reminded her of her vulnerability. In Vanessa's first days after childbirth, nursing her son seemed to heighten both her fear of disappearing into his needs and her need to see her son loved and cared for. The emptying and filling of her breasts mirrored her struggle to discern the right place for her child: to keep him with her or to place him with another. Even as his suckling told her she was his mother, her desire to escape his demands caused her to wonder if she could truly be his mother. Yet turning from her son was not possible for Vanessa in the face of her overriding need to respond to him. Between the risk of losing herself and the risk of losing him lay the root of her mothering pains, the difference between only wanting him and needing to see his needs met. Still, as Vanessa listened to her own voice, she recognized the need to be heard by others as herself. As she was heard, she saw what she understood herself to be as mother. As she was listened to, she no longer felt that as her son's mother she herself as woman would be irretrievably lost.

Vanessa's experience prompts us to ask if her inner dialogue corresponded with the conflicting needs experienced by many of the other women. Through and with their bodies, most of the women seemed to discover some of their innermost hopes and fears about their mothering experiences. Those discoveries were unique for each woman, and what came into view did not always lead toward connection. The yearning to hold her baby in her arms could be the same ache that told a woman her arms were empty. Until each woman found the way in which she could safely mother, her place of refuge had to be guarded, and connection with a self-other was tentative.

The tentative nature of connecting is well described in McGeary's research by the woman who welcomed uncomfortable signs of pregnancy, such as heartburn. She could let down her guard a bit, as did the women in Harris's study when the blood of menstruation did not arrive. At the same time, letting down one's guard was in and of itself a reminder that things could change, that one's guard might need to rise again. One's period might come tomorrow, and even if it didn't, it was possible that one's child might grow inside one and then die.

What was at stake for each mother from the first moment of entering uncertain motherhood? Reading across the women's stories, we note that feelings of loss seemed to occur frequently: with each drop of blood that signaled no baby or a lost one; with every time a fetus did not seem to move enough or a fragile preterm infant seemed to startle too easily; with each moment one lay on a table awaiting another exam, another test, another birth, another abortion. To open up to the possibility of motherhood was to allow both one's memories and one's fantasies a constant presence in one's body and to undergo what seemed like countless variations of one's hopes and fears.

This interpretation of the women's experiences suggests that the bodily imprint of uncertain motherhood reminds women that nothing is to be taken for granted. Anything can be taken away. The joy in what might be gained in uncertain motherhood seems matched, measure for measure, to the pain of what one may lose forever. Wanting to touch yet afraid to touch, yearning to hold yet afraid to hold, emptying breasts into a pump or nourishing one's infant at the breast: Different physical experiences let each woman know whether she was or was not yet a mother, or would not ever be. As the bodily aspects of her experience unfolded, the alternate moving toward and away from connecting with a possible fetus or child left each woman with her own realization of what was at stake, with her own unique and deeply personal mothering pains.

Mothering Pains: Responding to the Call of a Child

In Lever Hense's study, Grace said, "I know what it is like to give birth and to have a stillborn baby and, I mean, what is worse than that? Nothing." Grace voices every mother's ultimate fear when she names the pain of losing a child: the name of that pain is nothing. It is the pain you cannot go through and yet you will anyway. There is nothing to make it okay, nothing to be done, nothing to bring one's world back to what it is supposed to be. It is "the horror of it all." The words each woman shared about her experience do not suggest that the pains of miscarrying a hoped-for child, of not conceiving a child, of aborting a possible child, or of delivering a handicapped child are like each other, or like Grace's pain. All of these losses in childbearing may be more different than they are the same.

Perhaps considering pain as "problem" corresponds with describing these childbearing experiences as "loss," as both approaches provide only partial insight into the experience of uncertain motherhood. Pain and loss may take on different and fuller bodies of meaning in the context of the women's experiences as a whole. Katherine's description of her abortions and her miscarriage as "the same pain" invites us to consider whether there are aspects of mothering pains that each woman carries forward, aspects that become part of her experience every time she contemplates motherhood.

If we choose this more full-bodied perspective of the women's experiences, there may be other images of mothering pains found in the women's stories. Could it be that the ways in which a previously lost child accompanied a woman's understanding of her current pregnancy, or that repeated scheduled sex filled some women with a growing emptiness, or that mothering an infant not like a healthy one at home shook one's confidence, all touch the same body of pain in uncertain motherhood? Perhaps the core of mothering pains was reached for all of the women when they began to respond to the possibility of a child.

The response of each woman to the possibility or reality of a child was an experience of relationship with a fragile other. Each woman responded to that relationship in the ways that she could; that is, she moved to being a mother in the ways that felt safe. For Maggie, a safe relationship came only after her pregnancy, in the nonjudgmental care of a compassionate priest. For other women, safety built slowly as their pregnancies progressed, as ultrasounds and other tests turned out well, and as movements within reassured them of the growing presence of the unborn child. For the women in Lever Hense's study, safety was usually reached with the arrival of a healthy, live child, although for Grace, safety was not achieved until she had been at home for some weeks with her child.

It is critical to note, however, that the same details that held the promise of reassurance could also convey powerful messages that all was not well. For most of the women in Harris's study, successive tests were approached with a heightened sense of hope and dread, as each disappointing result reinforced a failure to achieve pregnancy. Even for women who achieved wanted pregnancies, neither technology nor their own experiences were always sources of comfort. Sometimes an ultrasound did not visualize the fetus, even when subsequent images affirmed the baby's progress; sometimes the baby did not seem to move. Books the women read for reassuring information could just as often produce confusion and anxiety. The same monitors that provided the reassurance of close observation for a preterm infant could induce terror for parents who witnessed their repeated alarms.

For Vanessa, it was precisely what *was* well that was not okay for her; she hated that pregnant glow (Marck, Chapter 3). Despite the apparently contrary nature of her experience, it provides the same insight as the responses of other women. One cannot assume what made each woman's experience "okay" or "not okay," "safe" or "not safe" for each one individually. For each woman, safety could be reached only when she located what her experience meant to *her,* when she reached her own understanding of mothering. To locate her own experience, each woman sought relationships with others who were interested in learning about her experience.

The Search for Care: Relationships Between Caregivers and Women

In her research with women becoming mothers for a first time, Bergum (1989) asked: What does it mean to move into motherhood? What is it like to imagine oneself as mother? What does it mean to encounter a new and unique relationship with a developing fetus within and then with a newborn child in your life? In answer, the women spoke of a unique experience, an inner dialogue that asked for a sharing of self with other, a relationship with a "self that is not oneself" (p. 55). This vulnerable relation of self-with-other took hold within each woman as she felt able to explore and develop her relationship with an imagined child-to-be. Each woman set out on her passage to motherhood and talked of her fears and hopes for her child and for herself as mother.

If we ask what capacities each woman in Bergum's (1989) research discovered in making the transformation to motherhood, it may give us insight into what is asked of women faced with less certainty of bearing a child and perhaps with less conviction about how they will find themselves as mothers. Even the women in Bergum's work voiced the terror that something could happen to their children-to-be or to their new babies: "Oh, my gosh, is this what having a kid is like? Terror like this? Will she be okay? Will she be okay tomorrow? Will she be the day after?" (p. 31). Realizing the potential of losing one's child may be part of what every woman who responds to a child comes to know; this is a part of how she understands what it is to mother. The presence of a real or imagined child brings with it the inevitable pain of mothering. Its presence holds the possibility of its absence, and with the commitment to respond to a child comes the real risk of loss of that child.

The questions asked in the studies explored in this book take Bergum's work further: What does it mean to move toward motherhood when that move is uncertain—uncertain in one's own imagination, uncertain in one's bodily experience, and uncertain in the life and health of the baby? This collective group of studies suggests that these latter questions seem uniformly relevant and reflective of the nature of uncertain motherhood for many of the women, if not all. All needed to come to their own sense of what becoming a mother in this experience meant to them, and all sought relationships with those who might help them attune to that sense.

Mothers and Caregivers: Divergent Knowledge

As each woman discovered her own sense of what was taking place within her, a sea of other all-knowing voices competed with her own. Expert others—doctors, nurses, technicians, friends, and family—gave pronouncements on her experience from their respective sets of "facts." Even technology itself, through ultrasound, monitors, charts, and thermometers, impressed upon the women other points of view, other facts that indicated what they were or were not as mothers.

Many of the women spoke of how they alternately sought out these external sources of "knowledge" about their experiences and wrestled with what they heard. In Harris's work, this experience was eloquently described by the women as "living under the microscope." While physicians and other caregivers explained the science of achieving pregnancy, each woman struggled to locate her own inner knowledge about her "infertility work." Gillian's awareness of her ovulation captures the contrast between scientific knowledge and personal knowledge with lucidity: "I know because I get very nauseated. I have mittelschmerz, pain in my side. My mucus is very thin and very stretchy. And my cervix is very soft and open" (Harris, Chapter 2). Gillian's knowledge was immediate, whereas scientific knowledge is abstract, objective, and uncertain. Scientific knowledge either affirmed or discounted her experience, depending on the content and the manner of its presentation.

Advice from experts about trying longer to achieve pregnancy, charting ovulatory periods, and scheduling sex thus needed to be balanced with attempts to make sense of this experience from a personal understanding of trying to become pregnant, an attunement to inner rhythms, hopes, and fears. Others could tell a woman when she should engage in sexual relations and even demand to know when she did so, but only she and those in her life could know whether sex seemed possible when it was mandated, whether her relationship could withstand the pervasive invasion of its intimacies. No caregiver or relative could make this project safe for her; no one could assure her that more would be gained than lost in the end.

This tension between the "facts" and "opinions" of others and the actual experience of uncertain motherhood permeates many of the women's stories. Every woman in Marck's study provided descriptions of choosing in unexpected pregnancy that differed radically from the words proffered by most of their caregivers, friends, and families. Women in McGeary's project referred to the contradiction between others' advice to read, sing, or talk to their unborn children and their own frequent inclination to stay apart and separate from developing fetuses whose loss they feared.

These divergent interpretations between the women's experiences and the advice of others are borne out in all the studies. Women held back while caregivers urged them to push in labor; or struggled to see how recommendations about support groups or respite from their preterm infant fit with their personal understanding of their own and their infants' needs; or tried to translate medical jargon about Down's syndrome into helpful understanding of how they would care for a handicapped baby. The dissonance between personal knowing and expert knowing seemed to reinforce for the women that there were no guarantees, no way to make and to keep everything right again, the way it was supposed to be.

Those people who failed to appreciate the disparate natures of the professional and the personal (the scientific versus private ways of knowing) held a frightening power to wound many of the women. Sally reeled at the brutal admonishment from house staff that her baby was not going to "die on the spot" (Diachuk, Chapter 7); Katherine could only conclude that both she and her pain did not matter to insensitive surgical staff (Marck, Chapter 3); Pam felt her fragile confidence crack as the pediatrician flatly announced her infant was "home too soon" (Brady-Fryer, Chapter 6). Not asked by such caregivers to describe her own experience, each woman suffered more uncertainty from such thoughtless acts and was led away from composing a useful sense of herself and her situation.

Knowledge from others was thus useful to each woman only as she filtered it through her experience in a way that brought her back to herself. Facts and opinions that others "knew" provided just one intimation of what each woman sought to understand: what this experience of uncertain motherhood meant to her and how it was that she could endure it, regardless of its outcome. For that knowledge to be unearthed, each woman had to cross over into her most private pain and hope that tactful others could be found to accompany her safely to the other side.

Providing Care:
Toward Professional Understanding

In these stories of uncertain motherhood, not every woman took home a child to nurture and raise. It was not even every woman's goal to do so, and for many of the women, it was an impossible goal. What every woman took out of this experience of uncertain motherhood was not a living child but the experience of having responded to the notion of mothering a child.

For each woman, responding to the possibility of motherhood was a unique and deeply personal struggle, one that brought pain and a need to make sense of her experience. Understanding came as each woman experienced her pain and as she found others who would witness and share in it honestly. Carla's frustration in her search for a caregiver who could acknowledge her fears of a second stillbirth underscores the importance of the recognition of the need to have one's pain acknowledged by others: "I couldn't find a doctor who could understand how concerned I was that it would happen again. The first family doctor that I came across said, 'Well, these things happen and it won't happen again' " (Lever Hense, Chapter 5).

At the same time, the women recognized and felt supported by efforts made by friends, family, and health professionals to be open to the presence of their pain. A husband who went with his wife to difficult procedures during infertility treatments or pregnancy, or who encouraged his wife to express breast milk for their preterm baby, was a source of strength in a time of need. A nurse or physician who said, "This must be hard for you" or who offered to stay and answer questions freely became a caregiver from whom to draw comfort and someone to trust with one's hopes and fears. Such caregivers were the ones women recalled as helping them care for their babies, teaching them how to breast-feed, showing them the way to hold a fragile newborn. To be in their care was a safe place to be, one that allowed for both the pain of their experiences and the possibility of mothering that each woman wanted.

Unfortunately, many examples of care that did not offer safe passage surfaced throughout the studies. Norma spoke of the doctor, "a stranger actually," who woke her up to tell her that her baby had Down's syndrome and then left, all in a "a two-minute deal" (Diachuk, Chapter 7). Katherine recalled the nurse after her third abortion who said, "You've had one in '88, '89, and '90; don't bother coming back in '91" (Marck, Chapter 3). The price such tactless caregivers could exact may have been most powerfully described by the mothers of preterm infants in Brady-Fryer's study. There, rather than risk antagonizing nurses who oversaw their infants' care, Jacky made expensive long-distance calls to family members and Sue "removed [herself] . . . and had a damn good cry" (Brady-Fryer, Chapter 6).

Acts of omission could wound as well. A partner who could not share the project of infertility work or who even sabotaged the possibility of pregnancy through his behavior was one who underscored the loneliness for women of seeking pregnancy through science. Family or friends who made their wishes about an unexpected pregnancy evident, or who wanted to talk with an anxious expectant woman only about how everything would go well, sent clear messages to women that their own personal experiences were not asked for and did not count.

The lack of dialogue a woman experienced at home was sometimes repeated in the health care setting. Technical expertise and information might be freely offered, but time to explore hopes and fears thoroughly was not always assigned similar value by the caregivers these women encountered. Yet, in the words not spoken, taboos not admitted into conversation, the women seemed to recognize some of their most deep-seated pain. The loss of a previous infant who was not acknowledged by others left a woman unable to connect freely with an infant to come. Unable to openly mourn possible children not conceived, women experiencing infertility talked of avoiding places where pregnancy and birth were celebrated while their hidden grief deepened. Throughout the studies, this theme of buried pain was repeated. What one could not talk about, one could not make sense of and move on from, so that safe passage through uncertain motherhood remained elusive.

In contrast, caregivers who encouraged women's concerns in their exchanges made real differences in the women's experiences. A nurse who "carried me through" and a doctor who showed "true concern, not just a medical concern" offered women the comfort, respect, and tactful presence that made their uncertainty endurable (Brady-Fryer, Chapter 6). The kind words of a nurse after Katherine's miscarriage (Marck, Chapter 3) and the "personal attention" of a nurse who had a Down's syndrome child of her own (Diachuk, Chapter 7) gave each woman space to voice her pain and allowed her to start the reparations needed to carry on past this loss and become whole again.

The intricacies of getting through uncertain motherhood were as unique for each woman as the deeply personal nature of the experience itself. Leah prepared for disappointment after a third attempt at in vitro fertilization with "a really nice pair of panties [that] had a pad in it already" (Harris, Chapter 2); Mary's daughters took to her bed with blankets, milkshakes, and tears after her miscarriage (Marck, Chapter 3). For the women in McGeary's study, the time of feeling safe to connect with the fetus differed, and in Lever Hense's research, the personalized grief for a child stillborn inevitably accompanied each woman as she took on motherhood with a new child safely born.

Caregivers who understood the distinctly individual nature of each woman's experience were deeply valued by the women and warranted special mention in their accounts of care. A physician who took the time to answer questions carefully and slowly, a nurse who helped a woman succeed in her breast-feeding, and a priest who listened without judgment all told the women who recalled them that their needs counted, their questions mattered. The tact and respect that their care conveyed laid the foundations for safe passage and told each woman that she could find the understanding she needed to grow from or live through the experience of uncertain motherhood.

Through phenomenological investigation in three separate perinatal contexts, K. Swanson (1991) has developed a middle-range theory of caring. She identifies caring as including knowing, being with, doing for, enabling, and maintaining belief. *Knowing* is "striving to understand the event as it has meaning in the life of others" (p. 162); *being with* is when the caregiver is emotionally present to the other. *To do for another* is to do what he or she would do for him- or herself if it were possible; *enabling* is facilitating passage through unfamiliar events; and *maintaining belief* is sustaining trust in the other person's capacity to get through an event and anticipate a future of fulfillment.

This description of caring practices suggests to us some of the qualities that seem central to those caregivers who might best help women through the experience of uncertain motherhood. These are health professionals who sense and respond to the vulnerability of the women in ways that communicate support and understanding. They respect the unique nature of the relationship between each woman and child or possible child, a relationship like no other that begins within each woman's imagination and that may not always lead to the birth of a mother and child. These caregivers recognize the nonlinear character of uncertain motherhood, in which past memories and future imaginings intermingle with each woman's present hopes and fears. Such caregivers also appreciate the physical experience of uncertain motherhood for each woman, including the powerful imprint of technology in her care; the central bodily experiences of yearning, hoping, fearing, or grieving for a child; and the vital difference a kind tone, tactful gesture, or tactful silence can make. They know that as each woman reaches her own understanding of her experience, she will find safe passage through it. From that perspective, the expert knowledge they offer is given in exchange for equally important personal knowledge of each woman's feelings, thoughts, and questions.

Living Through Mothering Experiences
When the Outcome Is Uncertain

Out of the vulnerability, inner dialogue, and search for care that each woman underwent, a way to survive her experience had to be discovered. The women's stories reveal the personal strength and self-understanding that eventually enabled each one to find some semblance of safe passage through uncertain motherhood. The insights and capacities required of each woman to cope with uncertain motherhood were as unique as the private nature and timing of her pain and of her understanding of self as mother. In living through the experience, many women described the discovery of strength they did not know they had, strength which enabled them to bear burdens and costs they had not imagined before the possibility of becoming a mother became real.

It was equally evident from the women's narratives that the experience of uncertain motherhood stayed with them in significant ways. Notably, caregivers received considerable mention in many of the stories, and the impacts of their careless or thoughtful actions seemed to be lasting ones.

As we develop the discussion of the women's survival below, the salient question for caregivers to ask is: How do we recognize or not recognize and assist women through uncertain motherhood, where everything can be threatened and there can indeed be everything to lose?

Identifying a Threat

Whether women could not become pregnant when they wished (Harris, Chapter 2), became pregnant unexpectedly (Marck, Chapter 3), had a pregnancy diagnosed as "at risk" (McGeary, Chapter 4), had experienced the loss of a baby (Lever Hense, Chapter 5), or had a preterm or less-than-perfect child (Brady-Fryer, Chapter 6; Diachuk, Chapter 7), the vision of pregnancy was altered by a threat to their images of motherhood. Although they might receive medical diagnoses, the recognition of the threat was confirmed by their own observations or concerns. As the goals of a normal pregnancy and healthy child became uncertain, the women became uncertain, as well, about their capabilities either to become mothers or to be mothers to those children. Although it can be argued that all pregnant women are vulnerable, the perception of threat led these women to see themselves as defenseless and exposed, as they frequently faced situations for which they were unprepared. Figure 8.1 presents the process the women used as they appraised and coped with the perceived threat to their becoming mothers.

Appraising the Threat

Once they perceived a threat, the women began to explore the need for assistance or considered the proffered medical interventions. At this stage they used information to consider the degree of threat to themselves or their babies, the process of "balancing the scales" (Harris, Chapter 2). During the process of threat appraisal they decided whether they needed to follow medical advice and treatment, whether information they received was accurate, and whether or not they needed to be concerned. One technique that was used was to compare themselves with other women or to compare their babies with other babies. If they could see themselves or their babies as "normal," this helped them to perceive a low threat that in turn decreased the level of anxiety. The women did not appraise threat in the same way as health professionals. For example, whereas a health professional appraised the threat as low in the case of a subsequent pregnancy following stillbirth, the mother might assess the risk as high.

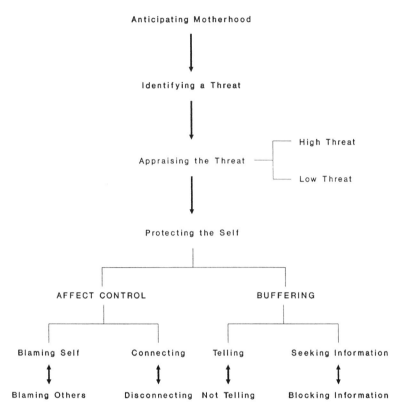

Figure 8.1. Model of Coping When the Outcome of Motherhood Is Uncertain

Threat appraisal included both physiological and psychological aspects of care. *Balancing the scales* was a problem-focused coping strategy that was related to managing the source of the distress. The women in Harris's study who changed physicians when they perceived a lack of individualized care were balancing the potential for cure against the need to receive tactful and personal care. Harris further describes how women balanced the scales as they made decisions about whether or not to continue with infertility treatment. In Lever Hense's work the mothers used a similar technique in deciding whether or not to risk another pregnancy, whereas the women in Marck's study balanced their own concerns in light of their relationships with others as they made their decisions.

Low Threat/High Threat

The women made decisions regarding the level of threat to themselves and their potential babies or their newborns based on their self-appraisals and available information. The mothers in both Brady-Fryer's and Diachuk's studies watched the placement of their babies in the NICU and used this as one measure of the improvement or deterioration of their children. They also used physical observations, such as learning to read the hospital's monitoring devices. The mothers in Diachuk's research compared their children with other babies as they looked for signs of physical abnormality or lack of growth. The quality of communication affected the stress level of the women but could not remove their sense of uncertainty.

The women in all the studies were vigilant regarding their own health and used their assessment as one indicator of the threat to motherhood. For example, in Harris's study the women put themselves "under the microscope" as they looked for signs of pregnancy or menstruation; in Lever Hense's work the mothers looked for signs of fetal movement to reassure themselves that all was well with their unborn children.

Family support or lack of support influenced the women in several ways. If there was perceived support they could talk to husbands, family members, or friends and so share their concerns. Two of the women in Harris's study felt unsupported by their husbands. In Lever Hense's work some mothers with previous stillbirths had not had the opportunity to explore the meaning of those experiences with professionals. Others had encountered professionals who failed to respond to their concerns; this increased their uncertainty about subsequent pregnancy and led to a raised perception of threat to themselves and their unborn babies.

Protecting the Self

Previous experience had an effect on whether a woman lowered or raised her guard in relation to perceived threat. Among the women who had chosen pregnancy, fetal movement was taken as a critical indicator that all was well with the pregnancy. Ultrasound allowed the mother to establish the reality of her baby, but if the risk appraisal was still one of high threat, most of the women talked about trying to avoid internalizing this information. Caregivers need to recognize that technology is not a substitute for the understanding that their presence, listening ear, and expert knowledge can provide. In the hands of professionals, technology has the power to reassure falsely as well as to disappoint sometimes, if we do not help women to fit the information into their overall experience in a way that is meaningful to them.

Most of the women used strategies to protect themselves from hurt. Harris, borrowing from Corbin (1986), describes this as "protective governing," Lever Hense as "self-protection," and McGeary as "guarding." Such strategies were also evident in Brady-Fryer's and Diachuk's work as women described their fears of becoming attached in case they lost their babies. In addition, all the women experienced pain; sometimes this pain seemed to envelope a woman's whole being. It might manifest itself in physical or emotional form, but it flowed through her whole life and involved the significant others who surrounded her. Corbin (1986) has described the strategy of protective governing as one whereby participants protect or shield themselves and/or others from perceived risk. They do this by controlling, assessing, and balancing, which, Corbin notes, are three interrelated processes. Protective governing can be described as taking action to protect oneself or one's child from harm; McGeary has called this process "guarding." It is evident that all the women, when faced with uncertain outcomes to motherhood, used protecting behaviors as they assessed and balanced the consequences of their own and other people's actions within their life situations.

The women also used protective strategies to shield themselves from further harm. If they perceived the threat as high, they used coping mobilization strategies that could be seen as both affect control and buffering. Affect control, or guarding one's emotions, is one means of protecting oneself; it can be accomplished by blocking emotional stimuli or by displacing one's feelings onto another. Morse and Johnson (1991) describe buffering as a form of protection in which an individual protects the self from concerns in order to provide him- or herself with the time and energy needed to get well. It can be argued that the women in these studies needed time to generate the energy required to cope with the event. Affect control involved both blaming self or others and connecting or disconnecting from the event. Buffering involved telling or not telling and seeking or blocking information.

Blaming self/blaming others. Many of the women initially blamed themselves for the events that precipitated their responses to motherhood as uncertain. One way of coping with anxiety was to place the control of the situation in the hands of another. That other could be God (Brady-Fryer, Harris, Lever Hense), health professionals (Diachuk), or previous family events that made it inevitable that the same thing would happen to the woman herself (Harris). Mothers interviewed by Brady-Fryer and Harris also talked of appealing to a divine being beyond themselves in the belief that this was a source of additional support.

Connecting/disconnecting. The process of connecting to or disconnecting from the event was evident as the women in Harris's study spoke of emotional letdown when their menstrual flows began. Marck describes how Maggie sought to find a relationship with the child she had once hoped for after she had an abortion. For the women in Lever Hense's and McGeary's studies there was a vacillation between detaching from and attaching to their unborn children during the course of their pregnancies. For the women who had previous stillbirths there was a need to pass the point at which their previous children were lost before they could trust in successful outcomes for their current pregnancies (Lever Hense). These women strove to remain detached until they assessed the threat of repetition to be decreased. In both Brady-Fryer's and Diachuk's research the mothers looked for ways to mother their babies, but it seemed increased hope was needed before they began to form close bonds. Mothering could be seen as providing physical care and visiting the child, as distinct from actually bonding with a fragile child.

Telling others/not telling others. Sometimes the threat of telling others about the event was greater than the support that could be obtained from sharing concerns. One of Harris's informants did not tell her partner of her infertility because she was afraid it would result in further loss in the form of breakup of the partnership. In addition, other women did not speak of their infertility in an effort to protect themselves from harm. Katherine and Maggie in Marck's study also withheld information from their partners. In Diachuk's study one family at first did not tell the grandfather that the child had Down syndrome because of the fear of rejection. This mechanism was not evidenced in all the studies, but when used it was to protect the self. In contrast, some women actually told others about their experiences in efforts to obtain support.

Seeking information/blocking information. The final behavior observed in these women was related to use of information. In the phase of threat appraisal, most mothers actively sought information. With mothers who perceived the threat as low, comparisons with others were used to confirm their assessment. One information-seeking behavior engaged in by some mothers was to compare their current newborns with their previous pregnancies so they could evaluate their current progress (Brady-Fryer, Diachuk). The women in Harris's study sought information to help them decide whether or not they wanted to undertake further treatment for their infertility and whether their bodies were similar or dissimilar to those of other women.

All the women constantly reappraised their own situations. When they perceived the threat to be low or decreased, they actively sought information. When the threat was perceived as high, they guarded against hurt by blocking information. Further, information alone did not necessarily help the women to assess their own experiences in meaningful ways. To make sense of any particular piece of information, the women needed to talk with caregivers, family, and friends to share their own hopes and fears. When such exchanges did not occur, new information was often not integrated into their experiences in ways that were helpful or meaningful.

Although Figure 8.1 depicts as linear the process involved in a mother's coping with an event that threatens her vision of becoming a mother, it should be noted that as new threats occur a woman may circle back to earlier phases of the process. Ultimately, for most of these women, resolution of the perceived threat occurred. When and how this happened were unique for each woman.

For some, such as Grace, who had a previous stillbirth, resolution of concerns about the loss of the current child did not end with that child's birth. For all the mothers who had previously experienced stillbirth, medical concern decreased before the concerns of the mothers themselves. For the others in Brady-Fryer's study, taking their babies home was frequently the event that reassured them that all would be well. For the women diagnosed as infertile, pregnancy reassured them, yet if they had had previous miscarriages, pregnancy alone was insufficient to assure them that they would become mothers in time. Some infertile women who believed they had exhausted all forms of treatment abandoned the goal of motherhood; they spoke of setting new goals for their lives. For some, resolution had not occurred by the time they spoke with the researcher; Vanessa, in Marck's study, was still searching for the best way to get on with her life. In some ways, it is possible that resolution has to be experienced again and again throughout a woman's life.

Discussion

The validity of the themes discussed above is supported by some of the recent research on a variety of women's experiences. In Beck's (1992) phenomenological study of postpartum depression, one woman echoes the desolation of the women who spoke about different postpartum losses. Speaking of her descent into depression, the woman told Beck that her biggest fear was that "I wasn't going to be the same person I was before the experience; that I never would quite get over it" (p. 169). It can be argued that postpartum depression constitutes another variation of uncertain motherhood, where a woman may well fear losing both herself and her baby. The theme that anything can happen, all is vulnerable, continues to fit.

Other studies on pregnancy after perinatal loss (Brost & Kenney, 1992), on the preterm labor experience (Mackey & Coster-Schulz, 1992), and on managing infertility treatment (Blenner, 1992; Phipps, 1993) reinforce the significance of caregivers' actions during the experience of uncertain motherhood. Physicians, nurses, and others were frequently seen as holding tremendous power to either allay or increase the stress of these women's situations; qualities such as warmth, patience, listening, and concern were recalled as making a genuine difference.

Further, the critical role of professional support may extend beyond emotional comfort. Mackey and Coster-Schulz (1992) and Iams, Johnson, O'Shaugnessy, and West (1987) speculate that some imp roved perinatal outcomes previously attributed to medical monitoring may be more closely related to the decreased stress levels experienced by women receiving recurrent nursing contact and close attention to preterm labor symptoms. The possibility that levels and frequency of nursing care may be significantly related to the outcomes of a variety of perinatal events bears further research, both for the sake of women and families and in the interest of cost-effective maternal-child care.

The themes drawn from the studies presented in this volume and elsewhere also support a call for outcomes research with broader agendas in these and other concerns of women. These concerns include but are not limited to menopause (Dickson, 1990), contraceptive management (Klitsch, 1991; Swanson, 1988), perinatal care (Bergum, 1989), breast-feeding (Bottorff,

1990; Morse & Bottorff, 1988), and family violence (Innes, Ratner, Finlayson, Bray, & Giovannetti, 1991; Ratner, 1991). Women who adopt their babies, women who place their babies for adoption, and young, unmarried women who keep their babies are also potential participants in for significant research (Bergum, 1994).

Another significant and controversial body of work that supports the need for a broader research agenda in women's health is located in the issues for women, their families, and society with respect to a wide variety of current scientific initiatives. These initiatives include prenatal diagnosis and fetal therapy, the use of fetal tissue for research, and the related research directions in genetic and new reproductive technologies (Bonnicksen, 1992; Field, 1989; Fletcher & Wertz, 1991; Gerrand, 1993; Hynes, 1989; Kearney, Vawter, & Gervais, 1991; Knoppers, 1991; Lippman, 1991; Macklin, 1991; Mullen & Lowy, 1993; Rothman, 1992; Royal Commission, 1993). These concerns and questions that scientists, ethicists, feminists, and others pose about these initiatives cannot be adequately addressed by any one group, discipline, or research methodology, and it is vital that the notion of uncertain motherhood, along with several other perspectives of women, gain far greater influence on the future direction of research in these areas. That direction should include both quantitative and qualitative methods of inquiry in order to broaden our notion of what should and could be scientifically investigated (Affonso, 1992; Bergum, 1989; Malterud, 1993; Sherwin, 1992).

It is also useful to reflect on the model of uncertain motherhood outlined in this work by comparing it with earlier work by Mishel (1988) on illness. Norton (1975) notes that uncertain events are based on vagueness, lack of clarity, ambiguity, the probability of an event occurring, and lack of information. For all the women in these studies one or more of these characteristics were present during this process of motherhood. Individual women had difficulty appraising the event and so began to lack certainty about the goal of motherhood. Mishel (1988) describes how individuals have difficulty appraising their experience. The women in these studies moved on to appraise their situations and to decide whether threats to themselves or their children were low or high. If the risk was high, they avoided relating to their children, became hypervigilant, and/or avoided information that indicated risk. These behaviors are coping behaviors, as suggested by Mishel's conceptual model. When the women believed information was being held back, their uncertainty increased.

The uncertainty related to motherhood led the women to engage in threat appraisal. This is a widely recognized process in which individuals assess the risk of events to themselves or to significant others. Risk assessment patterns include the scanning of potentially dangerous stimuli; risk assessment is thought to be more closely related to anxiety than to fear (Barbarin, 1990). It was evident that the outcomes of the risk assessments engaged in by these women frequently did not correspond with those of the professionals they consulted. The women used their understanding of symptom patterns (feeling well, comparing themselves or their babies with others), event familiarity (understanding of test and procedures), and event congruence (was motherhood threatened more or less than the physician told them?) to determine the degree of threat. These mechanisms have high congruence with Mishel's (1988) stimuli.

Mercer (1990) has also explored vulnerable families and their adaptation to threat and loss. She suggests that adaptation to a crisis leads to increased ability to cope through psychological and environmental readjustment. She defines threat as "any event or series of events that places a desired or valued person or outcome in jeopardy, thus creating disequilibrium for the individual" (p. 39). Mercer describes anxiety as being characterized by feelings of apprehension, nervousness, and uneasiness, all expressed by the women in these studies. Mercer further suggests that parents use "intellectualization to avoid the disturbing impact of the event through mastery of knowledge about the stressor" (p. 45). This may be part of the mechanism used by the women as they interpreted information in their own ways; yet their process of threat appraisal was very deliberate and their methods of acquiring data systematic. The women sought to rationalize the events by attributing them to an omnipotent being or family traits. To assess for themselves the severity of the threat they actively compared themselves with other women, compared this pregnancy with other pregnancies, and compared their babies with other babies.

The fact that the women felt their move to motherhood was uncertain created considerable disequilibrium. Their modes of coping appeared to be active and functional as they sought to make sense of the threat. It was also striking how frequently these women appraised the threat as different from that proposed by the professionals. One striking example is the medical diagnosis of infertility, which was frequently overshadowed by the potential parents' hesitancy to make public their private sexual lives.

Work by Morse and Johnson (1991) on an illness-constellation model identifies four stages: uncertainty, disruption, striving to regain self, and regaining wellness. There are strong similarities between Morse and Johnson's stages of uncertainty, in which patients suspect and read the body as they identify illness, and the initial experiences of the women in these studies. However, these women did not consistently move toward being overwhelmed by the events. As they perceived themselves or their babies as being at risk, they distanced themselves from their experience in some ways. The degree to which they relinquished control also varied, from a great lack of control in the case of frequent medical intervention, to relinquishing control only occasionally. Some women lost control over their bodies' function, whereas others lost control because they no longer believed in their bodies' ability to function. The support women received from partners and loved ones also influenced their perception of control.

Although the women did not see themselves as ill, they set goals and undertook monitoring activities as people with illness often do. Infertile women watched for blood; women uncertain of intrauterine survival set milestones by which they measured the potential for their unborn children's safe birth. In the NICU, mothers watched the progress of their babies from one area of the nursery to the next and used this as a gauge to measure when they would be able to take their babies home.

Throughout, the women tried to make sense of their experiences and to preserve themselves. They constantly renegotiated their anticipated roles of motherhood, seeking reassurance that they were making relevant choices. The women provided strong evidence that caregivers' assumptions did not in fact reflect the women's own reality. Caregivers did not always seek cues and become aware of the reality as seen by the women themselves. The women had a need to share their feelings with health professionals as well as other important people in their lives. They needed to be comforted and protected. For example, professionals needed to structure situations so the women could preserve their dignity, particularly where tests and procedures were involved (Swanson, 1991). Health professionals frequently fell short of providing adequate explanations in helping the women to generate alternatives or think through consequences. Enabling behaviors that would have assisted women in "balancing the scales" were frequently absent. Finally, the women needed health professionals to support them as women and as mothers. They needed to know they were held in esteem for themselves and not just for their reproductive capabilities. Nurses who "went the distance" were in turn esteemed by these mothers. Caring behaviors on the part of health professionals are a necessary part of providing effective care for women as they move toward motherhood in various ways.

Conclusion

The contributors to this volume have described and discussed the experiences of many women as they moved toward motherhood through many different experiences: unexpected pregnancy, infertility, high-risk pregnancy, livebirth after stillbirth, and the birth of children with disabilities. In this concluding chapter we have identified several themes that describe experiences that were shared, more or less, by women in all the studies. These include the journey into vulnerability, the inner dialogue with uncertainty, the search for care, and surviving the experience of possible motherhood. The women talked about their lives never being the same again, and expressed the need for caregivers and others in their lives to understand what they were going through. The desire to capture these experiences in a model led to our discussion of the women's processes of identifying the threat, appraising the threat, and protecting the self through various processes such as blaming self and others, connecting and disconnecting with the fetus/child, telling and not telling others about their experiences, and seeking and blocking information.

The strength of this discussion of experiential themes and an abstract model is that it provides ways in which women's experiences can be shared and understood so that caregivers can better assist and work with women as they go through these difficult mothering experiences. The weakness of both approaches is that they tend to generalize about experiences that are not generalizable. Each woman's experience is unique, and if this work effectively describes the differences as well as the similarities in women's experiences, then women and caregivers will be more informed as they enter into relationships with each other. Although we have discussed commonalities that can be used to explain, in part, the processes women use to live through experiences of uncertain motherhood, the way in which each woman proceeds is unique. The model can provide assistance for anticipating how a woman might react when she discovers that motherhood is not a given or that a baby may not be the final outcome, but there must be recognition of the need to understand how each woman perceives the threat in her own situation. Despite our attempts to understand these women's experiences, it is clear that each woman's experience is particular and true only for her, and that the task of the caregiver and other people involved in her life is to be attuned to the meaning that she individually brings to the situation.

Entering a relationship with a woman as she moves toward motherhood entails construction of meanings that are mutually agreed upon by the partners in the relationship—that is, both the caregiver as professional and the woman as patient. Both must be present as active participants, exploring, affirming, and confirming the meaning of the experience that each offers the other (Gadow, 1993). There can be few predetermined assumptions about experience, as each relationship clarifies the meaning of this experience in the life of a particular woman. Always in the foreground and respected must be the knowledge that each woman is unique, despite her similarities to others in similar circumstances. Having a relationship through conversation means that one explores all aspects of the experience: the time of ovulation as optimum for conception as well as how this affects the desire or wish to "make love"; knowledge of the usual progression of labor as well as the woman's need to progress at her own pace; knowledge about the physical well-being of the handicapped child as well as the needs of other children in the family.

Knowledge that is constructed through understanding the person not as a diagnosis (infertile, high risk, premature, pregnant) but as a living person going through experiences of uncertain motherhood reintegrates the body and self as a complex and dynamic being. As health care becomes more specialized and technological services more common, relationships and thoughtful interaction need to be given renewed attention. Viewing pregnancy, birth, and death as situations to be lived through instead of primarily as problems to be solved recognizes the complexity of human life. Through the process, coming to know something or somebody must always reject the use of power or force, including the use of powerful knowledge (medical, scientific, philosophical), a powerful position (doctor/nurse/patient), or even powerful technology (IVF, fetal monitoring, highly sophisticated perinatal care). Participation by both caregivers and patients in understanding and responding authentically to one another appears to involve personal knowledge, objectivity, and risk.

Relationships that focus on understanding, experience, and meaning do not have specific outcomes (e.g., care or cure), nor can outcomes be predicted. Rather, relationship is the engagement of subjects-in-process where living with vulnerability is made possible. Knowledge and understanding gained through listening, acknowledging, and supporting can be life-giving, and as such may ease vulnerability and pain. Relationship is the place where hope resides. The act of recognition and willingness to enter relationship might be initiated by asking, What is this experience like for you? Tell me about it! With these words and the talk that they bring, both caregivers and the women they care for may find better and more humane ways of understanding the experience of motherhood, in any form in which it occurs in women's lives.

References

Affonso, D. D. (1992). Postpartum depression: A nursing perspective on women's health and behaviors. *Image: Journal of Nursing Scholarship, 24,* 215-221.

Baier, A. (1986). Trust and antitrust. *Ethics, 96,* 231-260.

Barbarin, O. A. (1990). Adjustment to serious childhood illness. In B. R. Lahey & A. E. Kazdin (Eds.), *Advances in clinical child psychology* (Vol. 13, pp. 377-403). New York: Plenum.

Barnhart, R. K. (1988). *The Barnhart dictionary of etymology.* New York: H. W. Wilson.

Beck, C. T. (1992). The lived experience of post-partum depression: A phenomenological study. *Nursing Research, 41,* 166-170.

Bergum, V. (1989). *Woman to mother: A transformation.* South Hadley, MA: Bergin & Garvey.

Bergum, V. (1994). *Toward an ethic of nurturance: Responsibility to self and other.* Research in progress, Faculty of Nursing and Division of Bioethics, Faculty of Medicine, University of Alberta, funded by the Social Science and Humanities Research Council of Canada.

Blenner, J. L. (1992). Stress and mediators: Patients' perceptions of infertility treatment. *Nursing Research, 41*(2), 92-97.

Bonnicksen, A. (1992). Genetic diagnosis of human embryos. *Hastings Center Report, 22*(4), S5-S11.

Bottorff, J. (1990). Persistence in breastfeeding: A phenomenological investigation. *Journal of Advanced Nursing, 15,* 201-209.

Brost, L., & Kenney, J. W. (1992). Pregnancy after perinatal loss: Parental reactions and nursing interventions. *Journal of Gynecological and Neonatal Nursing, 21,* 457-463.

Corbin, J. (1986). Coding, writing memos, and diagramming. In W. C. Chenitz & J. M. Swanson (Eds.), *From practice to grounded theory: Qualitative research in nursing* (pp. 102-120). Menlo Park, CA: Addison-Wesley.

Dickson, G. L. (1990). The metalanguage of menopause research. *Image: Journal of Nursing Scholarship, 22,* 168-173.

Field, M. (1989). Controlling the woman to protect the fetus. *Law, Medicine & Health Care, 17*(2), 114-129.

Fletcher, J., & Wertz, D. (1990). Ethics, law, and medical genetics: After the human genome is mapped. *Emory Law Journal, 39*(3), 747-809.

Gadow, S. (1980). Body and self: A dialectic. *Journal of Medicine and Philosophy, 5,* 172-185.

Gadow, S. (1990, October). *Beyond dualism: The dialectic of caring and knowing.* Paper presented at the conference "The care-justice puzzle: Education for ethical nursing practice," University of Minnesota, Minneapolis.

Gadow, S. (1992). Existential ecology: The human/natural world. *Social Science and Medicine, 35,* 597-602.

Gadow, S. (1993). *Women's health care: Social, medical and ethical narratives.* Paper presented at the conference "Women, health care and ethics," University of Tennessee, Knoxville.

Gerrand, N. (1993). Creating embryos for research. *Journal of Applied Philosophy, 10*(2), 175-187.

Goldenberg, N. R. (1990). *Returning words to flesh: Feminism, psychoanalysis and the resurrection of the body.* Boston: Beacon.

Harris, R. E. (1992). *Pregnology: The process of getting pregnant through science.* Unpublished master's thesis, University of Alberta.

Hayakawa, S. I. (Ed.). (1968). *Use the right word: A modern guide to synonyms.* Montreal: Reader's Digest.

Iams, J. D., Johnson, F. F., O'Shaugnessy, R. W., & West, L. C. (1987). A prospective random trial of home uterine activity monitoring in pregnancies at increased risk of preterm labor. *American Journal of Obstetrics and Gynecology, 157,* 638-643.

Innes, J. E., Ratner, P. A., Finlayson, P. F., Bray, D., & Giovannetti, P. B. (1991). *Models and strategies of delivering community health services related to woman abuse.* Unpublished report of a National Health Research and Development Program funded project, University of Alberta.

Kearney, W., Vawter, D., & Gervais, K. (1991). Fetal tissue research and the misread compromise. *Hastings Center Report, 21*(5), 7-12.

Klitsch, M. (1991). How well do women comply with oral contraceptive regimens? *Family Planning Perspectives, 23*(3), 134-136, 138.

Knoppers, B. (1991). *Human dignity and genetic heritage.* Ottawa, Canada: Law Reform Commission of Canada.

Lippman, A. (1991). Prenatal genetic testing and screening: Constructing needs and reinforcing inequities. *American Journal of Law & Medicine, 27*(1 & 2), 15-50.

Mackey, M. C., & Coster-Schulz, M. A. (1992). Women's view of the preterm labour experience. *Clinical Nursing Research, 1,* 366-384.

Macklin, R. (1991). Artificial means of reproduction and our understanding of the family. *Hastings Center Report, 21*(1), 5-11.

Malterud, K. (1993). Strategies for empowering women's voices in the medical culture. *Health Care for Women International, 14,* 365-373.

Mercer, R. (1990). *Parents at risk.* New York: Springer.

Mishel, M. H. (1988). Uncertainty in illness. *Image: Journal of Nursing Scholarship, 20,* 225-263.

Morse, J. M., & Bottorff, J. L. (1988). The emotional experience of breast expression. *Journal of Nurse-Midwifery, 33,* 165-170.

Morse, J. M., & Johnson, J. L. (1991). Toward a theory of illness: The illness-constellation model. In J. M. Morse & J. L. Johnson (Eds.), *The illness experience: Dimensions of suffering* (pp. 315-342). Newbury Park, CA: Sage.

Mullen, M., & Lowy, F. (1993). Physician attitudes toward the regulation of fetal tissue therapies: Empirical findings and implications for public policy. *The Journal of Law, Medicine & Ethics, 21*(2), 241-250.

Norton, R. W. (1975). Measurement of ambiguity tolerance. *Journal of Personality Assessment, 39,* 607-619.

Phipps, S. A. A. (1993). A phenomenological study of couples' infertility: Gender influence. *Holistic Nursing Practice, 7*(2), 44-56.

Ratner, P. A. (1991). *The health problems and health care utilization patterns of wives who are physically and psychologically abused.* Unpublished master's thesis, University of Alberta.

Rothman, B. K. (1992). Not all that glitters is gold. *Hastings Center Report, 22*(4), S11-S15.

Royal Commission. (1993). *Proceed with care* (Final Report of the Royal Commission on New Reproductive Technologies). Ottawa, Canada: Canada Communication Group.

Sherwin, S. (1992). *No longer patient: Feminist ethics and health care.* Philadelphia: Temple University Press.

Swanson, J. M. (1988). The process of finding contraceptive options. *Western Journal of Nursing Research, 10,* 492-503.

Swanson, K. (1991). Empirical development of a middle range theory of caring. *Nursing Research, 40,* 161-166.

Author Index

Subject Index

About the Authors

Gwen Anderson, R.N., M.N., obtained a diploma in nursing at Mount Royal College in Calgary, Alberta, and a B.Sc.N. in 1983 at University of Victoria, British Columbia. She taught at a hospital-based school of nursing program for five years while completing a master's in nursing at University of Alberta in 1990. Currently, she is a Ph.D. candidate in nursing at Boston College and continues to work on a program of research aimed at better understanding of the impact of genetic testing on patients' decision-making processes and the ethical issues that arise when these tests are introduced into health care. She is committed to advancing the nurse genetic specialist role and to developing a research base to guide these advanced-practice nurses.

Vangie Bergum, R.N., Ph.D., received her B.Sc.N. from the University of British Columbia. Her work life has focused on public health nursing and health care ethics (university teaching, prenatal education, health care consultant) in many parts of Canada. In 1980 she completed a master's in adult education from St. Francis Xavier University and in 1986 completed her Ph.D. from the University of Alberta. She is a Professor at the University of Alberta, Faculty of Nursing, and a Professor Associate with the Division of Bioethics, Faculty of Medicine. Her postdoctoral study took her to the University of Colorado (with Dr. S. Gadow). In 1992 she was a Visiting Research Fellow at Oxford University. Her research focuses on the areas of mothering and bioethics, and she has published a number of books, book chapters, and journal articles on these subjects.

Barbara Brady-Fryer, R.N., M.N., received her B.Sc.N. degree from the University of Maryland and her M.N. from the University of Alberta in

Edmonton. She has worked for more than 15 years in a number of perinatal nursing roles, including staff nurse and clinical nurse specialist. She currently is employed as Coordinator–Research at the University of Alberta Hospitals. She has a strong commitment to excellence in health care and a belief in the value of challenging the status quo of nursing and medical practice to improve the outcomes of patient care. Her research interests include family relationships, lactation, pediatric pain management, and health care technology assessment.

M. Gail Diachuk, R.N., M.N., received both her B.Sc.N. in 1978 and her M.N. in 1989 from the University of Alberta. Her clinical experience includes oncology and pediatrics, and her community experience includes several years as a community health nurse, prenatal instructor, and genetics nurse specialist. She is currently teaching both nursing research and community health nursing through distance education at Athabasca University, Alberta.

Peggy Anne Field, R.N., M.N., Ph.D., received her basic nursing and midwifery education in the United Kingdom. Following immigration to Canada, she completed a B.N. at McGill University, her M.N. at the University of Washington, and a Ph.D. at the University of Alberta. She is a Professor in the Faculty of Nursing, University of Alberta, where she has been since 1964. In 1984 she received a Rutherford Award for Undergraduate Teaching and a McCalla Research Professorship. She has published widely in the areas of maternal-child nursing, midwifery, and qualitative research. In 1992-1993 she held a Killam Annual Professorship in recognition of outstanding scholarship and service to the community.

Rhonda E. Harris, R.N., M.N., received a Diploma of Nursing from the Misericordia School of Nursing in Edmonton and a B.Sc.N. degree from the University of Alberta. She also completed a master of nursing degree from the University of Alberta in 1992. Her clinical practice has primarily been in a neonatal intensive care unit. Her areas of interest include human sexuality and thanatology. She is currently a Research Affiliate of the HOPE Foundation of Alberta, in Edmonton, Alberta.

Ann Lever Hense, R.N., M.N., received her B.N. from Memorial University of Newfoundland and a diploma in advanced practical obstetrics and an M.N. from the University of Alberta. She coordinated the Perinatal Outreach Education Program for Newfoundland and Labrador for five years, and currently holds the same coordinator position for Northern and Central Alberta. Her clinical experience in labor and delivery and postpartum prompted an interest in helping women who experience the tragedy of perinatal loss.

Patricia Beryl Marck, R.N., M.N., received her B.Sc.N. and M.N. from the University of Alberta. She was a Research Associate in the Division of Bioethics, Faculty of Medicine, while in her graduate program and is currently an Adjunct Professor with the division. She has had extensive experience in clinical nursing and nursing education and is currently a Nursing Practice Consultant for the Alberta Association of Registered Nurses.

Karen McGeary, R.N., M.N., received her B.N. from the University of Manitoba and her M.N. and certificate in advanced practical obstetrics from the University of Alberta. Her clinical experience is centered in women's health, in which she has served in various roles, including community health nurse, staff nurse in obstetrics, lecturer in maternal-child health, and perinatal nurse researcher. She is currently an administrator in a women's hospital.